Whose Right It Is

A Handbook
of Covenantal Theology

Jero —

Be Blessed!

Heb 6:10

Kelly Varn

Whose Right It Is

A Handbook
of Covenantal Theology

by Kelley Varner

Destiny Image Publishers
P.O. Box 310
Shippensburg, PA 17257-0310

**"Speaking to the Purposes of God for this Generation
and for the Generations to Come"**

ISBN 1-56043-151-2

For Worldwide Distribution
Printed in the U.S.A.

Destiny Image books are available through these fine distributors outside the United States:

Christian Growth, Inc. Jalan Kilang-Timor, Singapore 0315	Vine Christian Centre Mid Glamorgan, Wales, United Kingdom
Rhema Ministries Trading Randburg, South Africa	Vision Resources Ponsonby, Auckland, New Zealand
Salvation Book Centre Petaling, Jaya, Malaysia	WA Buchanan Company Geebung, Queensland, Australia
Successful Christian Living Capetown, Rep. of South Africa	Word Alive Niverville, Manitoba, Canada

Inside the U.S., call toll free to order:
1-800-722-6774

Acknowledgments

To all the local churches and individuals whose gifts made this project possible.

To historian Dave MacPherson, for his courage to research and print the truth.

To Pastors Dale Frasier, Earl Moore, and Lloyd Willhite, for their insights and research.

To Dr. Mark Hanby, for his invaluable wisdom.

To the Holy Spirit, who is my Teacher.

Dedication

Amos 3:7, KJV

Surely the Lord God will do nothing, but He revealeth His secret unto His servants the prophets.

Before the glory of the Ark of the Covenant was brought into the view of the whole nation in Zion's tabernacle, it was carried aside into the house of a faithful man and his family (1 Chron. 13:13-14).

The most powerful messengers in biblical and ecclesiastical history have been men of obscurity, tucked away exclusively for the Master's good pleasure. Real prophets are uniquely forged on the anvil of misunderstanding, and even persecution. Their only crime: they fearlessly declare the truth in love.

Two such men have strengthened and blessed my life and ministry. We have been companions in tribulation for the sake of the revelation of Jesus Christ. For many decades, these brothers have been good stewards of the mystery of Christ, the gospel of glory. They have stood in the gap since the beginnings of the Latter Rain revival (1948) so that younger men like me could receive the benefit of their courage and devotion.

To Pastors Earl and Kandice Moore of Indianapolis, Indiana, and to Pastors Lloyd and Beverly Willhite of Porter, Oklahoma: We thank you.

About the Cover

Our rights seem to be the hot topic of the day. We expend our energy fighting about equal rights, civil rights, and the right to life. We are so busy being consumed with our *rights* that we forget our *wrongs*. Because of our wrongs, we have no rights. But there is one *whose right it is*, the Scepter, the King—Jesus Christ—who gives us the *right* to become sons and heirs. As we ascend and take our place as joint-heirs with Christ, His rights become our rights because we are transformed into His image. We become a part of Him and rule with Him as priests and kings over all our enemies.

Tony Laidig
Artist

Table of Contents

Part Three
The Dragon Still Has a Mouth

Foreword

I first met Kelley Varner more than seventeen years ago. It was obvious from the beginning that he was a man on a mission. After hearing him minister the Word of God, I was very impressed and desired fellowship with him. Clearly and without question, I found him to be a person who loves God and His Word. He stands for God and His Church. As the years have passed, I have noticed Pastor Varner's ministry to be balanced on both sides—the spiritual and the practical. Needless to say, he has made a lasting impression on me.

Pastor Varner was sent with a special message to the southeastern North Carolina region. His voice has been as an oracle crying in the wilderness for the Church to prepare the way of the Lord, to make His paths straight (Is. 40:3; Mk. 1:3). Old and young alike have heard a new sound; the Son, Jesus Christ, revealed Himself from the Most Holy Place. Many realized, although they were somewhat uncertain, that we had to follow on to know the Lord. The glory cloud led us away from our beloved

Feast of Pentecost. We became a region in upheaval, yet we pressed on toward the Feast of Tabernacles.

From this latter perspective, the Church has very few qualified scribes or scholars. Pastor Varner is both. After almost two decades of pastoring and traveling extra-locally in the Body of Christ, he is a man who has been tempered by the deep dealings of God and mature scholarship. This volume, *Whose Right It Is*, is the result of those processings. A Christo-centric treatise, it zooms in on many essential truths of Scripture, dislodging man-made traditions. Historical dispensationalism has robbed God's people of much needed enlightenment. The book before you demands men to rethink their values, to meditate on history, and then to refocus their vision as the Scriptures come alive.

Whose Right It Is will be an earthquake of enormous magnitude to many. I urge you to read it discerningly. Allow Pastor Varner to help restore Jesus Christ and His supremacy over all things as the basis and focal point of your theology. Like the Psalmist, you will rejoice at God's Word as one finding great spoils (Ps. 119:162).

I believe and pray that our Father will anoint you afresh with the Spirit of wisdom and revelation. May He cause you to walk the path of the just that shines more and more unto the perfect day. May *Whose Right It Is* dethrone every false hope in your life and re-establish your understanding of sound, foundational, biblical orthodoxy. Don't let this book become just another resource manual. Let it become a treasure chest revealing Christ to you and your family.

Stephen Everett, Pastor
Present Truth Ministries
North Fort Myers, Florida

Preface

A great Christian statesman once boldly testified, "Satan may be the god of this world, but he's not the god of my world." Like him, I believe in a real devil—a really defeated devil. Jesus conquered satan by His death and resurrection.

Eph. 4:27, KJV

Neither give place to the devil.

The marked duality of many Christians has two manifestations: the double-minded emphasis upon the old Adamic man and the new creation man; and the level of attention satan receives in song and sermon that is on par with the attention given Jesus. With regard to the latter, the Body of Christ needs an adjusted vision concerning our adversary. To this end, this book was commissioned by the Holy Ghost.

Theologically, the study of satan comes under the heading of angelology. Our purpose is not to do a thorough treatment of satan's origin, person, or work. Concerning the former, the Scripture has little to say. One is left to decide whether the earth's anointed cherub who fell in Isaiah 14 and Ezekiel 28 was the devil or the first man Adam. Pastor Karl Barden of Pullman, Washington, in his book, *The Enlightened Church: satan Who?* (Shippensburg, PA: Destiny Image Publishers, Inc., 1994) treats this issue squarely and fairly. This scholarly work is necessary reading for any serious Bible student.

Jesus Christ's finished work has given men power over the enemy. Are we to take back what the devil stole, or appropriate the eternal spoils of Calvary? This is not a book about satan; it is a book about Jesus and who we are in Him.

Ezek. 21:27, KJV

I will overturn, overturn, overturn, it: and it shall be no more, until He come whose right it is; and I will give it Him.

Gal. 3:19, NIV

What, then, was the purpose of the law? It was added because of transgressions until the Seed to whom the promise referred had come....

Whose Right It Is re-establishes the covenantal centrality and supremacy of the Lord Jesus Christ. It unmasks the angel of light and equips the Church to enforce his defeat. All spiritual warfare must be waged from the posture of Jesus' finished work. Our Lord rests within the rent veil, the enthroned Ruler over all enemies. Unless we stand and fight from the perspective of solid resurrection ground, we will continue to do no more than cover ourselves with sweat and beat the air.

To properly view our adversary, we must understand the clear teaching of biblical apostolic orthodoxy:

1. Satan is not God's adversary. He is ours (Is. 40:1-2; Col. 2:15).

2. Satan has never had legal jurisdiction in the earth (Ps. 24:1; Heb. 1:1-2).

3. Satan is not the thief of John 10:10 anymore (Jn. 10:1,8,10).

First, we have an adversary, but Jesus defeated him at the cross! We are engaged in spiritual warfare, the good fight of faith, ever confident in the complete triumph of our King. The warfare is accomplished; the victory was secured by the finished work of Messiah.

Second, throughout the Old Testament, God ruled the earth through prophets (not kings) until *the* Prophet, the Seed came. The devil, the god of this temporal world system, has never had legal authority on this planet. He is a liar, deceiver, outlaw, usurper, intruder—an illegal alien. The earth is the Lord's.

Third, the dragon has been defeated, but he still has a mouth (Rev. 12:15-16). Satan *was* the thief of John 10:10, but the outlaw was crucified! The "thieves" of John 10:8 are the "many antichrists" (1 Jn. 2:18) and religious traditions we put "before" God, those things we hold superior to the knowledge of Him (Ex. 20:3; Col. 2:8). The most prevalent example of this is the current stronghold of classical dispensationalism, a la Darby, Scofield, and Larkin. Our adversary is chained, but he still has influence. His purpose is to abort the Christ in us by robbing the Church of her God-given identity as the seed of Abraham and the seed of David (see Mt. 1:1; Rom. 2:28-29; Gal. 3:29; 1 Jn. 4:17).

Jn. 1:12, NIV

Yet to all who received Him, to those who believed in His name, He gave the right to become children of God.

Jesus Christ has been given all executive authority in Heaven and in earth. He and His Bride, as heirs together of the grace of life, have the legal, covenantal right to all things. The devil has no rights at all.

The Church must return to the simplicity that is in Christ. Many are like Apollos, an outstanding Christian in the early Church who knew only the previous order—the baptism of John (Acts 18:24-26). Our current information about satan and the endtimes is not necessarily wrong, just incomplete. For that reason, I have provided a fresh historical and biblical look at dispensationalism, devoting a complete chapter to exegete its grandfather clause—Daniel's prophecy of seventy weeks (Dan. 9:24-27).

Read this entire writing with an open mind like that of the Bereans (Acts 17:11). Above all, give yourself to the One *whose right it is*. The Spirit of the Son has been sent into our hearts. In these days of global harvest, He is not coming down...He is coming out! The Lion of Judah, *whose right it is*, now roars out of Zion, coming forth in the mature expression and manifestation of Christ fully formed in a people, His glorious Church!

Pastor Kelley Varner, Th.B., D.D.
Praise Tabernacle
Richlands, North Carolina

Chapter One

Introduction

"…whose right it is…."

Ezekiel 21:27

Whose Right It Is: A Handbook of Covenantal Theology is a fresh apostolic admonition to the Body of Christ, especially God's people in America. Brethren, we must return to sound orthodoxy, the expository preaching and teaching of the Scriptures. Jesus is the Word (Jn. 1:1). Preach the Word…preach Jesus!

Holding to and building on our evangelical and Pentecostal heritage, we are being apprehended for the upward calling to the Feast of Tabernacles (Deut. 16:16; Phil. 3:12-14). The Mosaic "pattern" (Ex. 25:40) with its three dimensions—Outer Court, Holy Place, and Most Holy Place—reveals our growth in grace, the development of the New Testament Christian as a babe, youth, and full-grown man (1 Jn. 2:12-14).

In the initial experience of regeneration (Jn. 3:7), expressed in the Feast of Passover, the emphasis is completely on man. This is followed by the firstfruits Feast of Pentecost, the earnest of our inheritance (Rom. 8:23; Eph. 1:13-14)—an outrageous, adolescent mixture of God and man.

Beyond the veil, where men seek His face (nature) not His hand (works), the total focus is on God. There, in the depths, His footsteps are not known (Ps. 77:19). The uncharted territory of the Feast of Tabernacles is the path that the vulture's eye has not seen (Job 28:7). There, in unapproachable light, is no darkness at all (1 Tim. 6:16; 1 Jn. 1:5), no jungle and no lion, no devil...there (Is. 35:9; 1 Pet. 5:8).

While we hold the vision of the third feast and the maturity of the Church before us, we are experientially Pentecostal—youthful in our understanding, living in an in-part realm marked by duality or double-mindedness (Jas. 1:8). This is evidenced by the current emphasis upon Jesus *and* the devil, the new man *and* the old man.

To see is to understand (Eph. 1:18). We become what we behold in worship (2 Cor. 3:18). Our vision—our focus and emphasis—must be adjusted away from the devil and placed back upon Jesus. The time has come for the Church to unmask our adversary and put him under our feet (Rom. 13:11-14; 16:20).

Heb. 12:2, NIV

> *Let us fix our eyes on Jesus, the author and perfecter of our faith....*

Not Wrong, Just Incomplete

The information that men have received to date with regard to the devil and the endtimes is not necessarily wrong, just incomplete.

Acts 18:24, KJV

And a certain Jew named Apollos, born at Alexandria, an eloquent man, and mighty in the scriptures, came to Ephesus.

The Living Bible says that Apollos was "a wonderful Bible teacher and preacher." Like this powerful man, many today are fluent orators, skilled in literature and the arts. Apollos had stores of learning and could use it convincingly; he was "mighty" or "capable" in the Word.

Acts 18:25, KJV

This man was instructed in the way of the Lord; and being fervent in the spirit, he spake and taught diligently the things of the Lord, knowing only the baptism of John.

Acts 18:25, TLB

...but that is all he knew. He had never heard the rest of the story!

The word describing Apollos' indoctrination is *katecheo* (compare the English *chatechism*). This earnest Christian leader was on fire, ministering the Scriptures he knew with exactness and accuracy (Lk. 1:3). But he knew only the baptism of John—the dynamics of a previous order.

Acts 18:26, KJV

And he began to speak boldly in the synagogue: whom when Aquila and Priscilla had heard, they took him unto them, and expounded unto him the way of God more perfectly.

Apollos preached frankly, confident in spirit and demeanor. The pastoral team of Aquila and Priscilla "expounded" or "exposed" the way of God more perfectly to this teachable man. The information that Apollos had received was incomplete, therefore inaccurate. He needed to hear the rest of the story.

No one has ever graduated from the school of the Holy Spirit. If one's theology or eschatology is ever challenged by new considerations, he should maintain a right spirit and respond with flexibility and openness. When it comes to picking between God's Word and man's tradition, there is no choice.

Whose Right It Is

Ezek. 21:25-27, KJV

And thou, profane wicked prince of Israel, whose day is come, when iniquity shall have an end,

Thus saith the Lord God; Remove the diadem, and take off the crown: this shall not be the same: exalt him that is low, and abase him that is high.

I will overturn, overturn, overturn, it: and it shall be no more, until He come whose right it is; and I will give it Him.

Ezek. 21:27, NIV

...until He comes to whom it rightfully belongs....

Ezek. 21:27, TLB

...until the Man appears who has a right to it. And I will give it all to Him.

Our primary text is prophetically addressed to wicked King Zedekiah and the evil spirit who energized him—satan, the god and prince of this world. The devil's day is about to end. Up till now, it appears that he has been free to roam loose while the Church has been in captivity. But the Day of the Lord is a day of reversals (Ps. 126); the wicked one will be bound and the people of God released!

In its historical context, Ezekiel 21:25-27 addresses Zedekiah, who was king of Judah from 597-586 B.C. (see 2 Kings 24:17-20; 25:1-7; Jer. 37:1-2; 2 Chron. 36:12). The last of 21 monarchs in the Davidic line, this evil man eventually fell under Jehovah's rod of correction, King Nebuchadnezzar of Babylon (2 Kings 25:7).

"Until He come...." This specific prophecy heralds the arrival of the Messiah. The Lord Jesus Christ is the one "whose right it is...." Moses, centuries before, bore witness to the Advent of Judah's Ruler and Zion's King.

Gen. 49:10, NIV

The scepter will not depart from Judah, nor the ruler's staff from between his feet, until He comes to whom it belongs and the obedience of the nations is His.

Whose Day Is Come

2 Cor. 2:11, KJV

Lest Satan should get an advantage of us: for we are not ignorant of his devices.

The Greek word for "devices" means "perception, purpose," and is translated in the King James Version as "device, mind, thought." The strategies and schemes concocted in the gates of hell will not overcome the true Church (Mt. 16:18). The prophet Ezekiel details Zedekiah's demise, reflecting satan's undoing.

Ezek. 21:25, KJV

> *And thou, profane wicked prince of Israel, whose day is come, when iniquity shall have an end.*

Ezek. 21:25, NIV

> *...whose time of punishment has reached its climax.*

Ezek. 21:25, TLB

> *O King Zedekiah, evil prince of Israel, your final day of reckoning is here.*

As with Zedekiah, the devil, the wicked prince of this world system (Jn. 12:31; Eph. 2:2), is "profane." This Hebrew word means "pierced (especially to death); figuratively, polluted." Translated over 30 times in the Book of Ezekiel as "slain," it comes from a primitive root meaning "to bore, to wound, to dissolve." It points to satan's day of reckoning at Golgotha, where Jesus "pierced" him through at the cross (Col. 2:15). On that awful day when the true Passover Lamb was sacrificed for us, Jesus bruised the king of darkness and dismantled his kingdom.

Like the courageous Jael who bored the workman's hammer through the head of Sisera (Judg. 4:18-21; 5:24-27), Jesus mortally wounded our adversary at the place of the skull (Hab. 3:13). In that historic moment, iniquity and perversity came to an end; it was literally "chopped off." This latter noun in Ezekiel 21:25 is used to denote the end of a person or a "death" (Gen. 6:13). The day has come, the seventh day from Adam and the third day from Jesus (Hos. 6:1-3; 2 Pet. 3:8), to fully understand and appropriate those spoils of His eternal triumph!

Remove the Diadem and Take Off the Crown

Ezek. 21:26, KJV

Thus saith the Lord God; Remove the diadem, and take off the crown: this shall not be the same: exalt him that is low, and abase him that is high.

Ezek. 21:26, NIV

...Take off the turban, remove the crown. It will not be as it was....

Ezek 21:26, TLB

...The old order changes....

The word for "diadem" in our root text means "a tiara, the official turban (of a king or high priest)," and it is translated in the King James Version as "diadem, mitre." It reveals the office of the High Priest (see Ex. 28:4,37,39; 29:6; 39:28,31; Lev. 8:9; 16:4). The "crown" speaks of the office of king. Together, they point to the Messiah, Jesus Christ, our great King-Priest after the order of Melchisedec (Heb. 5:1–8:6).

The power and authority of the Kingdom was taken from Zedekiah and retained by the heavenly Father until the day He sent His Son, made of a woman, made under the law (Gal. 4:4). The prophet Zechariah foresaw the time when Messiah would come, the one "whose right it is," who mingles the office of priest and king, rightly attired with both mitre and crown (Zech. 6:12-13; Heb. 2:9). Jesus would build the true temple, the Church of the New Covenant (Mt. 6:18).

"This [this government, administration, authority, way of things] shall not be the same" (Ezek. 21:26). In the coming of the promised Messiah, the order of the Old Testament would change. The Law and priesthood would never be the same (Heb. 7:12). Sin and death was swallowed up by the Spirit of life in Christ Jesus. Levi was superceded by Melchisedec.

Having prophesied these things, Ezekiel then sets forth the governing principle of the Messianic Kingdom, the criterion for being a king-priest, the key that unlocks all true spiritual authority (Mk. 10:44-45).

Ezek. 21:26, KJV

> *...exalt him that is low, and abase him that is high.*

This word for "exalt" means "to soar, be lofty." "Low" comes from a root meaning "to depress or sink, to humiliate," the same word translated in this verse as "abase." The word for "high" means "elevated, powerful, arrogant."

The excessive, unreasonable focus upon the devil must be abated. Jesus must be lifted up and exalted (Jn. 12:32). Just as ungodly King Zedekiah was publicly stripped, humiliated, and his crown removed, so the unwarranted attention given to satan must be severed from him and given to Him "whose right it is."

A Triple Overthrowing

Ezek. 21:27, KJV

I will overturn, overturn, overturn, it....

Ezek. 21:27, NIV

A ruin! A ruin! I will make it a ruin!...

This verse can be compared with the triple over-throwing mentioned in Haggai 2:22 (explained in Chapter Nine of my book *Unshakeable Peace* [Shippensburg, PA: Destiny Image Publishers, Inc., 1994]). The devil's purpose is to abort the seed—Christ in you (Col. 1:27; 1 Pet. 1:23). Man is a trichotomy—spirit, soul, and body (1 Thess. 5:23). The Father's purpose through the Son is to plunder and ruin satan...three times.

First, the traditional concepts and ideas regarding the devil must be "overturned," or "overthrown," in our spirits. As we learn the truth about our adversary, we are freed from his tyranny (Jn. 8:32). Truth must be birthed and written in our hearts by the Holy Ghost.

Second, our souls must be transformed, our minds "renewed" or "renovated" (Rom. 12:1-2; Phil. 2:5). Our problem is not the devil; it's what we have been taught, and consequently think, about the devil.

Third, the members of our bodies will come to ex-press what has been revealed in our spirits and souls. From a singleness of heart our mouths will speak only of Him (Mt. 12:34). Our hands and feet, once members of an unrighteous, unfocused vision, will become weapons of true righteousness (Rom. 6:13).

The Divine Right

Ezek. 21:27, NIV

...It will not be restored until He comes to whom it rightfully belongs; to Him I will give it.

Heb. 1:2, NIV

But in these last days He has spoken to us by His Son, whom He appointed heir of all things....

Jesus Christ is the legal covenantal owner of all things in Heaven, in earth, and under the earth—He is Heir of all things. The Spirit of the Son is the Spirit of the Heir!

Gal. 4:6-7, NIV

Because you are sons, God sent the Spirit of His Son into our hearts, the Spirit who calls out, "Abba, Father."

So you are no longer a slave, but a son; and since you are a son, God has made you also an heir.

Like the spirit of Elijah that fell upon Elisha (2 Kings 2:8-14), we have been made joint-heirs with Christ (Rom. 8:16-17). The mantle of our Lord, the power and anointing of the Holy Spirit, has been given so that His life might be worked out and expressed through us (see Acts 2:29-36; 1 Cor. 6:17; Phil. 2:13; 1 Jn. 4:17). The purpose of the Holy Spirit is to reveal Jesus, the Word of God (Prov. 1:22-23; Jn. 1:1).

The true Messiah, the Righteous One who is always right, is the one whose "right" it is. This key word in Ezekiel 21:27 is *mishpat* (Strong's #4941) and means "a verdict pronounced judicially, especially a sentence or formal decree; abstractly, justice, including a participant's right or privilege" (James Strong, *The Exhaustive Concordance of the Bible*, Peabody MA: Hendrickson Publishers, n.d.). *Vine's Expository Dictionary of Biblical Words* adds that *mishpat* means "judgment; rights" (Thomas Nelson Publishers, 1985). This word carries two main ideas: The first deals with the act of sitting as a judge, hearing a case, and rendering a proper verdict (Eccl. 12:14); the second refers to the "rights" belonging to someone (Ex. 23:6). This second sense conveys several particulars:

1. The sphere in which things are in proper relationship to one's claims (Gen. 18:19).

2. A judicial verdict (Deut. 17:9).

3. The statement of the case for the accused (Num. 27:5).

4. An established ordinance (Ex. 21:1).

This word for "right" in Ezekiel 21:27 is taken from the primitive root *shaphat* (Strong's #8199), which means "to judge, pronounce sentence (for or against); by implication, to vindicate or punish; by extension, to govern; passively, to litigate (literally or figuratively)." *Vine's* adds that *shaphat* means "to judge, deliver, rule." This speaks of the accomplishing of a sentence (Gen. 18:25; 1 Sam. 3:13) or to deliver from injustice or oppression (1 Sam. 24:15). *Shaphat* can also be used to describe a process whereby order and law are maintained within a group (Num. 25:5).

1 Tim. 2:5, KJV

For there is one God, and one mediator between God and men, the man Christ Jesus.

The contexts of these cross-references have a judicial sense expressing the activity of a third party who presides over two sides at odds with one another. Pure Christology reveals the Son of God to be Heaven's Arbiter, the Advocate who fully represented God and man (Job 9:33; 1 Jn. 2:1). Jesus Christ was fully empowered as "very God" and "very man." He bridged the chasm and impasse of sin, bringing reconciliation by arbitration. His word is binding; it is law (Jn. 6:63; Rom. 8:1-2)! His priesthood is immutable and permanent; there will not be "another" covenant. Jesus' blood is better than the blood of Abel's sacrifice, for it removes, rather than covers, sin (Jn. 1:29; Heb. 12:24). The righteous life of the Word made flesh is the standard by which all men are judged—He is the judgment personified.

Ezek. 21:27, KJV

...and I will give it Him.

This judicial right has been "given," or "ascribed, assigned, delivered, ordained, rendered, and restored" to Messiah, the New Testament king-priest. By extension, this dominion is ultimately shared with His overcoming Church, the corporate Man foreordained to judge the world and angels (Acts 17:31; 1 Cor. 6:1-3; Rev. 2:26-27).

This word for "give" in Ezekiel 21:27 also has a technical meaning in the area of jurisprudence; it means to "ascribe," or hand something over to someone, to "commit" it to his care (Gen. 9:2). This manifests the transfer of political power, such as the divine right to rule (2 Sam. 16:8). It is used especially in a military and judicial sense, meaning "to give over one's power or control," or to grant victory to someone (Deut. 7:24).

Psalm 72 powerfully states and prophetically overviews the Messiah's "right" to judge and rule the earth. Consider as well Psalm 110:1-3, Isaiah 42:1-5, Jeremiah 33:17, and Luke 1:30-33.

Is. 9:6, KJV

> *For unto us a child is born, unto us a son is given: and the government shall be upon His shoulder....*

To summarize, Jesus Christ is the only one with legal, contractual rights to all things, the one "whose right it is." Contrariwise, the devil has *no* rights to anything!

Until Christ Be Formed

The pragmatic application and manifestation of Jesus' reign is the Father's ultimate intention: a family of sons in the image of the Firstborn (Rom. 8:29). To accomplish this, He has sent forth the Spirit of His Son into our hearts (Gal. 4:6). The spirit of Moses was multiplied and placed upon the 70 elders (Num. 11:24-25); even so the New Testament Mediator has become a many-membered Man in His corporate Body (1 Cor. 12). "Christ in you" (Col. 1:27) is the Heir in you!

2 Cor. 10:13, NIV

> *We, however, will not boast beyond proper limits, but will confine our boasting to the field God has assigned to us, a field that reaches even to you.*

The King James Version of this verse notes each man's unique "measure," or *metron*, in Christ. Don't glory outside or beyond your measure, but boast within your assignment, your destiny—God's will for your life. Pursue your ministry, your place in His great Body. The one "whose right it is" has been birthed in your spirit. Loose Him and let Him go! The purpose of this writing is to awaken a bold, fresh awareness in every man to his covenantal right in Christ to open his mouth and prophesy the good news, to get up and go forth in the name of the Lord.

Gal. 4:19, NIV

My dear children, for whom I am again in the pains of childbirth until Christ is formed in you.

Gal. 4:19, TLB

...I am once again suffering for you the pains of a mother waiting for her child to be born—longing for the time when you will finally be filled with Christ.

"Until He come whose right it is..." prophesies concerning Jesus, then His Body, the Church—until He corporately comes, until Christ be formed in His Body! Our adversary, the devil, is after the seed to kill it. He wants the heir to remain a child and never be trained under real ministry (Gal. 4:1-2; Eph. 4:11).

The word used for "little children" in Galatians 4:19 is *teknion*, and can mean "infants." The apostle John used this word one time in his Gospel (Jn. 13:33) and 14 times in his first Epistle. Paul's "travail" is an apostolic burden for the maturity of the Body of Christ. The Greek word *odino* (Strong's #5605) means "to experience the pains of parturition," and is akin to *odin*, a "pang or throe, especially of childbirth," translated as "pain, sorrow, travail" in the King James Version (Gal. 4:27; Rev. 12:2).

"Until" He comes "whose right it is"—"until" the indwelling Heir (Son) be fully formed in a people—is illuminated by these Scriptures:

Gal. 4:2, KJV

> *But is under tutors and governors **until** the time appointed of the father.*

Eph. 4:13, KJV

> ***Till** we all come...unto a perfect man, unto the measure of the stature of the fulness of Christ.*

Phil. 1:6, KJV

> *...He which hath begun a good work in you will perform it **until** the day of Jesus Christ.*

Rev. 7:3, KJV

> *...**till** we have sealed the servants of our God in their foreheads.*

Compare Matthew 24:38, Luke 1:20; 19:13; 21:24, Acts 3:19-21; 20:11, Romans 11:25, First Corinthians 15:25, and Revelation 17:17.

"...Until Christ be *formed* in you" (Gal. 4:19). Until He comes—into our understanding, our mouths, our lives, our homes, our churches. This Greek word, used only here in Galatians 4:19, is *morphoo*, and means "to fashion." It is taken from *morphe* (Strong's #3313), which means "(through the idea of adjustment of parts); shape; figuratively, nature." *Vine's* adds that *morphoo* refers, not to the external and transient, but to the inward and real, expressing the necessity of a change in character and conduct to correspond with inward spiritual condition, so that there may be moral conformity to Christ.

Each of the members of His Body must personally experience this revolutionary work of the Spirit. Inwardly in vision and understanding, outwardly in life style, each of us must be refashioned. We must undergo an adjusted vision concerning satan. Our current information is not necessarily wrong, just incomplete.

It Becomes He, He Becomes Them

Hab. 2:3, KJV

> *For the vision is yet for an appointed time...it will surely come, it will not tarry.*

Heb. 10:37, KJV

> *...He that shall come will come, and will not tarry.*

The writer to the Hebrews quotes Habakkuk, moving the vision from abstract to reality, from type to antitype, from shadow to substance. Advancing from the Old Testament to the New Testament, we discover the "vision" to be a Person! *It* becomes *He*, and His name is Jesus.

Is. 52:7, KJV

> *How beautiful upon the mountains are the feet of him....*

Rom. 10:15, KJV

...How beautiful are the feet of them....

By New Covenant expansion and Holy Ghost illumination, the apostle Paul declares that the feet of "Him" become the feet of "them"—Christ in the fullness of His Church (Eph. 1:23)! The gospel proclaims that Jesus has come to bring forgiveness, life, and peace to all. This good news centers in His glorious Person, in "Him." Through the power of the Holy Ghost, the Spirit of Jesus Christ now resides in "them"—His glorious Body.

Ezek. 21:27, KJV

...until He come whose right it is; and I will give it Him.

Jn. 1:12, NIV

Yet to all who received Him, to those who believed in His name, He gave the right to become children of God.

"Whose right it is"—it belongs first to Jesus, then to the Spirit of the Son in His Body—first *Him*, then *them*! *It* becomes *He; He* becomes *them*, those who believe in His name. The divine, covenantal right is His, then ours!

This foundational, introductory truth is based on King Jesus having been given all authority in Heaven and earth (Mt. 28:18). God is omnipotent; He has no enemies. They all lay defeated under His mighty feet. The warfare is accomplished. The devil is not God's adversary—he is ours.

Part One

The Warfare
Is Accomplished

"...her warfare is accomplished...."

Isaiah 40:2

Chapter Two

Satan Is Defeated

"…the Lord rebuke thee, O Satan…."

Zechariah 3:2

Jesus Christ, the Lord of all, has been crowned with glory and honor (Heb. 2:9). Our risen King is the sole object of our affections and devotion as we refocus our vision and look unto Him, the Author and Finisher of our faith (Heb. 12:1-2). Consequently, the apostle Paul admonished us:

Eph. 4:27, KJV

Neither give place to the devil.

Eph. 4:27, NIV

And do not give the devil a foothold.

The Greek word for "place" used here is *topos* (compare the English word *topography*), and it means "a spot; figuratively, condition, opportunity." It is rendered in the King James Version "as coast, licence, place, quarter, room." Throughout the nations, men continue to give the devil "place."

Positions have polarized, and camps have formed. On one side, satan is all-important; on the other, he is not important at all. One man preaches, sings, and testifies constantly about the devil; another ignores him, perhaps to the point of denying his existence as an literal entity. One thing is certain: satan is not God's adversary; God has no enemies. They are all under the feet of Jesus Christ (Eph. 1:20-23)! The devil is not God's adversary— he is *yours*!

Your Adversary

1 Pet. 5:8, KJV

Be sober, be vigilant; because **your** *adversary the devil, as a roaring lion, walketh about, seeking whom he may devour.*

1 Pet. 5:8, TLB

Be careful—watch out for attacks from Satan, **your** *great enemy. He prowls around like a hungry, roaring lion, looking for some victim to tear apart.*

In serious times, the Body of Christ, as sons of the day (1 Thess. 5:6-8), must be "sober," or "free from the influence of intoxicants." Men naturally abuse their bodies with alcohol and nicotine. Others, drunk on their favorite doctrines and experiences, frustrate the grace that comes with the revelation of Jesus Christ (1 Pet. 1:13).

Peter further instructs us to be "vigilant," to "keep awake, watch." The root of this word means "to collect one's faculties; to rouse (from sleep, from sitting or lying, from disease or death); figuratively, to rouse from obscurity or inactivity." Jesus used this word in Gethsemane when He admonished the apostles to watch and pray (Mt. 26:41). Compare First Corinthians 16:13, Colossians 4:2, and First Peter 4:7.

Satan is not God's "adversary"—he is ours. *Antidokos* (Strong's #476) means "an opponent (in a lawsuit); satan, the arch-enemy," and it is taken from two Greek words: *anti*, meaning "opposite; instead of," and *dike*, meaning "right; justice."

Our adversary is the enemy of the Kingdom whose scepter is righteousness (Rom. 14:17; Heb. 1:8). He is anti-God, against the one "whose right it is."

He is the "devil," or *diabolos* (Strong's #1228), meaning "a traducer" and rendered in the King James Version as "false accuser, devil, slanderer." *Webster's New Universial Unabridged Dictionary* says that a *traducer* is "one who defames, maligns, or slanders" (Second Edition, New York, NY: Simon & Schuster, 1983). The diabolical one hurls his evil accusations and fiery darts at the brethren (Eph. 6:16; Rev. 12:9-10). Unlike God, who is omnipresent, the devil is limited in his goings as he walks about (Job 1:7) seeking whom he may "devour," or swallow.

Satan seeks whom he *may* devour. He requires permission, but he has to find us first! The believer has died to sin, and his life is hidden with Christ in God (Col. 3:1-3).

Who Is Satan?

The Hebrew word transliterated "satan" (Strong's #7854) means "adversary, satan" and is found 24 times in the Old Testament, including 11 times in Job 1:6-12; 2:1-7.

1 Chron. 21:1, KJV

And Satan stood up against Israel, and provoked David to number Israel.

Ps. 109:6, KJV

Set thou a wicked man over him: and let Satan stand at his right hand.

Zech. 3:1, KJV

And he showed me Joshua the high priest standing before the angel of the Lord, and Satan standing at his right hand to resist him.

The Greek word for "satan" is *satanas* (Strong's #4567). It means "the accuser, the devil." *Vine's* adds, "adversary." This word refers to a slanderer or false accuser. "Satan" is mentioned by name 34 times in the New Testament:

1. The Synoptic Gospels: Matthew 4:10; 12:26; 16:23, Mark 1:13; 3:23, 26; 4:15; 8:33, Luke 4:8; 10:18; 11:18; 13:16; 22:3; 22:31.

2. The Gospel of John: John 13:27.

3. The Book of Acts: Acts 5:3; 26:18.

4. The Pauline Epistles: Romans 16:20, First Corinthians 5:5; 7:5, Second Corinthians 2:11; 11:14; 12:7, First Thessalonians 2:18, Second Thessalonians 2:9, First Timothy 1:20; 5:15.

5. The Book of Revelation: Revelation 2:9, 13, 24; 3:9; 12:9; 20:2, 7.

The various names given to satan in the Scriptures indicate his nature and work:

1. Accuser (Rev. 12:10)—prosecutes the brethren.

2. Adversary (1 Pet. 5:8)—the meaning of "satan."

3. Angel of light (2 Cor. 11:14)—deceives by wrapping himself with the Word of God.

4. Beelzebub (Mt. 10:25)—the unclean "lord of the flies, lord of the dunghill."

5. Belial (2 Cor. 6:15)—"worthless" and vile.

6. Deceiver of the whole world (Rev. 12:9)— through the medium of the spirit of fear.

7. Destroyer (Ps. 17:4)—"apollyon."

8. Devil (Mt. 13:39)—"slanderer."

9. Dragon (Is. 51:9)—grew up from the serpent.

10. Enemy (Mt. 13:39)—ours, not God's.

11. Father of lies (Jn. 8:44)—he cannot tell the truth.

12. Fowler (Ps. 91:3)—snares those who live in the heavenlies.

13. God of this world (2 Cor. 4:4)—invented all religions.

14. Leviathan (Is. 27:1)—the serpent in the sea.

15. Murderer (Jn. 8:44)—full of hate.

16. Prince of the power of the air (Eph. 2:2)—ruler of demons.

17. Prince of this world (Jn. 12:31)—see the three principles of First John 2:15-17.

18. Roaring lion (1 Pet. 5:8)—intimidates.

19. Serpent (Job 26:13)—"whispers" perverted wisdom.

20. Sower of discord (Prov. 6:14)—subtracts and divides.

21. Tempter (Mt. 4:3)—through the power of suggestion.

22. Wicked one (Eph. 6:16)—cruel and pernicious.

23. Wolf (Jn. 10:12)—rapacious, preying upon the sheep.

Much more could be said, but the focus of this writing is not the devil; rather it is on Him "whose right it is." Satan's assaults on the patriarch Job (Job 1:6–2:13) reveal much about his purposes and tactics. See my notes on *Principles of Present Truth From Job*, pages 37-46 (Richlands, NC: Tabernacle Press, 1984).

The Warfare Is Accomplished

Satan is not God's adversary—he is *ours*. Both Testaments proclaim Jesus' complete triumph over satan. As a man filled with the Holy Ghost, the Pattern Son defeated the evil one on his own turf (Acts 10:38). Our Lord's victory over the devil disintegrated the devil's kingdom, denied him power over death, and divested him of all his authority.

Is. 40:1-2, KJV

Comfort ye, comfort ye My people, saith your God.

Speak ye comfortably to Jerusalem, and cry unto her, that her warfare is accomplished, that her iniquity is pardoned....

Liberal theologians and proponents of higher criticism speculate an Isaiah I (chapters 1-39) and Isaiah II (chapters 40-66), supposing that the authorship or authenticity of these sections of the book differ.

Indeed! Any Sunday School student knows that there are 66 chapters in Isaiah and 66 books in the canon of Scripture. Isaiah is a miniature Bible; its first 39 chapters capture the essence of the Old Testament, and its last 27 chapters the spirit of the New. More to the point, the opening verses of Isaiah 40 prophesy the beginnings of the New Testament and the coming of John the Baptist!

Is. 40:2, NIV

Speak tenderly to Jerusalem, and proclaim to her that her hard service has been completed, that her sin has been paid for....

The New King James Version says in Isaiah 40:2, "her warfare is ended." The Living Bible adds, "her sad days are gone." The gospel is the good news that Jesus has defeated sin and satan, reconciling the creation back to God (2 Cor. 5:19; Eph. 2:14-18; Col. 1:19-23).

To speak "comfortably" to God's people literally means to speak "to the heart." Religious tradition is what men and demons teach. The mind, apart from the power of the Holy Ghost, cannot understand or receive spiritual realities (1 Cor. 2:9-16). But this is the day of the Spirit.

The word for "cry" in Isaiah 40:2 is *qara* (Strong's #7121) and means "to call out to, to address by name, to call out loudly, to get someone's attention." Above all, *qara* signifies the specification of a name. Every true prophet who speaks to the heart of the Church declares the name of the Lord unto her, projecting the nature of the Lord over her. Christians are called and baptized into His name (Acts 2:38-39). Our predetermined destiny is to be a people for His name (Acts 15:14). We refuse to emphasize the bad news about the devil and his crowd. With our eyes fixed on Jesus, we preach the Word.

The warfare is "accomplished." This is the primitive root *mala* (Strong's #4390), which means "to fill or be full of." It is translated in the King James Version as "accomplish, confirm, be at an end, fill, fulfil, fulness." The warfare has been fulfilled. It is finished!

Jn. 19:28-30, KJV

After this, Jesus knowing that all things were now accomplished, that the scripture might be fulfilled, saith, I thirst.

Now there was set a vessel full of vinegar: and they filled a sponge with vinegar, and put it upon hyssop, and put it to His mouth.

When Jesus therefore had received the vinegar, He said, It is finished: and He bowed His head, and gave up the ghost.

The New Testament word for "accomplished" and "finished" is *teleo* (Strong's #5055). It means "to end, complete, execute, conclude, discharge (a debt)." It comes from the root *tello* (Strong's #5056), which means "to set out for a definite point or goal; the conclusion of an act or state; result (immediate, ultimate, or prophetic)." *Teleo* is rendered in the King James Version as "accomplish, make an end, expire, fill up, finish, go over, pay, perform" (Phil. 1:6; 2 Tim. 4:7). Jesus was determined to fulfill the Father's will.

Lk. 12:50, NIV

> *But I have a baptism to undergo, and how distressed I am until it is completed!*

Lk. 18:31, KJV

> *Then He took unto Him the twelve, and said unto them, Behold, we go up to Jerusalem, and all things that are written by the prophets concerning the Son of man shall be accomplished.*

The war of the ages was fought and won 2,000 years ago. We must acknowledge and appropriate the bounty of His victory. To fight the good fight of faith is to arm ourselves with a settled conviction that the warfare is accomplished. To participate in spiritual warfare apart from the revelatory truth that our adversary has been defeated is asking for defeat.

The Hebrew and Greek words for "faith" speak of things that are certain, settled, established. Be assured that Jesus has finished the work. The weapons of our warfare are mighty "through God" (2 Cor. 10:3-6)— through what He did! This is not the Joshua syndrome of "taking the land," but it is the higher ground of

Ephesians that *He* took! In Christ we sit, walk, and stand postured in the heavenlies with His victory (Eph. 2:6; 4:1; 6:14). We are not fighting to beat the devil. The good fight of faith is to believe, receive, and appropriate Calvary's spoils!

The only battles the enemy has won are those in which we did not engage him. We have the *right* to come against satan in the name of the Lord, standing on the solid resurrection ground of Jesus' finished work. Otherwise, as stated earlier, we will do no more than cover ourselves with sweat and beat the air (1 Cor. 9:26).

The Old and New Testaments are filled with examples of our Lord's victory over the king of darkness. Messiah went forth to crush the serpent's head (Gen. 3:15; Hab. 3:13). He subdued the leader of the land of wickedness, stripping him from head to foot. The Bible reveals eight absolutes about our glorious King, declaring that:

1. Jesus triumphed over principalities and powers.
2. Jesus bound the strong man.
3. Jesus slew the dragon.
4. Jesus killed the giant.
5. Jesus judged the prince.
6. Jesus dismantled satan's kingdom.
7. Jesus abolished death.
8. Jesus divided the spoils.

Jesus didn't go to hell (Eph. 4:9-10; 1 Pet. 3:18-19) to finish the victory. He went there to announce it! The complete and total triumph of our Lord is best summed up in His own words, uttered just prior to His epochal achievement at the cross. The ancient serpent left no trailing influence upon the Rock (Prov. 30:19)!

Jn. 14:30, AMP

I will not talk with you much more, for the prince (evil genius, ruler) of the world is coming. And he has no claim on Me. [He has nothing in common with Me; there is nothing in Me that belongs to him, and he has no power over Me.]

Jesus Triumphed Over Principalities and Powers

2 Cor. 2:14, KJV

Now thanks be unto God, which always causeth us to triumph in Christ....

Col. 2:15, KJV

And having spoiled principalities and powers, He made a show of them openly, triumphing over them in it.

Col. 2:15, NIV

And having disarmed the powers and authorities, He made a public spectacle of them, triumphing over them by the cross.

Jesus "spoiled" our adversary at the cross. This word, which carries the thought of becoming divested of clothing or armor, is used in Colossians 2:11 to describe the "putting off" of the old man. Our Lord literally exhibited, or exposed, the enemy.

The Greek word for "triumph" is *thriambeuo* (Strong's #2358), and means "to make an acclamatory procession; to conquer or to give victory." Its root *throeo* means "to clamor; by implication, to frighten," and could be rendered as "to lead in triumph." Picture winning the Super Bowl or leading a ticker-tape parade ending World War II. The conquered host's leader would be stripped, shackled, and shamed, then paraded before the multitudes; his spoils—total embarrassment and humiliation (Is. 49:25; Ps. 68:18; Eph. 4:8). A Roman captain (Heb. 2:10) in such a parade would follow the defeated leader in his chariot, often accompanied by other great warriors. On such occasions, the captain's sons, with various officers, would ride behind him (Rev. 3:21; 17:14). Then came the troops in quick-step, shouting, "Triumph! Triumph! Triumph!"

Strong's Concordance says that *thriambeuo* is a "noisy *iambus*," which is a certain meter of verse used in satire. The picture is clear: Jesus defeated the devil. Praise the Lord! Make a joyful noise! Let's go to the parade! Let's mock the enemy. Jesus whipped him at the cross.

Col. 1:13, KJV

Who hath delivered us from the power of darkness, and hath translated us into the kingdom of His dear Son.

Col. 1:13, AMP

[The Father] has delivered and drawn us to Himself out of the control and the dominion of darkness and has transferred us into the kingdom of the Son of His love.

We have been delivered, rescued, and preserved by the finished work of Jesus Christ. Our Lord has delivered us from the "power," or "authority," of the kingdom of darkness and sin (2 Cor. 1:10; Eph. 2:1). We have been translated, or transferred, from darkness to light, changed, and made able to stand in the righteousness of Christ.

Jesus Bound the Strong Man

Jer. 31:11, KJV

For the Lord hath redeemed Jacob, and ransomed him from the hand of him that was stronger than he.

Mt. 12:29, KJV

Or else how can one enter into a strong man's house, and spoil his goods, except he first bind the strong man? and then he will spoil his house.

Mt. 12:29, TLB

One cannot rob Satan's kingdom without first binding Satan. Only then can his demons be cast out!

On Calvary, the stronger Man prevailed. The Greek word translated as "strong" in Matthew 12:29 means "forcible." Its root, *ischus*, is translated as "ability, might, power, and strength" in the King James Version. Jesus is stronger than the devil. He bound the enemy and then began to seize and plunder his goods. The original language is intensive, "He will completely spoil his house."

Lk. 11:22, KJV

But when a stronger than he shall come upon him, and overcome him, he taketh from him all his armour wherein he trusted....

This verse bears witness that Jesus has overcome or subdued the adversary. More powerful and better-armed, the Conqueror stripped the devil of his weapons and carried off his belongings. The Greek word for "armor" is *panoplia* (English *panoply*) and means "all armor, full armor; all weapons." The cross took away the whole armor of satan and made provision for the whole armor of God (Eph. 6:11-13). "Trusted" is *peitho*, the verb form of *pistis*, the Greek word for "faith." On Golgotha's hill, the devil's faith was destroyed and the faith of God was inaugurated (Heb. 12:1-2). *Peitho* means "to rely by an inward certainty." Satan's whole world caved in—around the father of insecurity and instability.

But Jesus, the Rock of ages, is stronger than the devil. Everything about our King is superior. Not even death was able to hold Him down! It could not seize or retain the one who is the resurrection and the life.

Acts 2:24, TLB

> *...death could not keep this man within its grip.*

Jesus Slew the Dragon

The battle of the ages is the battle for the seed. Jesus Christ was the Seed of the woman, the Seed of Abraham, and the Seed of David (Mt. 1:1). Therein is revealed His pain, His promise, and His power as He relates to mankind racially, redemptively, and royally.

Gen. 3:15, NIV

> *And I will put enmity between you and the woman, and between your offspring and hers; he will crush your head, and you will strike his heel.*

The Hebrew word for "enmity" means "hostility; to hate (as one of an opposite tribe or party)." This first promise of the Messiah's coming prophesies of Mary's son who would come and bruise or overwhelm the serpent's head. The devil was predestined to be put under the feet of the Lamb of God (Eph. 1:22; Heb. 2:8-9).

The Hebrew word for "serpent" in Genesis 3:15 is *nachash* (Strong's #5175) and means "a snake (from its hiss)." It's root means "to hiss; to whisper a magic spell; to prognosticate." Our adversary operates his ministry by the spirit of fear. His weapon is suggestion: "Hath God said?" (Gen. 3:1)

Every thought (like seed) has its source in one of three spirits—God's, man's, or the devil's. Man's soul (*psyche*) or mind is like a womb, wherein conception (of thoughts) takes place. When fiery darts come, we must not receive or meditate them. Faith comes by thinking upon the Word of God (Rom. 10:17). Fear comes by contemplating the voice of the devil. The birth canal for this fertilized seed is the mouth; our words—the baby—are the fruit of our lips (Mt. 12:34). Every word we speak has its source in the realm of spirit. We must learn to agree with the Father (Amos 3:3).

The adversary's primary tactical purpose is abortion—to kill the son, the seed, the heir. That seed (the Greek word is *sperma*) is the living Word—what God has said. Doubt is the wedge of sin. The enemy encourages us to imagine things that are not real. He wants to separate us from the Word and the source of that Word.

Gen. 3:14, KJV

And the Lord God said unto the serpent…upon thy belly shalt thou go, and dust shalt thou eat all the days of thy life:

Is. 65:25, KJV

…and dust shall be the serpent's meat….

1 Cor. 15:49, AMP

And just as we have borne the image [of the man] of dust, so shall we and so let us also bear the image [of the Man] of heaven.

How did the serpent of Genesis 3 become the dragon of Revelation 12? His influence has enlarged because men have ignorantly worshiped and magnified him with their words. Originally, the serpent was cursed to go on his belly. Men have made him what he is, giving him mobility—arms and legs—weapons of unrighteousness (Rom. 6:18-20).

Ancient Israel handed down the bronze serpent (Num. 21:1-9) from generation to generation for over 700 years! Finally, godly King Hezekiah destroyed the idol, knowing it to be *Nehushtan*, just a "piece of brass" (2 Kings 18:4). May God's leaders today do the same with the present, undue emphasis on the devil.

The first man Adam was earth-minded, a man of dust. The only place that satan can live, move, and have his being is in the carnal minds of men. As our minds are renovated, we can put satan under our feet (Rom. 12:1-2;

16:20). We have the mind of Christ (1 Cor. 2:16). Jesus the serpent-bruiser is also the dragon-slayer!

Is. 27:1-2, KJV

In that day the Lord with His sore and great and strong sword shall punish leviathan the piercing serpent, even leviathan that crooked serpent; and He shall slay the dragon that is in the sea.

In that day sing ye unto her, A vineyard of red wine.

Is. 27:1, NIV

...Leviathan the gliding serpent, Leviathan the coiling serpent; He will slay the monster of the sea.

"In that day" points to *this day*, the New Testament day. The "sore and great and strong sword" is Jesus, the Word made flesh (Jn. 1:1,14; Heb. 4:12). The sea symbolizes the nations that are restless, teeming masses of unregenerate humanity (Is. 57:20-21). Jesus slew the sea monster. The sweet, lowly Savior was also the "sore" or "cruel, hard" secret weapon of the Father who "punished" the devil. "Punished" means "to visit with hostile intent." That's why Jesus came to this planet, to defeat the devil on his own territory (Lk. 4:1-14; Heb. 4:14-16). He accomplished this by pouring out the "red wine" of His precious blood.

The devil is called "leviathan" in Isaiah 27:1. This Hebrew word (Strong's #3882) is *livyathan* and means "a wreathed animal, a serpent (especially the crocodile or some other large seamonster); figuratively, the constellation of the dragon; also a symbol of Babylon." It comes from a primitive root that means "to twine" (leviathan is the "twisted one"), and is mentioned six times (the number of man) in the Bible (see Job 41:1; Ps. 74:14; 104:26; in Job 3:8, it is translated "mourning"). In extra-biblical Canaanite literature, "Leviathan" is the well-known mythological serpent Lotan that has seven heads (Rev. 12:3). He belonged to the forces of chaos personified by the sea and its monsters, which were conquered by the gods of order.

Job 41:1, KJV

> *Canst thou draw out leviathan with an hook? or his tongue with a cord which thou lettest down?*

Ps. 104:26, KJV

> *There go the ships: there is that leviathan, whom thou hast made to play therein.*

The fortieth and forty-first chapters of the ancient Book of Job furnish a detailed portrait of Behemoth and leviathan, respectively. In my book *Principles of Present Truth From the Book of Job* (Richlands, NC: Tabernacle Press, 1984), I show that *Behemoth* points to the Lord Jesus Christ and His brethren (Rom. 8:29; Heb. 2:6-13)—the corporate Son (Head and body) of the New Testament. In contrast, *leviathan* speaks of satan and all his ministers (seed).

Behemoth is the "chief" or the "first" of the ways of God (Job 40:19), revealing the principle of firstfruits. *Leviathan* is "king over all the children of pride" (Job 41:34). Behemoth has seven specifics: loins, navel, tail, stones, bones, eyes, and nose. Leviathan has nine features: scales, neesings, eyes, mouth, nostrils, breath, neck, flesh, and heart (Job 41:18). This chart, taken from my notes on the Book of Job, is helpful to show their contrast:

Behemoth	Leviathan
God	satan
Christ (Son of God)	antichrist (son of satan)
The truth (light)	the lie (darkness)
Chief of the ways of God	king over all the children of pride
Domesticated (Job 40:15)	wild (Job 41:1)
Peaceful (40:20)	destructive (41:19)
Mouth swallows death (40:23)	mouth spews out death (41:19)
Strength in loins (40:16)	strength in neck (41:22)
Covered by shady trees (40:21)	covered with scales and flakes of flesh (41:23)
Flexible heart (40:23)	heart of stone (41:24)

In Isaiah 27:1, leviathan is the "piercing" serpent, literally, "the serpent that flees or bolts suddenly." That's what happened when Jesus pierced him at the cross. That happens today when men submit to God and resist the devil (Jas. 4:7).

Satan is also called the "crooked" serpent in Isaiah 27:1. This word means "tortuous; to wrest." Jesus tortured him for three-and-one-half years (Acts 10:38), and then wrestled him to the death in Gethsemane and on the cross. The Messiah came to do the will of the Father, to "slay" the dragon. This word means "to smite with deadly intent; to kill, slay, destroy," expressing the idea of a slaughter. The words *sacrifice* and *altar* (with regard to the sacrificial Lamb) convey the same truth.

The Hebrew word for "dragon" in Isaiah 27:1 is *tanniyn* (Strong's #8577), and means "a marine or land monster, sea-serpent or jackal." It comes from an unused root, probably meaning "to elongate; a monster; a sea-serpent (or other huge marine animal); also a jackal (or other hideous land animal)." Jesus defeated the devil and broke the power of his demonic heads (Eph. 6:12; Col. 2:15).

Ps. 74:13, NIV

It was You who split open the sea by Your power; You broke the heads of the monster in the waters.

Ps. 91:13, KJV

Thou shalt tread upon the lion and adder: the young lion and the dragon shalt thou trample under feet.

Leviathan, or the dragon, is often connected with Pharaoh and the land of Egypt—a type of sin and bondage (Ezek. 29:3). Pharaoh, the god and prince of Egypt, typifies the one who is the god and prince of this world system. Jesus has dealt with the old, ancient serpent (Rev. 12:9), mortally wounding the dragon! Jesus is the right hand and holy arm of the Father, the one who got the victory (Ps. 98:1).

Is. 51:9, KJV

...Art Thou not it that hath cut Rahab, and wounded the dragon?

Is. 51:9, NIV

...Was it not You who cut Rahab to pieces, who pierced that monster through?

Jesus triumphed over the devil and the kingdom of darkness. The *stronger* Man bound the strong man. He slew the dragon in the sea. Satan is defeated!

Chapter Three

Jesus Is Lord

"...King of kings, and Lord of lords."

Revelation 19:16

Chapter Two introduced the first three of eight absolutes concerning our victorious Lord, declaring:

1. Jesus triumphed over principalities and powers.

2. Jesus bound the strong man.

3. Jesus slew the dragon.

This chapter concludes that outline and sets forth the supremacy and lordship of our Savior and King:

4. Jesus killed the giant.

5. Jesus judged the prince.

6. Jesus dismantled satan's kingdom.

7. Jesus abolished death.

8. Jesus divided the spoils.

Jesus Killed the Giant

Jesus' once-and-for-all blood sacrifice triumphed over satan, bound the strong man, and slew the dragon. The greatest Son of David also killed the "giant." Throughout the Old Testament, the Philistines were perpetual enemies of Israel, thus typifying demon forces. Goliath, their mouthy champion, is a type of satan. Like the "giants," or *Nephilim*, in Noah's day (Gen. 6:4), who were "bullies or tyrants," Goliath was an intimidator, a spiritual terrorist.

1 Sam. 17:51, KJV

> *Therefore David ran, and stood upon the Philistine, and took his sword, and drew it out of the sheath thereof, and slew him, and cut off his head….*

Ps. 24:8, KJV

> *Who is this King of glory? The Lord strong and mighty, the Lord mighty in battle.*

Psalm 24 was King Jesus' coronation song as He passed through the heavens and ascended the throne of David (Heb. 4:14). Christ had just come from the bloody battlefield—Gethsemane, Calvary, and the empty tomb. The giant lay slain, his head removed, his army scattered and beaten.

To fully appreciate the story of David and Goliath, one must know the events of First Samuel 1–16 that led up to this momentous confrontation. The Book of First Samuel opens with an existing Eli and a growing Samuel. A corrupt priesthood, heavy of flesh, without restraint, and going blind had become *Ichabod*; "the glory had departed." Then to be like the heathen nations, Israel clamored for a king. Chosen by the people, Saul was a head-and-shoulders man who emphasized human wisdom and strength. He was anointed, but when it came to dealing with the Amalekites (the flesh), Saul held back the part that he liked. So it is with those who stop at the Feast of Pentecost, and go no further. David was anointed by the prophet Samuel with a ram's horn full of oil, preparing him for the day of battle.

1 Sam. 17:1-4, KJV

> *Now the Philistines gathered together their armies to battle, and were gathered together at Shochoh, which belongeth to Judah, and pitched between Shochoh and Azekah, in Ephes-dammim.*
>
> *And Saul and the men of Israel were gathered together, and pitched by the valley of Elah, and set the battle in array against the Philistines.*
>
> *And the Philistines stood on a mountain on the one side, and Israel stood on a mountain on the other side: and there was a valley between them.*
>
> *And there went out a champion out of the camp of the Philistines, named Goliath, of Gath, whose height was six cubits and a span.*

Shococh means "hedge" and *Ephes-dammim* means "boundary of blood." Satan can go so far, and no further. The armies were camped on two separate mountains, representing two opposing kingdoms—the Kingdom of God and the kingdom of darkness. Goliath drew near and taunted the people of God for 40 days, the Bible number denoting trial and testing.

1 Sam. 17:8-9, KJV

And he stood and cried unto the armies of Israel, and said unto them, Why are ye come out to set your battle in array? am not I a Philistine, and ye servants to Saul? choose you a man for you, and let him come down to me.

If he be able to fight with me, and to kill me, then will we be your servants....

Jesus Christ, the servant of Jehovah, the seed of David, was chosen for the contest of the ages (Is. 42:1; Mt. 1:1). The terms were clearly set. Whichever champion prevailed would win the day.

1 Sam. 17:38-40, NIV

Then Saul dressed David in his own tunic. He put a coat of armor on him and a bronze helmet on his head.

David fastened on his sword over the tunic and tried walking around, because he was not used to them. "I cannot go in these," he said to Saul, "because I am not used to them." So he took them off.

Then he took his staff in his hand, chose five smooth stones from the stream, put them in the pouch of his shepherd's bag and, with his sling in his hand, approached the Philistine.

Saul's armor, the strength of flesh, could not prevail in this battle. Likewise, Jesus overcame the evil one by the Word of God and the power of the Spirit (Lk. 4:4; Acts 10:38). The "five smooth stones" prefigure the fivefold ascension-gift ministries of our Lord to His Church (Eph. 4:8-13). Jesus smote the enemy and then apportioned His governmental ministry among His apostles, prophets, evangelists, pastors, and teachers. Theocratic government and divine order will smite the thinking of the enemy in the forehead.

1 Sam. 17:51, KJV

...And when the Philistines saw their champion was dead, they fled.

David killed Goliath. Jesus overcame the wicked one. Let us arise in prophetic praise and prayer to declare unto principalities and powers that their champion is dead!

Eph. 3:10-11, NIV

His intent was that now, through the church, the manifold wisdom of God should be made known to the rulers and authorities in the heavenly realms,

according to His eternal purpose which He accomplished in Christ Jesus our Lord.

Jesus Judged the Prince

The warfare is accomplished. The giant has been slain. When Jesus died for our sins according to the Scriptures and rose again for our justification, He also judged the prince of this world.

Jn. 12:31, KJV

Now is the judgment of this world: now shall the prince of this world be cast out.

Jn. 12:31, NIV

...now the prince of this world will be driven out.

The Greek word for "judgment" is *krisis* (Strong's #2920). It means "a decision; by extension, a tribunal; by implication, justice (especially, divine law)." Compare this with the English words *crisis* and *criterion*. The word for "world" is *kosmos* (English *cosmetic*) and means an "orderly arrangement; decoration; by implication, the world."

There is a difference between the "earth" and the "world." The earth is forever the Lord's (Ps. 24:1). The world is a temporary order, a system, an arrangement of things. Satan is the prince of this world (Eph. 2:2; Jas. 4:4). John 12:31 says that when Jesus finished him at the cross, satan was "cast out," also translated in the King James Version as "cast out, drive out, expel, thrust out, put forth, send away." Jesus, knowing in John 12 that His hour of being offered was near, declared the time of satan's judgment to be "now"—"now" was 2,000 years ago. He then announced that the Holy Spirit would come to convince us of this truth.

Jn. 16:8-11, NIV

> *When He comes, He will convict the world of guilt in regard to sin and righteousness and judgment:*
>
> *in regard to sin, because men do not believe in Me;*
>
> *in regard to righteousness, because I am going to the Father, where you can see Me no longer;*
>
> *and in regard to judgment, because the prince of this world now stands condemned.*

Most of contemporary Christendom has only been acquainted with one-third of the Comforter's ministry. The

Holy Ghost is the one who convinces men of sin and their need of a Savior. He is the one who reveals Jesus, the sacrificial Lamb. But the same Spirit also desires to convince us that we have been made the righteousness of God in Christ (2 Cor. 5:21). We have begun to understand our identity in Him. But few have considered that the Spirit will further assure our hearts concerning God's judgment, His criterion.

Paul unfolds this mystery in the first chapter of Romans. In verse one he mentions "the gospel of God"; in verse nine, "the gospel of His Son"; and in verse sixteen, "the gospel of [the] Christ."

The "gospel of God" is the judgment written—the Scriptures, the Word of God. The Bible is God's criterion for righteousness, His standard of living for all men. The "gospel of His Son" is the judgment personified—the Word was made flesh (Jn. 1:14). The life of Jesus Christ is now the gauge, the *krisis*, by which all men are judged. Just as Noah condemned his world by his righteous life (Heb. 11:7), so Jesus condemned the devil and cast Him out. The "gospel of [the] Christ" is the execution of the judgment that He is—the Body of Christ arising to appropriate Jesus' victory over the devil, to enforce the law of satan's defeat, and to become salt and light, a people of influence (Mt. 5:13-16).

As with the principle of resurrection, judgment is past, presently progressive, and future. The devil has been judged and cast out, and our sins have been judged in Christ. As we learn the truth, grow in grace, and judge ourselves righteous in Christ, we will progressively cast satan out of our thinking, preaching, and singing. Finally, the day will come when even the memory of our adversary shall perish (Neh. 2:20; Is. 26:13-14). In that day, the Church will execute the judgment that He is!

Jesus Dismantled Satan's Kingdom

Humpty-dumpty sat on a wall,
Humpty-dumpty had a great fall,
All the king's horses and all the king's men,
Couldn't put the devil back together again!

Heb. 2:14-15, NIV

Since the children have flesh and blood, He too shared
in their humanity so that by His death He might destroy
him who holds the power of death—that is, the devil—
and free those who all their lives were held in slavery
by their fear of death.

Jesus "destroyed" the devil (1 Cor. 15:26). This Greek word *katargeo* (Strong's #2673) means "to be (render) entirely idle (useless)." *Vine's Dictionary of New Testament Words* adds that *katargeo* means "to reduce to inactivity" and is taken from two Greek words: *kata*, meaning "down," and *argos*, meaning "inactive."

Jesus put the devil down and rendered his kingdom inoperative, without authority. *Katargeo* is translated in the King James Version as "abolish, cease, destroy, do away, become (make) of no (none, without) effect, fail, loose, bring (come) to nought, put away (down), vanish away, and make void." Compare Romans 6:6, Ephesians 2:15, and Second Thessalonians 2:8.

Our glorious Lord brought about the demise of the one who had previously held men captive to the fear of death by abolishing death itself (2 Tim. 1:10). Satan and his demons knew that Jesus had come to dismantle their kingdom (Mk. 5:1; Jas. 2:19).

1 Jn. 3:8, KJV

> *He that committeth sin is of the devil; for the devil sinneth from the beginning. For this purpose the Son of God was manifested, that He might destroy the works of the devil.*

Here the Greek word for "destroy" is *luo* (Strong's #3089) and means to "loosen." *Vine's* adds, "to dissolve, sever, break, demolish." It is rendered in the King James Version as "break (up), destroy, dissolve, loose, melt, and put off." Jesus pulverized, wrecked, and dismantled satan's kingdom and "works." This is the word *ergon*; it means "toil (as an effort or occupation); an act." Jesus put the devil in the unemployment line. How sad that the traditions of men have given him place again.

Jesus came to open our eyes that we might live in the light of God instead of satan's darkness (Acts 26:18). Because of His finished work, the devil has been annihilated and robbed of any authority in our lives.

Jesus Abolished Death

The crescendo of Jesus' defeat of satan reaches its apex in the truth that the one who is the resurrection and the life confronted the last enemy and abolished death itself!

Is. 25:8, KJV

> *He will swallow up death in victory; and the Lord God will wipe away tears from off all faces; and the*

rebuke of His people shall He take away from off all the earth: for the Lord hath spoken it.

Hos. 13:14, KJV

I will ransom them from the power of the grave; I will redeem them from death: O death, I will be thy plagues; O grave, I will be thy destruction....

The prophet Isaiah predicted Jesus' victory over sin and death. The Hebrew word for "swallow" means "to make away with; destroy." The Lamb was slain to wipe away or erase the tears from all men (Is. 43:25). He removed the rebuke or disgrace of His people. According to Hosea 13:14, our Redeemer came to plague death, to be its "destruction" or extermination.

Rom. 6:9, NIV

For we know that since Christ was raised from the dead, He cannot die again; death no longer has mastery over Him.

The Lord of all abolished death. All enemies are under His mighty feet. The King James Version of Romans 6:9 says that death no longer has "dominion" over Jesus (compare Rom. 6:14). This Greek word *kurieuo* means "to rule," and it is taken from *kurios*, which means "supreme in authority; controller; by implication, Mr. (as a respectful title)." Settle it. Death is a spirit, an enemy that deserves no respect. That has been reserved for the Lord Jesus alone (Rom. 14:9; 1 Tim. 6:15).

First Corinthians 15 is the resurrection chapter of the Bible. The apostle Paul makes a powerful declaration with regard to the spirit of death:

1 Cor. 15:26, KJV

The last enemy that shall be destroyed is death.

1 Cor. 15:26, TLB

...This too must be defeated and ended.

Death is called the last, or final, enemy. Jesus abolished death, defeating the last "enemy." The word *echthros* means "hateful, odious, hostile; an adversary (especially satan)," and it is perhaps associated with the word *ekos*, which means "outside." Death and the devil are outsiders to the victorious King and His Kingdom.

Jesus swallowed up death in victory (1 Cor. 15:54). The word for "destroyed" in First Corinthians 15:26 is *katargeo*, the same word used in Hebrews 2:14 (see above) and Second Timothy 1:10.

2 Tim. 1:10, KJV

But is now made manifest by the appearing of our Saviour Jesus Christ, who hath abolished death, and hath brought life and immortality to light through the gospel.

2 Tim. 1:10, TLB

...who broke the power of death....

Jesus Divided the Spoils

The devil is defeated! Jesus is Lord! The warfare is accomplished! All satan has left is his roar of suggestion. He is a barking dog on a leash, a mouse with a microphone.

These two chapters have stressed one point: satan is not God's adversary because Jesus defeated him at the cross. The devil is "your" adversary. Jesus triumphed, binding the strong man. He is the dragon-slayer and the giant-killer. He judged the prince of this world and dismantled his kingdom. He took on every enemy, including the last one. Jesus abolished death!

What glory! What a victory! What spoils! Jesus became the Victor so that we don't have to be victims! The New Covenant is His last will and testament. The Benefactor of all things is the Testator who died that we might become heirs of salvation, then rose from the dead to become the Executor of His own will! As in the days of the four courageous lepers, the enemy has been defeated, and the table is spread with divine spoil (2 Kings 7:3-10). All things are now ready (Lk. 14:17). Come and dine!

Like King David who recovered all that the Amalekites had carried away and then sent a present, or blessing, of all the spoils to the elders of Judah (1 Sam. 30:18,26), our Lord Jesus Christ has determined to share His inherited wealth with His people. We are joint-heirs with Christ, heirs together of the grace of life (Rom. 8:17; 1 Pet. 3:7). By His blood, we have become partakers of the commonwealth of Israel (Eph. 2:11-12). The grandest poetic Old Testament chapter detailing the crucifixion of Jesus makes mention of His mighty spoil:

Is. 53:12, KJV

Therefore will I divide Him a portion with the great, and He shall divide the spoil with the strong; because He hath poured out His soul unto death....

The Hebrew word for "spoil" is the primitive root *chalaq* (Strong's #2505), which means "to be smooth; by implication (as smooth stones were used for lots) to apportion or separate." *Vine's* adds, "to divide, share, plunder, assign, distribute." These are unprecedented days of harvest when the Church is receiving Calvary's plunder. The prey of a great spoil is being divided (Ps. 2:8; Is. 33:23; 34:17).

"Therefore will I divide *Him*..." (Is. 53:12). After His victory at the cross, Jesus ascended and measured Himself into five ministries: the apostle, prophet, evangelist, pastor, and teacher (Eph. 4:8-11). He has apportioned His great name among His brethren. As with the priests of the Old Testament, our portion is the Lord Himself (Num. 18:20; Deut. 10:9). This day of great harvest is a day of great joy.

Is. 9:3, NIV

You have enlarged the nation and increased their joy; they rejoice before you as people rejoice at the harvest, as men rejoice when dividing the plunder.

Zech. 14:1, KJV

Behold, the day of the Lord cometh, and thy spoil shall be divided in the midst of thee.

Isaiah 53:12 adds that the Messiah will receive the portion of the great and that He will divide the spoil with the strong. The word for "great" means "abundant (in quantity, size, age, number, rank, quality)." It indicates the scope of His victory over all enemies. *Vine's* adds that "great" means "chief," an indication of "military rank" similar to our word "general." Jesus is the Captain of our salvation (Heb. 2:10). Our General has divided the spoil with His army of followers, those who are "strong," literally, the "powerful and numerous."

Lk. 11:22, NIV

But when someone stronger attacks and overpowers him, he takes away the armor in which the man trusted and divides up the spoils.

The Greek word for "divides" is *diadidomai*, meaning "to give throughout a crowd, deal out; also to deliver over (as to a successor)." We are heirs of God. The New Testament word for "spoils" is *skulon* (Strong's #4661), which means "something stripped (as a hide), booty." It comes from *skullo*, a primary verb that means "to flay, (figuratively) to harass." Jesus skinned the devil. It's time for the Church to recognize and appropriate His victory, then harass our adversary.

Rom. 16:20, KJV

And the God of peace shall bruise Satan under your feet shortly. The grace of our Lord Jesus Christ be with you. Amen.

This word for "bruise" means "to crush completely, to shatter." *Vine's* adds, "to rub together," and so "to shatter, shiver, break in pieces by crushing" (Mk. 5:4; Rev. 2:27). Our putting the devil under our feet will be "shortly," or in "a brief space (of time), in haste." This comes from a word that means "fleet, prompt or ready." God is always ready for us to spoil the enemy's house.

Our swift and complete victory over our adversary will be a quick work (Rom. 9:28).

The Day of the Lord has dawned. Everything is accelerating. As the Church becomes increasingly aware of our Lord's complete victory over satan and death, we will arise and enforce the law.

Never come into the house of the Lord with your tail between your legs, downcast and defeated. Come in shouting, clapping, and dancing! Celebrate the victory of our King. Arise with God's kind of faith, and soar into the heavenlies on eagles' wings of prophetic prayer, praise, and worship. Announce His triumph *there* in the face of principalities and powers (Eph. 3:10). Then go to the darkest places of the earth (Ps. 2:8). Tell the good news of Jesus' victory *there*—through anointed intercession and evangelism. For too long men have made the right declaration, "Jesus is Lord," in the wrong location—inside the four walls of a church building prophesying to each other.

When Peter and John entered the empty tomb on resurrection morning, the napkin that had graced the Head of the Church lay in a place by itself, neatly folded (Jn. 20:7). By Eastern custom, this meant that Jesus would not pass by that way any more! Death had been conquered one time. The warfare was accomplished. For His victory to be established in the earth, a second witness must step forward. Arise to the prey!

Men have made the devil what he is by believing religious tradition rather than the Bible. Let us arm ourselves with truth and then finish him off. Like the Ark of the Covenant housed in the temple of Dagon for three days (1 Sam. 5:1-5), Jesus ripped away the devil's arms and legs. After our Lord's death and resurrection, all that was left of our adversary was a stump. Men who don't know the Bible prop up what Jesus knocked down.

Somebody has to enforce the devil's defeat. Jesus locked him up and has the keys (Rev. 1:18). Get up in Jesus' name and rid the earth of satan's influence. In the Old Testament, King David made full provision so that Solomon could build the temple (1 Chron. 29:1-5). In the New Testament, King Jesus bound the strong man so that we could spoil his house.

Mt. 28:18-19, KJV

> *And Jesus came and spake unto them, saying, All power is given unto Me in heaven and in earth.*
> *Go ye therefore....*

Jesus Christ is Lord! The warfare is accomplished, the battle won. Our mighty Sovereign has given us the legal *right*—the authority and privilege—to receive the Kingdom and become the sons of God (Jn. 1:12). The earth is the Lord's. It belongs to the Seed of Abraham and David. It is the rightful inheritance of our Lord and His Church, Mr. and Mrs. Jesus Christ!

Part Two

The Earth Is the Lord's

"The earth is the Lord's...."

Psalm 24:1

Chapter Four

Jesus Is the Seed of Abraham

"…Jesus Christ…the son of Abraham."

Matthew 1:1

The glorious Church is refocusing her attention upon her victorious Husband, the one alone "whose right it is" to wear the priestly diadem and kingly crown. Chapters Two and Three testified that the "warfare is accomplished." Satan is *not* God's adversary; he is ours. Jesus has no enemies. They were all conquered in His death, burial, and resurrection. The righteous King who has victoriously ascended the throne of grace is the Word forever settled in Heaven who sits and laughs!

Chapters Four and Five expose a second popular notion, that Adam committed high treason and turned the earth over to the devil. That is only half true. Adam did transgress, but the earth is the Lord's.

One source of this concept is the writings of E.W. Kenyon. In his basic Bible course, *The Bible in the Light of Our Redemption*, he stated: "Adam turned this legal dominion over into the hands of God's enemy, Satan" (Lynnwood, WA; Keyon's Gospel Publishing Society, 1969, p. 26).

Did satan seize the earth from Adam, or did God retain His own authority to be given to Him "whose right it is?"

Ps. 24:1, KJV

> *The earth is the Lord's, and the fulness thereof; the world, and they that dwell therein.*

Ps. 24:1, NIV

> *The earth is the Lord's, and everything in it, the world, and all who live in it.*

Ps. 24:1, TLB

> *The earth belongs to God! Everything in all the world is His!*

Jesus defeated the devil and divided the spoils with the strong (Is. 53:12). Now we consider His plunder—the inheritance of the *land* and the *throne*—the earth and the right to rule it.

Jesus is the Heir of all things (Heb. 1:2). He and His Church are the Seed of Abraham (Gal. 3:29; 4:1-2), the authorized recipients of the covenantal promise. Jesus Christ is the only one with legal right to all things. Stop giving the devil place. He has *no* rights to anything!

God of This World, Not the Earth

The earth is the Lord's. The devil has no real lawful authority on this planet. He is a liar, deceiver, outlaw, usurper, intruder—an illegal alien.

2 Cor. 4:3-4, KJV

> *But if our gospel be hid, it is hid to them that are lost:*
>
> *In whom the god of this world hath blinded the minds of them which believe not, lest the light of the glorious gospel of Christ, who is the image of God, should shine unto them.*

The devil's purpose is to abort the seed of God. The prince of this world wants to detain men in darkness and ignorance. He is content to have the things of the Spirit hid or veiled from men's understanding lest they perceive the gospel of God's glory and power—Christ formed in a people (Gal. 4:19).

The word for "blinded" in Second Corinthians 4:4 means "to obscure." It is derived from a word that means "to envelop with smoke"; figuratively, "to inflate with self-conceit." Its root means "to make a smoke, to slowly consume without flame." The verb is used metaphorically here, as well as in John 12:40 and First John 2:11 to describe the dulling of the intellect. Where the Word is never taught, there is more smoke than fire. The renewing of our minds brings the wind of His Spirit to blow away the spiritual fog that we might see our stance in Christ.

The word for "minds" in Second Corinthians 4:4 is *noema* (Strong's #3540), and means "a perception, purpose, or (by implication) the intellect, disposition." *Vine's* adds "thought or design." *Noema* is translated in the King James Version as "device, mind, thought." Consider its particular usage in the letter of Second Corinthians

(2 Cor. 2:11; 10:5; 11:3). We don't have to be ignorant of satan's schemes, taking captive every thought.

The devil has never had legal jurisdiction over the earth. In John 12:31, he is called the prince of this "world," or "age." In Second Corinthians 4:4, satan is named the god of this "world," not the earth—there is a great difference.

This latter word for "world" is kosmos (Strong's #2889). Compare it with the English word *cosmetic* (that which melts in the heat). *Kosmos* references the temporal, and means "an orderly arrangement, decoration; by implication, the world." *Vine's* adds that the *kosmos* is an "order, arrangement, ornament, adornment" (1 Pet. 3:3).

The "world" of which satan is god is an order, a system, an arrangement of things, especially men's concepts. It is a mind-set, a mentality. Above all, it is temporary, passing away (1 Jn. 2:15-17).

In Matthew's account of the temptation, the devil offered Jesus all the kingdoms of the transient cosmos, not the earth (Mt. 4:8-9). Luke's parallel passage (Lk. 4:5-7) uses the word *oikoumene*, which refers to the habitable earth. Through centuries of ignorance, men, not God, have given the devil power and glory.

Paul revealed that the cosmos has a spirit that is contrary to the Spirit of God (1 Cor. 2:12). Our lives were governed by the course and direction of that spirit prior to our salvation and the renewing of our minds (Eph. 2:2). Let every Christian say, "The devil may be the god of this world, but he's not the god of my world!"

The Prophets and the Son

Satan has never ruled this planet. The government of the earth was administered by prophets (not kings) until *the* Prophet came "whose right it is"—Jesus, the Son of God.

Heb. 1:1-2, KJV

God, who at sundry times and in divers manners spake in time past unto the fathers by the prophets,

Hath in these last days spoken unto us by His Son, whom He hath appointed heir of all things....

Throughout the Old Testament, God spoke through prophets—men like Noah, Abraham, Samuel, David, Elijah, and Elisha. The Hebrew Bible divides the Old Testament into the Law, the Prophets, and the Writings. The King James Version notes the Major Prophets (Isaiah, Jeremiah, Ezekiel, and Daniel) and the Minor Prophets (Hosea, Joel, Amos, Obadiah, Jonah, Micah, Nahum, Habakkuk, Zephaniah, Haggai, Zechariah, and Malachi). Jehovah spoke in "sundry times," or in many parts or portions—each prophet had a piece of the message. They prophesied in "divers manners," or in many ways, as to method or form. Two verses in particular reveal the power and rule of the Old Testament prophets.

Jer. 1:10, NIV

See, today I appoint you over nations and kingdoms to uproot and tear down, to destroy and overthrow, to build and to plant.

Amos 3:7, KJV

Surely the Lord God will do nothing, but He re-vealeth His secret unto His servants the prophets.

But in these New Testament days, God has spoken to us through His Son. Jesus *was* and *is* the Word, the *Logos*, the Sum of all the parts. He has been "appointed," or "placed," as Heir of all things. This word in Hebrews 1:2 is translated as "ordained" in the King James Version of John 15:16. It is the Greek word *kleronomos* (Strong's #2818), and means "a sharer by lot, inheritor, possessor."

God ruled the earth through prophets, not kings, until *the* Prophet came "whose right it is" (Gal. 3:19).

The Land and the Throne

In the spring of 1984, the Lord gave me a fresh under-standing of covenantal theology, although I had known since 1969 that the Church was the Seed of Abraham. *The Land and the Throne* was placed in written form and sent all over the world (Richlands, NC: Tabernacle Press, 1984). This chapter and the next encapsulate that booklet (the original four tapes are still available through the ministry of Praise Tabernacle).

Do you know who you are (in Christ)? Do you know what you have? Do you know how to get it?

The New Testament teaches that Jesus Christ is the Son or Seed of Abraham and David (Mt. 1:1). The Seed of Abraham has been given the land, and the Seed of David has been given the throne. The "land" is the earth, and the "throne" is the legal right to rule it!

Jesus Christ isn't going to become King of kings and Lord of lords; He already is! Our glorious Savior, not the devil, is alive and well on planet earth, having obtained legal ownership to all things. Many key Scriptures declare *His* dominion (see Ps. 2:8; 72:1-20; Mt. 1:1; 5:5; Lk. 1:30-33; Gal. 3:16; Eph. 1:19-23; Phil. 2:5-11; Rev. 1:5).

Jesus Christ is either Lord of all or not Lord at all. One verse summarizes this truth and constitutes the basis of the Great Commission. The verb is in the aorist tense, which denotes action in a point of time, especially the past.

Mt. 28:18, NIV

Then Jesus came to them and said, "All authority in heaven and on earth has been given to Me."

The Heir of all things, the incorruptible Seed, was planted in death and came forth in the increase of resurrection (Jn. 12:24). By extension, the Church, His Bride, shares the glory and authority of the one "whose right it is," being heirs together of the grace of life (Rom. 8:17; 1 Pet. 3:7). His Body, His Bride, is Mrs. Jesus Christ.

The Seed of Abraham Is Christ

Gal. 3:16, KJV

Now to Abraham and his seed were the promises made. He saith not, And to seeds, as of many; but as of one, And to thy seed, which is Christ.

The Seed of Abraham is Christ. The apostle did not mention "seeds," a natural seed and a spiritual seed. The only seed that counted with the Lord and Paul was a *spiritual* Seed—Christ! In the same way in which man is both male and female (Gen. 1:26-28), the true Israel of God is made up of Jew and Greek (Gal. 3:27-29; Eph. 2:11-16).

Abraham the Chaldean was not a Jew. Elijah the Tishbite was not a Jew. In any era, the only thing that matters to God is faith! The Israel of God is one covenantal people throughout the ages who have come to God by faith (Heb. 11), regardless of nationality. We are now favored to live in the extremities of that singular covenantal purpose (1 Cor. 10:11). The key issue is identity, the nature of the seed. The seed is not determined by nationality, race, gender, or culture—the seed of Abraham has always been spiritual!

Rom. 11:23, NIV

And if they do not persist in unbelief, they will be grafted in, for God is able to graft them in again.

The truths of Romans 11 are unlocked by the understanding that the "olive tree" is the tree of faith, our new nature in Christ. The "olive tree which is wild by nature" is the tree of unbelief, the untamed, Adamic nature (Rom. 11:17,24; Eph. 2:1-3; 4:22-24).

The glorious, anticipated outpouring of the Spirit upon national Israel is taking place in the context of the global outpouring of the Spirit upon "all flesh" (Joel 2:28-32)—Israeli flesh, African flesh, Russian flesh, Chinese flesh, and even American flesh! That they will be grafted in "again" reveals that they (and all men) were grafted in to begin with (Rom. 11:23)! The ongoing Messianic family, the Body of Christ, is comprised of covenantal men and women from every nation and era.

Rom. 9:33, KJV

...Behold, I lay in Sion a stumblingstone and rock of offence: and whosoever believeth on Him shall not be ashamed.

I love the natural descendants of Abraham enough to tell them the truth—salvation is by Jesus Christ or not at all. Men who are offended by these truths are offended by His cross (Gal. 5:11). When the Jews are grafted in again, it will be by the blood of Christ, not by the blood of bulls and goats which could never take away sin (Heb. 9:13-14; 10:4). That is why God is raising up key ministries with a special burden for the Jewish people (just as He is mandating others to sow in other parts of His glorious end-time harvest).

Acts 10:34-35, NIV

Then Peter began to speak: "I now realize how true it is that God does not show favoritism

but accepts men from every nation who fear Him and do what is right."

The Law, not the Church, was parenthetical, added because of the transgression (Gal.3:19). The Church is not an afterthought in the back of God's mind, but is His eternal purpose and program. God's chosen people are Christians, whom the New Testament doctrinal epistles designate to be:

1. Jews.

Rom. 2:28-29, NIV

A man is not a Jew if he is only one outwardly, nor is circumcision merely outward and physical.

No, a man is a Jew if he is one inwardly; and circumcision is circumcision of the heart, by the Spirit, not by the written code. Such a man's praise is not from men, but from God.

2. The children of the promise who are counted for the seed (Rom. 9:6-8).

Rom. 9:8, NIV

In other words, it is not the natural children who are God's children, but it is the children of the promise who are regarded as Abraham's offspring.

3. The chosen people (generation) (1 Pet. 2:1-10).

1 Pet. 2:9-10, NIV

But you are a chosen people, a royal priesthood, a holy nation...

...now you are the people of God....

4. The holy nation (Mt. 3:7-10; 21:42-43; 1 Pet. 2:9-10).

Mt. 21:43, KJV

Therefore say I unto you, The kingdom of God shall be taken from you, and given to a nation bringing forth the fruits thereof.

5. The circumcision.

Phil. 3:3, KJV

For we are the circumcision, which worship God in the spirit, and rejoice in Christ Jesus, and have no confidence in the flesh.

6. The new (heavenly) Jerusalem (see Jn. 4:19-24; Gal. 4:21-31; Heb. 12:22-24; Rev. 21:1-11).

Heb. 12:22-23, KJV

But ye are come unto mount Sion, and unto the city of the living God, the heavenly Jerusalem, and to an innumerable company of angels,

To the general assembly and church of the firstborn....

7. The Israel of God.

Gal. 6:16, KJV

And as many as walk according to this rule, peace be on them, and mercy, and upon the Israel of God.

Furthermore, Paul's allegory within Galatians 4:21-31 clearly differentiates between the earthly and heavenly Jerusalems, which symbolize two covenants. Focusing on a natural city, temple, and people "gendereth to bondage" (Gal. 4:24) or "bears children destined for slavery" (WEY). The natural mind cannot understand the things of the Spirit of God (1 Cor. 2:9-16). As noted above, the heavenly Jerusalem, the city of the living God, is the New Testament Zion—the Church, the Bride of Christ.

Rev. 21:9-10, KJV

> ...*Come hither, I will show thee the bride, the Lamb's wife.*
>
> *And he carried me away in the spirit to a great and high mountain, and showed me that great city, the holy Jerusalem, descending out of heaven from God.*

Everything said about Jesus Christ with regard to His being the Seed of Abraham can be applied to the Church (Rom. 4:13-16). He is the true Vine and we are the branches (Jn. 15:1-5), the seed that prolongs His days (Is. 53:10; Acts 1:1). We are His offspring, His generation, conformed to His image and likeness. The apostle John succinctly summed up these truths:

1 Jn. 4:17, KJV

> *Herein is our love made perfect, that we may have boldness in the day of judgment: because **as He is**, so are we in this world.*

An Israelite Indeed

The word *Hebrew* is a man-given term, and it refers to one who is a descendant of Eber (Gen. 10:21-25; 14:13; Phil. 3:5). The word *Jew* is a man-given term, and it pertains to one who is a descendant of Judah (see Gen. 29:35; Esth. 2:5; Jn. 4:9; Acts 22:3). But the word *Israel* is a God-given word, and relates to any person in any age who has met God face-to-face, overcoming himself by experiencing a change of name or nature—an Israelite indeed (Jn. 1:47).

Gen. 32:28, KJV

And he said, Thy name shall be called no more Jacob, but Israel: for as a prince hast thou power with God and with men, and hast prevailed.

Rom. 9:6, AMP

...For it is not everybody who is a descendant of Jacob (Israel) who belongs to [the true] Israel.

The first mention of the term "Israel" is found in Genesis 32:24-32. What happened that night to Jacob takes place in the life of every man who encounters the living God. The patriarch went through the time of his "trouble" the night he met God one-on-one (Jer. 30:7).

The pattern is clear. Jacob was "left alone" (Gen. 32:24). God will let a man believe anything to get him into the birthing position. Jacob had run from God and Esau for 20 years, but finally both caught up with the schemer. No crowds. No noise. No Mom. No Dad. No pastor. Just the man and his God, face-to-face, confessing his real name, or nature. God is going to trouble us until the "breaking." The Daystar will arise out of the night seasons to reveal the Israel or Christ, nature (Col. 1:27; 2 Pet. 1:19). In Genesis 32:25, God "touched," or "smote, struck violently," Jacob's thigh (2 Chron. 26:20; Job 1:19; Is. 53:4).

Gen. 32:27-28, AMP

[The Man] asked him, What is your name? And [in shock of realization, whispering] he said, Jacob [supplanter, schemer, trickster, swindler]!

And He said, Your name shall be called no more Jacob [supplanter], but Israel [contender with God]; for you have contended and have power with God and with men and have prevailed.

The old man, the Jacob nature, must be smitten by the Lord. God wants each of us to be overcomers, to prevail, to endure. The divine nature (2 Pet. 3:4) is displayed when God strikes our thigh—the place of human strength, man's ability to reproduce or create. He must increase; we must shrink or decrease (Gen. 32:32; Jn. 3:30).

Have you met God? Has He touched you? True Israelites are betrayed by their walk (Gen. 32:31). There is a familiar limp in the life and ministry touched by the Lord. Made patient through tribulation, we are not so quick on the trigger. The sun has arisen upon us as we walk in the light of His countenance. It is better to go into the Kingdom maimed than not to go in at all (Mt. 18:8). He must cripple our desires. An Israelite indeed has experienced this change of heart, having been delivered from hypocrisy and brought into the reality of the overcoming life. The Lord wants us to have power with God and men; He wants us to prevail.

Rev. 3:21, KJV

To him that overcometh will I grant to sit with Me in My throne....

No Longer Gentiles

The second chapter of Ephesians is a panorama of redemption's plan, beginning with man as a sinner (Gen. 3) and ending with man as the habitation of God through the Spirit (Rev. 21). Ephesians 2:11-12 particularly describe unregenerate, untamed, unsaved man.

Eph. 2:11-12, KJV

Wherefore remember, that ye being in time past Gentiles in the flesh, who are called Uncircumcision by that which is called the Circumcision in the flesh made by hands;

That at that time ye were without Christ, being aliens from the commonwealth of Israel, and strangers from the covenants of promise, having no hope, and without God in the world.

Popular eschatology (based primarily on Scofield's distinction between national Israel and the Church) leaves us in the same predicament. According to that view, Christians are still called "gentiles" and the "uncircumcision." Practically speaking, we are still without Christ, because we are told that the Holy Ghost anointing is not for us today, having ceased with the 12 apostles and the Book of Acts. Therefore we remain alienated from the wealth we have in common with Abraham, Isaac, and Israel, and strangers to the blessings and benefits of the Abrahamic and Davidic covenants.

To compensate, men have replaced the real hope of First John 3:1-3 with a false one. These teachings leave us without God in the world. The distant, external God of the old order is no better than the impersonal God of deistic philosophy who created this universe and wound it up like a clock, only to walk away to watch it run by natural law.

But the Emmanuel principle (Mt. 1:23) reveals the Church to be the ongoing incarnation of the living Word—He *is* come in the flesh of His Body. To deny that is to oppose the anointing, to offer some humanistic substitute for the truth (1 Jn. 4:1-3). We are not strangers and pilgrims just passing through. There is a generation of overcomers who have come to stay.

Moreover, the Greek word for "gentiles" in Ephesians 2:11 is *ethnos* (Strong's #1484). It means "a race (as of the same habit), a tribe; especially a foreign one (usually by implication, pagan)." *Vine's* adds that *ethnos* means "heathen; a multitude of people of the same nature or genus; a nation, people." Compare the English words *heathen* and *ethnic*. Surprisingly, *ethnos* is used in the King James Version to speak of the Jewish nation (Lk. 7:5; 23:2; Jn. 11:48-52)! It is translated in the King James Version a total of 164 times as:

1. "Gentiles" (93 times, mostly in the Book of Acts and Romans).

2. "Nation" (64 times, mostly in the Book of Acts and Revelation).

3. "Heathen" (5 times, in Acts 4:25; 2 Cor. 11:26; Gal. 1:16; 2:9; 3:8).

4. "People" (2 times, in Acts 8:9; Rom. 10:19).

Jesus is the Seed of Abraham. Abraham is our brother in Christ! As stated, the Law was temporary until the coming of the promised seed—Jesus and His Church, made up of Jew and Greek (Gal. 3:16-19,27-29). The New

Testament Church is God's chosen people. We are not second-class citizens, and there is no plan "B." We do not have to be evacuated from the planet or from history so that God can renew His program with the natural Jews.

The Old Testament prophets repeatedly warned God's people about idolatry, that He would root them out of the land (1 Kings 14:15). With the coming of John the Baptist and Jesus (Mt. 3:7-10), Jehovah laid the "axe" of truth to the root of Israel's tree, and planted a new Vine in the earth—His Son! The branches of that planting are men and women from "every nation" (Acts 10:34-35). God is no respecter of persons!

Men have tried to sew up the veil that He rent, but the middle wall of partition has been abolished (Eph. 2:13-18). Now that Jesus has come, there is neither Jew nor Greek (Gal. 3:28). There are no national distinctions, no physical advantages (or disadvantages) in Him.

Phil. 3:3, AMP

> *For we [Christians] are the true circumcision, who worship God in spirit and by the Spirit of God, and exult and glory and pride ourselves in Jesus Christ, and put no confidence or dependence [on what we are] in the flesh and on outward privileges and physical advantages and external appearances.*

The natural Jew has no privilege over me, and I have no advantage over him; we *both* must be born again! The Body of Christ is made up of men from every race and nation. Child of God, the New Testament spiritual Jew is you! This revelation of our true Biblical identity brings many New Covenant blessings, including the restitution of fellowship, promises, and authority.

We are in fellowship with the saints of the ages (Jn. 4:38; Heb. 11:39-40). We are to complete the Israel of God, carrying the bones of Joseph, the hopes and dreams of previous generations (Gen. 50:1-13; Ezek. 37:1-14).

We cannot claim our promised inheritance until we know who we are in Christ (2 Pet. 3:1-4). We must arise and possess the land (the earth), which has been previously relegated to another time (the future) and people (the natural Jews).

With the appropriation of the promises comes a new authority and boldness, a new anointing. We are no longer robbed by philosophy and vain deceit (Col. 2:8).

The Principle of Inheritance

To know who we are in Christ is to know what we have in Christ. The biblical principle of inheritance is revealed throughout both testaments.

The Hebrew word for "inheritance" is *nachalah* (Strong's #5159). It means "something inherited, (abstractly) occupancy, or (concretely) an heirloom; generally an estate, patrimony or portion." Its primitive root means "to inherit; causatively, to bequeath, or (generally) distribute, instate." This word is used most often in the Old Testament books of Numbers, Deuteronomy, Joshua, Psalms, Jeremiah, and Ezekiel.

The Greek word for "inheritance" is *kleronomia* (Strong's #2817), and means "heirship; a patrimony or possession." The inheritance is partitioned, apportioned, and distributed among the heirs. *Vine's* adds that the verb *kleronomeo* means "to receive by lot; to possess one-self of, to receive as one's own, to obtain." *Kleronomia* comes from two Greek words: *kleros*, meaning "to assign a privilege (this is probably taken from *klao*, which means 'to break [bread]')," and *nomos*, meaning "to parcel out; law." Compare *nomos* with the English word *name*.

The inheritance of the believer is not a mansion or golden streets. God has taken His name—all that He is, has, and does—and fulfilled it in His Son, the Heir of all things. Jesus, the Bread of life, has broken and shared His glorious name and nature with every believer.

In the New Testament, *inheritance* is mentioned in Matthew 21:38, Mark 12:7, Luke 12:13; 20:14, Acts 7:5; 20:32; 26:18, Galatians 3:18, Ephesians 1:11, 14, 18; 5:5, Colossians 1:12; 3:24, Hebrews 1:4; 9:15; 11:8, and First Peter 1:4.

For further consideration, the word "inherit" or "inherited" is found in Matthew 5:5; 19:29; 25:34, Mark 10:17, Luke 10:25; 18:18, First Corinthians 6:9-10; 15:50, Galatians 5:21, Hebrews 6:12; 12:17, First Peter 3:9, and Revelation 21:7.

The Greek word for "name" is *onoma*. We thereby perceive that the principle of inheritance has to do with the apportionment of the *name* of God. This is essential to Paul's teaching concerning our adoption or placement as full-grown sons. The son (especially the firstborn) received the father's inheritance, the birthright and blessing. In the Old Testament, God placed His *name* upon or in His sanctuary. In Revelation 14:1-5, we see a firstfruits company unto God and the Lamb who have the *name* of God written *in* their foreheads—the full mind of Christ.

The devil has no legal right to this planet—the earth is the Lord's. Jesus alone has obtained the covenantal right to all things. He *has* all things. He *is* all things. To possess Him is to possess all things (1 Cor. 3:21; Eph. 1:3; 2 Pet. 1:3-4).

Deut. 10:9, KJV

> *Wherefore Levi hath no part nor inheritance with his brethren; the Lord is his inheritance, according as the Lord thy God promised him.*

The Old Testament priesthood had no earthly inheritance, as the Lord Himself was their portion (see Num. 18:20; Deut. 14:27; Josh. 13:14; Ezek. 44:28). To inherit the Lord is to inherit life, to come into a living union with all that He is and all that He has. He is in us and we are in Him (Jn. 17). This is the crux of the Song of Songs, written for the Holy of holies (Song 7:10).

This glorious inheritance is in the saints (Eph. 1:18). We have been made worthy and fit to partake of this glorious estate (Col. 1:9-13). Our covenantal inheritance is in light, the Word of God (Ps. 119:105; Col. 1:12-13); it is in the heavenlies—the realm of spirit (Eph. 1:3,14; 2:1-6; 6:10-12). The divine endowment is His nature (life) made available through the promises (2 Pet. 1:3-4; 1 Jn. 4:17).

Our inheritance is being revealed through the fivefold ministry, especially the apostles and prophets (see Eph. 2:20; 3:1-5; 4:8-16; 2 Pet. 1:12). The Pentecostal experience is the key, the door into this entitlement. The Holy Ghost Baptism is the *earnest* (pledge, foretaste, down payment, guarantee) of our full possession (which includes the redemption of our bodies). The earnest is of the same substance and nature as the fullness (see Num. 13:20; Rom. 8:14-25; 2 Cor. 1:22; Eph. 1:13-14). Finally, this inheritance is to be revealed in the last time (1 Pet. 1:3-5).

Rev. 21:7, KJV

He that overcometh shall inherit all things; and I will be his God, and he shall be My son.

What About My Mansion?

Jn. 14:2, KJV

In My Father's house are many mansions: if it were not so, I would have told you. I go to prepare a place for you.

Jesus' words, "I go to prepare a place for you," were not spoken at His Ascension. He wasn't on His way to Heaven. The Lamb of God was on His way to Calvary!

Few other verses of Scripture have gendered more sermons or songs than this one. But the subject of John 14 is not Heaven. Heaven is real, but it is not mentioned once in that chapter. However, the *Father* is mentioned about 20 times. The word for "mansions" is only found one other place in the whole Bible, where it is translated as "abode."

Jn. 14:23, KJV

Jesus answered and said unto him, If a man love Me, he will keep My words: and My Father will love him, and We will come unto him, and make Our abode with him.

The Greek word for "mansions" and "abode" is *mone* (Strong's #3438). It means "a staying, residence (the act or the place)." It is akin to the primary verb *meno* (Strong's #3306), which means "to stay (in a given place, state, relation or expectancy)." *Vine's* compares it with the English words *manor* or *manse* and notes that there is nothing in the word to indicate separate compartments in Heaven.

First of all, Jesus was the house that the Father lived in—all the fullness of the Godhead in a body (Col. 1:19; 2:9). In Him, the "Father's house," there is a place for each of us as members of His Body in particular.

Second, the Church is the house of the Father (Heb. 3:5-6). The "mansion," or dwelling-place, is for the Lord, not man (1 Chron. 29:1). Beloved, we *are* His mansion. Our inheritance is not a mansion, or pearly gates, or golden streets. The inheritance of the believer is incorruptible (1 Pet. 1:4). Gold is corruptible and perishes (1 Pet. 1:7,18). How can that which is corruptible have anything to do with our incorruptible inheritance?

So what did Jesus actually inherit?

Rom. 15:8, KJV

> *Now I say that Jesus Christ was a minister of the circumcision for the truth of God, to confirm the promises made unto the fathers.*

The word for "confirm" speaks of that which is "stable"— firm, of force, steadfast, sure. Its root is *basis*, and it means "a pace; the foot." Jesus is the Seed of Abraham. He owns the land, the earth. He is the one "whose right it is" (Ezek. 21:27). He confirmed, or secured, the promises made to the fathers. In the program of the ages, Jesus is the basis and foundation of every covenantal purpose. All of the covenants consummate in Him who is the Heir and Sum of all things (Heb. 1:2; 8:1). Just as Joshua caused others to inherit, Jesus our Redeemer has shared His wealth with His Bride (Ruth 2:1; Phil. 4:19; 1 Pet. 3:7).

We discover the promises by asking, "Who are the fathers?"

Acts 3:13, KJV

The God of Abraham, and of Isaac, and of Jacob, the God of our fathers, hath glorified His Son Jesus; whom ye delivered up, and denied Him in the presence of Pilate, when he was determined to let Him go.

Jesus secured the promises made to the fathers—Abraham, Isaac, and Jacob. Concerning Abraham, study Genesis 12:1-3; 13:14-17; 15:1-7; 17:1-18; and 22:15-18. The initial passage lists the promises made to Abraham and His seed—Jesus and the Church:

1. I will make of thee a great nation.

2. I will bless thee.

3. I will make thy name great.

4. Thou shalt be a blessing.

5. I will bless them that bless thee.

6. I will curse them that curse thee.

7. In thee shall all the families of the earth be blessed.

Concerning the seventh promise, the Abrahamic Covenant is to affect the whole world (Rom. 4:13; Gal. 3:1-9).

Abraham's seed was to be innumerable, like dust, sand, and stars (Gen. 13:16; 22:17).

Regarding the promises made to the other two fathers, Isaac and Jacob, consider Genesis 26:1-5 and 35:9-12. The fathers did not receive the promise (see Acts 7:1-5; Rom. 4:13; Heb. 11:8-9,13,39-40). But Jesus did! A new nation in Him now arises to possess the land, to appropriate the spoils of His eternal victory (Mt. 12:29; Lk. 11:22). But there are specific requirements for all those who so walk by faith.

The Seven Separations of Abraham

Jesus and the Church are the Seed of Abraham. The most important Scriptures concerning the famous patriarch are found in Joshua 24:3, Nehemiah 9:7-8, Isaiah 51:2, Acts 7:1-8, Romans 4:1-25, and Hebrews 6:12-15; 11:8-17. The father and pattern of all those who live by faith was the friend of God (2 Chron. 20:7; Is. 41:8; Jas. 2:23).

This famous progenitor made *seven* critical decisions. Following the seventh and final separation, God revealed Himself to Abraham as *Jehovah-Jireh*, the God who sees and provides (Gen. 22:14). There is an unlimited provision (in Christ) awaiting those who follow the man whose trek was marked by this underlying principle: *Separation brings revelation, which leads to worship.* When Abraham made a separation, Jehovah would speak to him, prompting the prophet to build an altar and worship. The father of all those who walk by faith separated himself from:

1. *Country* (Gen. 12:1). The first separation deals with our immediate locale and surroundings. A country has

boundary lines or limitations, the familiar and comfortable things that restrict our walk in God. Ur of the Chaldees was a land governed by moon-worship (picturing the powers of darkness). Teachings and traditions that restrict, allowing us to go just so far (but no further), must be left in the land of Babylon. The heart that makes this choice says to God, "I put no limits on You."

2. *Kindred* (Gen. 12:1). Such radical discipleship will immediately impact one's natural and spiritual family. Our father's house can be a strong tie. The land of our nativity—the church, system, or doctrine under which we were born—may keep us from fully following God (Ruth 2:11; Ps. 45:10; Heb. 11:6). Sincerely misinformed family members expect the child of faith to stay in Ur of the Chaldees. These first two separations determine that nothing, and no one, will keep us from God's perfect will.

3. *Egypt* (Gen. 13:1). God interceded for a liar (Gen. 12:12-20). We thankfully leave Egypt—the world and all that is in it (1 Jn. 2:15-17); it is the place of servitude and bondage—the lust of the flesh, the lust of the eyes, and the pride of life. We refuse to use the anointing for our own gain, to make money with the gifts of God, or to become a hot commodity, such as somebody's favorite preacher.

4. *Lot* (Gen. 13:11). Lot typifies the carnal ones who want to walk with us; those who lust after God's presents, but not His presence. Abraham's nephew fancied the blessing without the procedure—covenant with God on his own terms. This one is along for the ride, desiring the benefits without the responsibility, the blessing without the birthright. He is a monkey on your back, Abraham.

5. *A Desire to Get Wealth* (Gen. 14:21-24). The fifth separation is most critical in our walk—the love of money (1 Tim. 6:10). The man of faith cannot be bought; he is under exclusive covenantal contract to the Lord. As the bondslave of Christ, he refuses to become the possession of another, settling for nothing less than the Father's full provision.

6. *Ishmael* (Gen. 17:18; 21:9-14). Ishmael, a product of the works of the flesh, reveals the principle of the mark of the beast. He was a product of Sarah's *head* and Abraham's *loins*—human wisdom and strength, the forehead and right hand. The last thing Abraham needed was a good idea, a man-made attempt to bring forth the promise of God. This is the sixth separation, and six is the number of *man*—the carnal mind, untamed and wild.

7. *Isaac* (Gen. 22:1-14). This is the ultimate test, the final separation. Afterward, Jehovah put no further requirements upon Abraham. The promise had become a reality. Abraham had held it in his arms and watched it grow. Now the divine demand is for that promise, which he loves. Do we love the gift or the giver, the promise of God or the God of the promise? This is worship in the purest sense. Finally, Jehovah could say to Abraham, "Now the promise is not yours or Mine...he is ours!"

The Lord Jesus walked these things out in perfect, covenantal obedience, ever delighting to do the will of the Father. The Abrahamic Seed to whom the promise was made is the one "whose right it is." But the Messiah is not only the Seed of Abraham. Jesus is also the greatest Son of David!

Chapter Five

Jesus Is the Seed of David

"...Jesus Christ, the son of David...."

Matthew 1:1

Covenantally, the earth is the Lord's. In the previous chapter, we learned that Jesus Christ, the Heir of all things, is the Seed of Abraham. The one "whose right it is" holds the title deed to this planet. But few have realized that King Jesus is also the Seed of David!

The rightful Seed of Abraham has obtained legal right and ownership of the land. Love constrains Him to share His wealth. Jesus came to bring many sons unto the same glory (Heb. 2:6-13). All born-again Christians are the seed of Abraham. The Body of Christ, the corporate heir of God, is lord of all, or owner of everything (Gal. 3:29; 4:1-2).

So what? Someone must arise and walk in what Jesus died for!

The creation is groaning for real deliverance, not some deeper teaching or higher concept. The invisible must be made visible. Heaven must come to earth. The gospel of the Kingdom must be translated into a life style that all men can read and understand. In days of inflation, talk is still cheap. We must be what we say we are and have, not shrink back in fear (Lk. 9:62; Heb. 10:38-39).

It is not enough to know that Jesus is the Seed of Abraham, or to know about our rightful spiritual estate. We must also know that we have a legal right to it, and we must experience the authority to go ahead and possess our possessions. We must know that Jesus Christ is also the Seed of David!

It's All Right

The land is His...the land is ours. The earth is His...the earth is ours. He is ours, and we are His.

Once a man begins to grasp the reality of His spiritual entitlement, he is bombarded by the fiery darts, or "bullets" in modern terms, of the accuser (Eph. 6:16; Rev. 12:9-11). Satan has three favorite lies. These bullets are all blanks, evil suggestions, lying vanities. The serpent whispers:

"You cannot have these promises (the inheritance)."

"If you can have these promises, you cannot have them now."

"If you can have these promises now, they won't last."

But King Jesus is the Seed of David, the one "whose right it is." He has been given the *throne*, the legal jurisdiction to rule the land (the earth).

Put into action what you now know. The duality and vacillating of His offspring must give way to Bible-based faith and power (Jas. 1:5-8). Wavering must give way to decisiveness—access with boldness. Still we ask and think:

"Is it all right to preach this?"
"Is it all right to lay hands on that person?"
"Is it all right to execute righteous judgment?"

To you who are being nudged by the Holy Ghost to do what you've never done before...to you who are being prompted by the Lord to say what you've never said before...To you I say:

"It's all right. Go ahead!"

It's all right because He's all righteous (1 Cor. 1:30; 2 Cor. 5:21). Jesus' uprightness gives every Christian the privilege to move forward, to push on. The Seed of David is the King of righteousness (Heb. 7:2). Because of His finished work, we have the legal prerogative to appropriate the Abrahamic covenant. John the revelator summed it up this way:

Rev. 12:11, NIV

They overcame him by the blood of the Lamb and by the word of their testimony; they did not love their lives so much as to shrink from death.

Jesus' blood has made us partakers of His righteousness. We have been forgiven and now have a legal right to speak forth in the name of the Lord. The testimony of

Jesus is the spirit of prophecy (Rev. 19:10). Prophecy is anointed utterance. We have been given the right to declare the Word of the Lord to our generation. We speak boldly, not loving our "lives," or "souls." We no longer hesitate because of what men will think or say, including ourselves. Fearlessly, boldly, unashamedly, we are becoming the Word made flesh.

Ps. 107:2, KJV

> *Let the redeemed of the Lord say so....*

Prov. 28:1, KJV

> *...the righteous are bold as a lion.*

The Davidic Covenant

Jesus Christ is the royal Seed according to the Davidic Covenant of Second Samuel 7 and First Chronicles 17.

David's desire to build a house for God furnished the revelation through the prophet Nathan that the Lord would indeed build David a house! David worshiped in humility and awe. Having expressed his unworthiness of all the mercies of God, and his high regard for the greatness and supremacy of God, he prayed with confidence in the veracity and promises of God. This great covenant of *Kingship* centers in and focuses upon the Lord Jesus Christ and provides:

1. *A house*—a posterity, family (Mt. 1:1,16).

2. *A throne*—a royal position and authority (Rev. 3:21).

3. *A kingdom*—a sphere of rule (Rom. 14:17; Eph. 1:20-23).

4. *Forever*—without cessation (Is. 9:6-7; Lk. 1:31-33).

Other Old Testament Scriptures to consider when studying the Davidic Covenant are First Kings 2:4, First Chronicles 22:8-10, Second Chronicles 7:17-18, Psalms 89 and 132, Isaiah 11:1-10, Jeremiah 23:5-6; 33:20-21, Amos 9:11-12, and Zechariah 3:8-9; 6:12-13; 9:10; 12:8; 13:1.

It is also noteworthy that David was anointed three times (Prov. 22:20) in his covenantal pursuit of God:

1. As exalted son (1 Sam. 16:13).

2. As king over Judah (2 Sam. 2:4).

3. As head over all things (2 Sam. 5:3).

Jehovah is a covenant-making and covenant-keeping God. A divine covenant is a sovereign disposition of God whereby He establishes an unconditional or declarative compact with man, obligating Himself, in grace, by the unshackled formula, "*I will*," to bring to pass of Himself definite blessings for the covenanted ones; or, a proposal of God, wherein He promises, in a conditional or mutual contract with man, by the contingent formula, "*If ye will*," to grant special blessings to man, provided he fulfills perfectly certain conditions, and to execute definite correction in case of man's failure.

The Old Testament word for "covenant" is *beriyth*, and means "to cut." The Lord Jesus was cut on Calvary to provide the New Covenant. The Greek word for "covenant" is *diatheke*. It has to do with the imposition of the will of a superior Being upon that of an inferior; that is, of God upon man. Man can accept or reject the divine compact, but he cannot alter the terms of the contract (Ps. 127:1).

The great covenants in effect prior to David's day were...

1. The Edenic covenant (Gen. 1).

2. The Adamic covenant (Gen. 3).

3. The Noahic covenant (Gen. 8–9).

4. The Abrahamic covenant (Gen. 12,15,17,22).

5. The Mosaic covenant (Ex. 19–24; Deut. 4–5).

6. The Palestinian covenant (Deut. 29–30).

The Davidic Covenant is the *seventh* and last covenant of the Old Testament, made to Israel's witness, leader, and commander (Is. 55:4). The ultimate fulfillment of the Davidic Covenant is found in Jesus Christ, David's greatest *Son*, and then the brethren who are conformed to His image (Rom. 8:14-29; Heb. 2:6-13). Jesus Christ is the one who established the New Covenant. He is the Head of the Church, which is the true spiritual Israel of God. The Davidic Covenant establishes Jesus Christ as the ultimate ruler of the earth and the universe, the King of kings and Lord of lords!

The Abrahamic Covenant gave Jesus the *land*, the earth. The David Covenant gives Him the *throne*, the right to rule the earth! The throne of the Davidic Covenant is the legal authority to rule in the name of the Lord Jesus Christ. The throne is not a chair or seat somewhere beyond the Milky Way or someplace in the Middle East. The Greek word transliterated "throne" is *thronos*, and it means "a place or seat of authority"—it is the right to rule. To rule from His throne is to speak in the authority of Jesus' name!

The Abrahamic Covenant, the Davidic Covenant, and the New Covenant (New Testament) are interrelated; each one is an extension of the other. God confirmed the New Covenant with an oath (Ps. 110:4; Heb. 7:20-28). Thus the Davidic Covenant is essentially a Kingdom covenant based upon the intertheistic pact—the relationship between the Father and the Son!

The house of the heavenly David is the Church, made up of Jew and Greek (Eph. 2:11-12; Heb. 3:5-6). His Kingdom is heavenly and spiritual (Jn. 18:36). Jesus now sits at the Father's right hand, and He will remain there until His enemies become His footstool (Heb. 10:12-13). The sure mercies of David (Is. 55:3; Acts 13:34) will consummate with the resurrection of the dead.

Jesus Christ is also the key of David (Is. 22:20-25; Rev. 3:7), the one who opens and shuts every door, every situation. The Anointed one, the Messiah, is the Horn of David (see Ps. 18:2; 89:20,24; 92:10; 132:17; Lk. 1:69) who has been anointed with the Spirit without measure (Jn. 3:34)—the "seven spirits of God" (the fullness of the Spirit) mentioned in Revelation 1:4; 3:1; 4:5; 5:6. Revelation 5:6 reveals Jesus to have "seven horns,"— representing all power and authority (Mt. 28:18-20). The Church, His Body, is the Tabernacle of David, a people for His name (see 1 Chron. 16:1; 17:1; Is. 16:5; Amos 9:11-12; Acts 15:13-18).

The Davidic covenant was fulfilled in the Lord Jesus Christ and His Church; it was fully realized in the New Covenant, the New Testament, in His blood.

An Exegesis of the Davidic Covenant

King David had been given rest from all his enemies (2 Sam. 7:1; 8–10; 1 Chron. 18–19). The Ark of God remained within or under curtains (2 Sam. 7:2). Second Samuel 7:5 is a statement in First Chronicles 17:4. It literally reads, "Thou shalt not be *he* who shall build Me a house." David is called Jehovah's servant 11 times in Second Samuel 7:5, 8, 20, 21, 25-29. Until this time God had walked in a tent or tabernacle (see 2 Sam. 7:6; 1 Chron. 17:5; Ps. 84:7; Rom. 1:17; 2 Cor. 3:18).

2 Sam. 7:8-9, KJV

> *Now therefore so shalt thou say unto My servant David, Thus saith the Lord of hosts, I took thee from the sheepcote, from following the sheep, to be ruler over my people, over Israel:*
>
> *And I was with thee whithersoever thou wentest, and have cut off all thine enemies out of thy sight, and have made thee a great name, like unto the name of the great men that are in the earth.*

David was chosen, appointed, accompanied, preserved, promoted, and honored by God. He was taken from the sheepcote to become ruler of Israel, their commander, chief, captain, governor, and prince (see 1 Sam. 25:30; 2 Sam. 6:21; 1 Kings 1:35; Mt. 2:6). God made David's name great and established it forever through his anointed Seed (Acts 4:12; Phil. 2:9-11).

2 Sam. 7:10, KJV

> *Moreover I will appoint a place for My people Israel, and will plant them, that they may dwell in a place of*

their own, and move no more; neither shall the children of wickedness afflict them any more, as beforetime.

2 Sam. 7:10, NIV

And I will provide a place for My people Israel and will plant them so that they can have a home of their own and no longer be disturbed. Wicked people will not oppress them anymore, as they did at the beginning.

This important verse reveals five major features of the Davidic covenant, consummated in the New Testament:

"I will appoint a place for My people...": This is the *throne* of God, the sphere of dominion and authority that centers in the name of Jesus Christ (see Ex. 33:21; Jn. 14:1-3; 17:20-24; Heb. 1:2; Rev. 3:21).

"...and will plant them...": This word means "to set or establish; drive a nail" (Ps. 1; Jn. 15:1-5). We are rooted in Him and seated in the heavenlies with Him (Eph. 2:6). Buried with Him in baptism, we have died, and our lives are hid with Christ in God (Rom. 6:5-6; Col. 2:11-12; 3:1-3).

"...that they may dwell in a place of their own...": We are members in particular of His Body (1 Cor. 12:12-27; Rom. 12:1-8; 1 Pet. 4:10-11). Each of us, as a joint of supply, shares the authority of His throne, His name (Eph. 4:16).

"...and move no more...": The old realm of double-mindedness is swallowed up in the singleness and simplicity found in Christ (see Mt. 6:22-24; 2 Cor. 11:2-3; Jas. 1:6-8; Heb. 12:1-2). The overcoming Christian who walks in the authority of the Davidic covenant is a pillar in the temple of God, steadfast, immovable (Rev. 3:12).

"...neither shall the children of wickedness afflict them any more, as beforetime...": Sin, sickness, poverty, and death must bow to the name of King Jesus (Is. 26:13-14; Gal. 3:13-14). The parallel passage in First Chronicles 17:9 says that the enemy will not "waste" or "wear out" the people of God any more.

2 Sam. 7:11-12, KJV

> *And as since the time that I commanded judges to be over My people Israel, and have caused thee to rest from all thine enemies. Also the Lord telleth thee that He will make thee an house.*
>
> *And when thy days be fulfilled, and thou shalt sleep with thy fathers, I will set up thy seed after thee, which shall proceed out of thy bowels, and I will establish his kingdom.*

David wanted to build God a house of devotion, but Jehovah declared that *He* would build David a house (Ps. 127:1; Mt. 16:18). First Chronicles 17:10 promises that God would subdue or humble all enemies (Ps. 110:1). Second Samuel 7:12 is a principal prophecy concerning David's Seed, the Messiah (see also Ps. 2; 72; 105; Mt. 1:1; Lk. 1:30-33).

Second Samuel 7:13-17 details the Davidic Covenant. The basis of the Messianic Kingdom would be the *Father-Son* principle established upon the resurrection of David's greatest Son. Note these principles:

"He shall build an house for My name..." (2 Sam. 7:13): This refers to Jesus, not Solomon. That name is *El-elyon*, the Most High God, Possessor of Heaven and earth (Gen. 14:22). The New Testament Church is that house (Mt. 16:18; Eph. 2:19-22; Heb. 3:1-6).

"...and I will establish the throne of his kingdom forever" (2 Sam. 27:13): This is the throne of the Son, the Lamb (see Is. 9:6-7; Lk. 1:30-33; Heb. 7:16; Rev. 3:21).

"I will be his Father, and he shall be My son" (2 Sam. 7:14): This is crucial to our understanding the Davidic covenant, which points to and focuses upon the sonship of Jesus and His brethren (Rom. 8:29; Heb. 2:10).

"If he commit iniquity..." (2 Sam. 7:14): This refers to Solomon, not Jesus; Jesus bore our iniquity (1 Kings 11:9-40; Is. 53; Heb. 7:26). However, it is interesting that some translators render the word "commit" as "bear."

"...I will chasten him with the rod of men, and with the stripes of the children of men" (2 Sam. 7:14): Every son, including the Firstborn, is to be trained and disciplined (Heb. 12:5-11). The Messiah literally bore the stripes of men as part of His suffering (Is. 53:5; 1 Pet. 2:24-25).

"But My mercy shall not depart away from him..." (2 Sam. 7:15): Jesus Christ *is* our propitiation or mercyseat (Rom. 3:25). In Him, the throne of judgment has become the throne of grace (Heb. 4:14-16).

Second Samuel 7:16 promises that the *house*, the *kingdom*, and the *throne* of David would be established *forever*. This is fulfilled in the Lord Jesus Christ. The parallel passage in First Chronicles 17:14 declares that David's Seed would be settled or stand forever. All this was by the vision of the Lord (2 Sam. 7:17; 1 Chron. 17:15).

Then David went into God's tabernacle and sat before the Lord (contrast 2 Sam. 7:1,18). The Messiah, who would come through the *nation* of Abraham, would now come through the *family* of the house of David. God assured David of a position, presence, protection, prominence, place, planting, peace, and prosperity. His was a unique relationship (father-son), kingdom (of Christ), and sequence (fulfilled in a Body of people).

There were several qualities in this sweet Psalmist of Israel, the man after God's own heart, which prompted the Lord to bring these covenantal results. A brief study of David's life reveal the principles of:

1. Decision (2 Sam. 2:1).

2. Government (2 Sam. 5:3).

3. Worship (2 Sam. 6:14).

4. Right motives (2 Sam. 6:21).

5. Humility (2 Sam. 7:18).

6. Desperation (2 Sam. 12:16).

7. Prophetic song (2 Sam. 22:1).

8. Sonship (2 Sam. 24:17).

For further consideration of the Davidic covenant and David's greatest Son, the Lord Jesus, consider these New Testament verses that speak of King David:

1. The Gospels (see Mt. 1:1,20; 9:27; 12:23; 15:22; 20:30-31; 21:9,15; 22:42-48; Mk. 2:25; 10:47-48; 11:10; 12:35-37; Lk. 1:27,32,69; 2:4, 11; 3:31; 6:3; 18:38-39; 20:42-44; Jn. 7:42).

2. The Book of Acts (see Acts 1:16; 2:25,29,34; 4:25; 7:45; 13:22,34; 15:16).

3. The Epistles (see Rom. 1:3; 4:6; 11:9; 2 Tim. 2:8; Heb. 4:7; 11:32).

4. The Book of Revelation (Rev. 3:7; 5:5; 22:16).

All Authority

Jesus is the Seed of Abraham and David. He owns the land and the throne. The earth is the Lord's. He alone has the right to rule it.

Our Captain is uttering His mighty voice before His army (Joel 2:1-11). He has not called us to evacuate the conflict or to escape our place in His redemptive plan. We must *activate* His dominion in the earth. The spiritual tribe of Judah, those who praise the Lord, have acknowledged the heavenly David (2 Sam. 2:4). Soon the entire holy nation will crown Him king (2 Sam. 5:3; 1 Pet. 2:9)!

Mt. 28:18-20, NIV

> *Then Jesus came to them and said, "All authority in heaven and on earth has been given to Me.*
>
> *Therefore go and make disciples of all nations, baptizing them in the name of the Father and of the Son and of the Holy Spirit,*
>
> *and teaching them to obey everything I have commanded you. And surely I am with you always, to the very end of the age."*

This treatise is most practical and especially evangelical, for the Great Commission is based upon the Davidic covenant! His jurisdiction is over all! Jesus' name has been exalted far above all things. There is no place in the universe that escapes the sphere of His rule (Ps. 139).

Why do we wait? Why do we hesitate? There is a time and season for all things (Eccl. 3:1-8), but the Day of the

Lord has dawned. For six days man has labored in the sweat of his own wisdom and strength (see Ex. 20:9; Is. 55:1-3; Mt. 11:28-30; 2 Pet. 3:8). The *seventh* day (sabbath) from Adam and the *third* day from Jesus has arrived (Hos. 6:1-3). It is time for King Jesus to manifest Himself in and through His sons.

Why do we procrastinate? Is it our improper response to the dealings of the Father as the Sauls of this age hound us day and night on the way to the throne? Every son must be disciplined and trained (Heb. 12:5-11). There is Adullam's dark cave, Michal's railings, and Shimei's cursings for each of us. The pressure of Samuel's oil is often weightier than the crown that shall fit over it. Could this be a result of self-pity, bitterness, or anger? But the Spirit of the Son of David lives within to encourage us (1 Sam. 30:6).

Then why do we delay? Is it because we have no control over the matters before us? Life was simple when we sang the song of the Lord to a few sheep. Now a nation beckons for a man to rule in righteousness. While waiting by the waters of En-gedi, we have visions of a permanent habitation of living stones. By the Spirit, we have seen one holy flock, one sheepfold, one Shepherd—even though our present companions are the owls and pelicans of the wilderness and the wild goats of the rocks.

You and I know why we hold back—we are *afraid* of being a failure (consider 2 Sam. 11–12 and Ps. 51). But our fear only betrays our selfishness and pride. A dead man has no apprehensions, no reputation to keep propped up with lame excuses. He has become a fool for Christ, a prisoner of the Lord, a slave to the will of God.

Great Is Thy Faithfulness

1 Thess. 5:24, NIV

The one who calls you is faithful and He will do it.

2 Tim. 2:13, KJV

If we believe not, yet He abideth faithful: He cannot deny Himself.

Jesus Christ is the Seed of David. He is the Surety and Guarantee of the New Covenant, the true and faithful Witness (Rev. 1:5). Psalm 89 is the coronation song of David and his Seed: Jesus and His Church. This Messianic psalm, the song of the Lord's oath, has as its theme the endless throne of David through Jesus Christ (Lk. 1:30-33). Its keynote is the *faithfulness* of God: the words "faithfulness" and "faithful" appear seven times (Ps. 89:1,2,5,8,24,33,37). Psalm 89 is related to Psalm 110, which contains Jehovah's oath or covenant with His Son Jesus concerning the perpetual throne of Melchisedec's priesthood (Heb. 7:16; 13:20).

In this poem and hymn of great beauty, the singer sets forth the praises of God (Ps. 89:1-37), telling of the covenant made with David. Then he surveys the present condition of the people, and so creates a contrast (Ps. 89:38-52). Yet all this is declared to be the work of Jehovah, the key phrase to this section being "Thou hast...."

The word "covenant" is found four times (Ps. 89:3,28, 34,39) and the word "throne" five times (Ps. 89:4,14,29, 36,44) in this song of the sure mercies of David, fulfilled in Jesus Christ, the King of the New Testament.

Ps. 89:1-4, KJV

I will sing of the mercies of the Lord for ever: with my mouth will I make known Thy faithfulness to all generations.

For I have said, Mercy shall be built up for ever: Thy faithfulness shalt Thou establish in the very heavens.

I have made a covenant with My chosen, I have sworn unto David My servant,

Thy seed will I establish for ever, and build up thy throne to all generations. Selah.

These prophetic verses are Messianic and Christological, telling of Jesus, the Seed of David. Compare Isaiah 42:1-5, Matthew 1:1, Ephesians 1:3; 2:6, and Revelation 3:21.

Ps. 89:19-23, KJV

Then thou spakest in vision to Thy holy one, and saidst, I have laid help upon one that is mighty; I have exalted one chosen out of the people.

I have found David My servant; with My holy oil have I anointed him:

With whom My hand shall be established: Mine arm also shall strengthen him.

The enemy shall not exact upon him; nor the son of wickedness afflict him.

And I will beat down his foes before his face, and plague them that hate him.

Jesus was the chosen of the Father, anointed with strength and power. Not even death, the last enemy, could defeat our King. See also Luke 4:18, Acts 10:38;

13:22-23, Ephesians 1:20-23, Second Timothy 1:10, and Hebrews 5:1-5; 10:12-13.

Ps. 89:24-29, KJV

But My faithfulness and My mercy shall be with him: and in My name shall his horn be exalted.

I will set his hand also in the sea, and his right hand in the rivers.

He shall cry unto Me, Thou art my father, my God, and the rock of my salvation.

Also I will make him My firstborn, higher than the kings of the earth.

My mercy will I keep for him for evermore, and My covenant shall stand fast with him.

His seed also will I make to endure for ever, and his throne as the days of heaven.

Jesus, the exalted Horn of David, introduced the Father to this planet. The Church, His seed, will prolong His days (Is. 53:10; Rev. 21:7-8). His "hand," the fivefold ministry, has been set in the earth (1 Cor. 12:28; Eph. 4:11). He is the Firstborn among many brethren (Rom. 8:29; Rev. 14:1-5). Compare Psalm 125:1-2, Galatians 4:1-7, Philippians 2:9-11, Hebrews 2:9; 5:7, and Revelation 5:6.

Ps. 89:35-37

Once have I sworn by My holiness that I will not lie unto David.

His seed shall endure for ever, and his throne as the sun before Me.

It shall be established for ever as the moon, and as a faithful witness in heaven. Selah.

David's Seed—Jesus and His Church—shall "endure," or "be," forever. The throne of God and the Lamb are as the "sun" (Ps. 19:4-5; Rev. 3:21). So rejoice in the *faithfulness* of God. He has sworn and will not repent. His purposes center in and rest upon Himself.

The Operation of David's Throne

Another great covenantal passage essential to understanding the Davidic covenant is Psalm 132, the revelation of the sweet psalmist's determination motivated by desire. It is the song of Messiah, David's Son, *enthroned* (compare Psalms 15; 24; 68). Psalm 132 was written to commemorate the day when the Ark of the Covenant was brought to Jerusalem and placed in David's tabernacle in Zion (2 Sam. 6; 1 Chron. 13–16). This prophetic song, the thirteenth song of degrees (Ps. 120–134), anticipates the glorious ascension and coronation of Jesus Christ as King of kings!

Ps. 132:11-14, KJV

The Lord hath sworn in truth unto David; He will not turn from it; Of the fruit of thy body will I set upon thy throne.

If thy children will keep My covenant and My testimony that I shall teach them, their children shall also sit upon thy throne for evermore.

For the Lord hath chosen Zion; He hath desired it for His habitation.

This is My rest for ever: here will I dwell; for I have desired it.

Zion is God's resting place. *Here,* in Zion—in Jesus and His brethren—God dwells in fullness (see Ps. 133; Eph. 4:13; Col. 1:19; 2:9). Compare John 16:13, Acts 5:30, Ephesians 2:19-22; 3:18-20, and Hebrews 2:6-13.

Psalm 132:15-18 then declares six things that happen once God has settled down into Zion. They constitute the governmental operations of David's throne that work through the one new Man of the New Testament. This prophetic river flows out from the throne to bless all the nations of the earth in the name of Jesus (Jn. 7:37-39; Rev. 22:1).

"I will abundantly bless her provision..." (Ps. 132:15): The priesthood after the order of Melchisedec is a blessing order (Heb. 7:1-6). This Zion company will walk in the name, or nature, of Jehovah-Jireh ("the Lord will see and provide"), ministering the resurrection life of the Holy Ghost (Jn. 10:10).

"...I will satisfy her poor with bread" (Ps. 132:15): The golden pot of manna (Heb. 9:4) is revealed in the "hidden manna" of Revelation 2:17. Those who have been partakers of the divine nature, the bread of life, have been broken to feed the nations. As in the days of Gideon, this "one bread" will destroy the works of the enemy (Judg. 7:13; Mk. 7:27; 1 Cor. 10:17).

"I will also clothe her priests with salvation: and her saints shall shout aloud for joy" (Ps. 132:16): Those who fully rule and reign with Him in Zion will have put on Christ. The power of His resurrection life and immortality is the consummation of the sure mercies of David revealed in Jesus Christ (Jn. 11:25; 1 Cor. 15:51-58).

"There will I make the horn of David to bud…" (Ps. 132:17): The horn is a symbol for power and authority. Jesus has been given all power; it will blossom and bring forth through His Church, the planting of the Lord (Mt. 28:18; Rev. 5:6). His resurrection will produce a joint-heir—the overcoming, glorious Church (Rev. 21:7).

"…I have *ordained* a lamp for Mine anointed" (Ps. 132:17): This Hebrew word means "to set in successive order, to appoint." This is the Man whose name is the Branch, anointed with the seven spirits of God—the fullness of the Spirit without measure (see Is. 4:1-6; 11:1-2; Jer. 23:5-6; Zech. 6:12-13; Jn. 3:34; 15:1-5; Rev. 1:4; 3:1; 4:5; 5:6).

"His enemies will I clothe with shame; but upon Himself shall His crown flourish" (Ps. 132:18): All enemies, even death, have been clothed with disgrace, put under the feet of the heavenly David. Jesus is the Victor, crowned with glory and honor; His crown will ever flourish or shine. This is the mitre and golden plate on the head of the high priest (Ex. 28:36-38)—the full mind of Christ and the name of the Father sealed in the forehead of those who overcome (see Ezek. 9:4; 1 Cor. 2:16; Phil. 2:5; Rev. 7:3; 14:1-5; 22:4).

All the promises of the Davidic covenant were made to Jesus Christ, David's true seed. These blessings are now offered to Jesus' family, the Church. Our Savior and King is the Son of Abraham and the Son of David. His is the *land* and the *throne*—the earth and the right to rule it. He now summons His people to share that responsibility.

Chapters Four and Five have highlighted the benefits of the Abrahamic and Davidic covenants. They are legally and permanently ours in Christ. The devil doesn't fit into this picture; the earth is the Lord's.

God cannot deny Himself. He remains faithful to His covenantal word. There are no excuses. Abraham gave us the promise. David gave us the right to appropriate and administer the promise. Jesus Christ is the Seed of Abraham and the Seed of David. To deny Him is to deny yourself.

What About the Lease?

Some teach that the devil has a 6,000-year lease on this planet given to him by Adam. The traditional thought is that once the lease expires, the Lord will return and catch away the Church, followed by a seven-year period known as the tribulation.

However, first of all, the earth is the Lord's. The devil has never had any kind of jurisdiction here. God ruled this planet through prophets until the Seed came to whom the promise was made. Now the earth belongs to Mr. and Mrs. Jesus Christ.

Second, if there were a lease that was running out, why should we leave?

The warfare is accomplished. The earth is the Lord's. But satan, our adversary even though subdued, has prolonged his influence in our inheritance. Although the dragon is defeated, he still has a mouth!

What is it that the dragon is saying? What is his underlying motivation and purpose? How has he covered his tracks?

Part Three

The Dragon Still
Has a Mouth

"...the flood which the dragon cast out of his mouth."
Revelation 12:16

Chapter Six

Eschatological Perspectives and Terminology

"...that ye all speak the same thing...."

First Corinthians 1:10

This message began by declaring Jesus Christ, the Messiah, to be the only one "whose right it is" (Ezek. 21:27).

Chapters Two and Three introduced an adjusted vision with regard to satan: The devil is not God's adversary—he is ours. Jesus defeated him. The warfare is accomplished (Is. 40:2)!

Chapters Four and Five further established that Adam's transgression did not turn the earth over to satan. God ruled this planet through prophets until *the* Prophet, the promised Seed, the Son of Abraham and David, came to receive all authority (Mt. 28:18; Heb. 1:1). A biblical overview of the Abrahamic and Davidic covenants established that the earth is the Lord's! It belongs to Mr. and Mrs. Jesus Christ. The strength of this Christological view is that the Old Testament is explained in the light of the New Testament, especially the Pauline Epistles.

Rev. 12:15-16, KJV

And the serpent cast out of his mouth water as a flood after the woman, that he might cause her to be carried away of the flood.

And the earth helped the woman, and the earth opened her mouth, and swallowed up the flood which the dragon cast out of his mouth.

To summarize, we have an adversary. Satan is defeated, but there is still a flood gushing from the dragon's mouth. To fully unmask his influential wiles, the remainder of this volume will re-evaluate popular eschatology, his favorite subject.

The section before us (for the sake of communication and clarity) will note familiar eschatological perspectives and vocabulary. Chapter Seven will take a fresh historical look at dispensationalism, tracing its roots to Darby, Scofield, and Larkin. Chapters Eight and Nine will investigate the Scriptures that are used to support their futurist view, and Chapter Ten will exegete its only real foundational clause—Daniel's prophecy of seventy weeks.

Jn. 10:10, KJV

The thief cometh not, but for to steal, and to kill, and to destroy....

The prophetic Church, the voice of the Lord, must be thoroughly equipped to rid the earth of the influence of satan. Notwithstanding, men continually give place to the devil (Eph. 4:27). Perhaps no other verse in the Bible has helped fuel this ignorance more than John 10:10. We have exposed the weakness of two commonly held views concerning satan, that he is God's adversary and that he received the earth from Adam. Now we come to the third, and boldly declare: Satan is *not* the thief of John 10:10 anymore! The criminal was crucified on Golgotha's hill.

Three Men Crucified

Our root text (Ezek. 21:25-27) was addressed to King Zedekiah of Judah, and, more pointedly, to the evil spirit who energized him. For a fuller exegesis of those verses, review Chapter One.

Ezek. 21:25, KJV

And thou, profane wicked prince of Israel, whose day is come, when iniquity shall have an end.

As with King Zedekiah, the devil is "profane"; he is the wicked prince of this world system (Jn. 12:31; Eph. 2:2). This Hebrew word means "pierced (especially to death); figuratively, polluted." Translated over 30 times in the Book of Ezekiel as "slain," it comes from a primitive root meaning "to bore, to wound, to dissolve."

It points to satan's day of reckoning at Golgotha (Col. 2:15), where there were three men crucified—the man on the middle cross was Jesus Christ the Messiah, God Almighty in the flesh. The thief on the right who repented, was re-membered (put back together), and entered paradise with Jesus was Adam, man in the flesh. The other thief, who had returned that day to be dealt with, was satan in the flesh. His calling card?—"If Thou be the Son of God…."

Lk. 4:3, KJV

And the devil said unto Him, If Thou be the Son of God, command this stone that it be made bread.

Lk. 4:9, KJV

And he brought Him to Jerusalem, and set Him on a pinnacle of the temple, and said unto Him, If Thou be the Son of God, cast Thyself down from hence:

Lk. 4:13, KJV

And when the devil had ended all the temptation, he departed from Him for a season.

Lk. 23:39, KJV

And one of the malefactors which were hanged railed on Him, saying, If Thou be Christ, save Thyself and us.

After a season, satan returned to complete the temptation but failed. In one grand, finished work, the cross of Jesus Christ destroyed the power of satan and the first man Adam! After Calvary, Christians are not to give place to either (Eph. 4:22-27).

Col. 2:15, NIV

And having disarmed the powers and authorities, He made a public spectacle of them, triumphing over them by the cross.

On that awful day when the true Passover Lamb was sacrificed for us, Jesus bruised the king of darkness. Like courageous Jael who put the hammer to the head of Sisera (Judg. 4:18-21; 5:24-27), Jesus mortally wounded our adversary at the cross. Iniquity came to an "end" (Ezek. 21:27); literally, it was "chopped off." This word is used to denote the end or death of a person (Gen. 6:13). The thief perished!

Heb. 2:14-15, KJV

> *Forasmuch then as the children are partakers of flesh and blood, He also Himself likewise took part of the same; that through death He might destroy him that had the power of death, that is, the devil;*
>
> *And deliver them who through fear of death were all their lifetime subject to bondage.*

1 Jn. 3:8, KJV

> *He that committeth sin is of the devil; for the devil sinneth from the beginning. For this purpose the Son of God was manifested, that He might destroy the works of the devil.*

The day has come, the seventh day from Adam and the third day from Jesus (Hos. 6:1-3; 2 Pet. 3:8). It is time to fully understand and appropriate the spoils of His eternal triumph!

The Thieves of John 10

Jn. 10:1, KJV

> *Verily, verily, I say unto you, He that entereth not by the door into the sheepfold, but climbeth up some other way, the same is a thief and a robber.*

Carnal men always look for the alternative, some other, or different, way. Jesus described such a one as a "thief," a "stealer." Moreover, he is a "robber," a "brigand," one who plunders openly and violently. Preachers are quick to quote John 10:10, but they rarely note that there is more than one thief mentioned in that chapter. In John 10:8, the Good Shepherd warned us about "thieves."

Jn. 10:8, KJV

> *All that ever came before Me are thieves and robbers: but the sheep did not hear them.*

Jesus declared that these thieves came "before" Him. This Greek word *pro* (Strong's #4253) means "fore, in front of, prior (figuratively, superior) to," and is also translated in the King James Version as "above." By Jesus' definition, a thief can be anyone or anything men put before or above Him. The first commandment reveals these to be other gods—"thieves" are idols!

Ex. 20:3, KJV

> *Thou shalt have no other gods **before** Me.*

These other gods are anyone or anything that means more to us than Jesus. This includes all thoughts and ideas that disagree with His Word. Our idols can be readily identified: the things we think about the most, the things we talk about the most, and the things for which we spend the most.

A man always finds time for what he really wants to do. He always has enough money for what he really wants to buy. Excuses are idols. The real issue has to do with the objects of our affection, the desires of our hearts—what we worship. Jesus must be first (Mt. 6:33). These critical times necessitate the recognition of the many thieves of John 10:8 to be the "many antichrists" of First John 2:18 and the "deceivers" of Second John 1:7.

1 Jn. 2:18, KJV

Little children, it is the last time: and as ye have heard that antichrist shall come, even now are there many antichrists; whereby we know that it is the last time.

"Antichrist" is transliterated from *antichristos* (Strong's #500), and it is made up of two words: *anti* (Strong's #473), meaning "opposite, instead of," and *christos* (Strongs #5547), "meaning anointed."

The latter is traced to the root *chrio*, which means "anoint." *Vine's* adds that *antichristos* denotes either "against Christ" or "instead of Christ," or perhaps, combining the two, "one who, assuming the guise of Christ, opposes Christ." This word is used to show contrast or substitution, or both. It is used five times, exclusively in John's epistles (1 Jn. 2:18 [twice],22; 4:3; 2 Jn. 1:7).

2 Jn. 1:7, KJV

For many deceivers are entered into the world, who confess not that Jesus Christ is come in the flesh. This is a deceiver and an antichrist.

The word for "deceiver," is *planos* (Strong's #4108). It means "roving (as a tramp); impostor, misleader." *Vine's* adds "wandering, or leading astray, seducing." It is used in Matthew 27:63 and Second Corinthians 6:8 to show the attitude of religious spirits against apostolic ministry and the Lord Himself. More pointedly, *planos*, the spirit of antichrist, is mentioned in First Timothy 4:1.

1 Tim. 4:1, NIV

The Spirit clearly says that in later times some will abandon the faith and follow deceiving spirits and things taught by demons.

These "seducing spirits" (1 Tim. 4:1, KJV) constitute a spirit of error and are "against the truth" (1 Tim. 4:1, TLB). Other Greek words related to *planos* can mean "to cause to roam from truth and safety; a straying from orthodoxy or piety; a rover, an erratic teacher."

To retrace our steps, the thieves of John 10:8 are antichrists and deceivers. These liars deny the Father and the Son, refusing to confess that Jesus Christ "is come" in the flesh (1 Jn. 2:22; 4:3). These religious spirits and concepts operate through vagabonds, spiritual bums who roam from church to church, preying upon ignorant pastors and unsuspecting saints. Such impostors are not covered by the Word of God or apostolic orthodoxy.

The aim of these demonic forces is threefold:

1. To stifle man's creativity, keeping him silent.

2. To foster man's immaturity, keeping him undeveloped.

3. To narrow man's consciousness, keeping him prejudiced.

God is sick and tired of all the griping and whining that goes on in the name of Christianity. We cannot face the world with the same countenance that the world already wears. People who need real answers don't need to see weak, defeated Christians. Young people want something they can sink their teeth into, something relevant that will work. A Christ-centered message is one of hope and victory. Lift Jesus up. He will do the rest.

Jn. 12:32, KJV

And I, if I be lifted up from the earth, will draw all men unto Me.

The powers of darkness tremble at the thought of the power of the Holy Ghost—the same Spirit that raised Jesus from the dead—being released from our lives and ministries. We are to overcome the devil by the word of our testimony, the spirit of prophecy (Rev. 12:11; 19:10). Paul admonished us to be men in our understanding of New Covenant realities (1 Cor. 14:20). The more excellent ministry of Jesus Christ, the New Testament priesthood after the order of Melchisedec, is a ministry without prejudice (Jn. 3:16; Heb. 8:1-6). We are not to be narrow-minded, focusing on one nation (the natural Jew), culture (black or white), gender (male or female), or denomination (our own), but on all men.

Jn. 10:10, NIV

The thief comes only to steal and kill and destroy….

This verse was written *before* the cross. The devil is no longer the thief…he has been crucified. The real culprit here is traditional teaching—what we have been taught about the devil. The Greek word for "destroy" is *apollumi* (Strong's #622) and means "to destroy fully." It is used to speak of a marred wineskin (Lk. 5:37), a lost sheep, a lost son (Lk. 15:4-6). *Vine's* adds that the idea behind *apollumi* is not extinction but ruin and loss, not of being, but of well-being. Religious customs, including the cherished belief that the devil is still the thief of John 10:10, make spiritual men sick.

Mk. 7:13, NIV

> *Thus you nullify the word of God by your tradition that you have handed down....*

Col. 2:8, KJV

> *Beware lest any man spoil you through philosophy and vain deceit, after the tradition of men, after the rudiments of the world, and not after Christ.*

Col. 2:8, TLB

> *...their wrong and shallow answers built on man's thoughts and ideas....*

Many have been carried off as spoil, led captive by their previous teachings. Men are lovers of human wisdom and empty deceit or delusion. *Vine's* says that this deceit gives a false impression, whether by appearance, statement, or influence (Mt. 13:22; Eph. 4:22; 2 Thess. 2:10). These spots and blemishes sport themselves with their own deceivings while they feast with you (2 Pet. 2:13; Jude 1:12). Behind the pulpit and in the pew, vain deceit has infiltrated the churches of America.

Such men are lovers of "tradition." This word in Colossians 2:8 means "to surrender, yield up, intrust, transmit" —to hand over, to hand down (Mt. 15:2; Gal. 1:14). Man-made teachings are based on the rudiments of this world system, this cosmos. These "principles" (compare Heb. 5:12) and systematic errors proposed by men are orderly in arrangement, as exampled by Scofield's eschatology, which is discussed in Chaper Seven (compare Gal. 4:3,9; Col. 2:20; 2 Pet. 3:10,12).

The real "thief" of John 10:10 is no longer the devil. The actual killer and destroyer of the Church's true purpose and destiny is *what men are still teaching about the devil*!

The Dragon Still Has a Mouth

The only way to overcome the mouth of the dragon is with the mouth of the Lord—a prophetic Church full of the living Word. The Greek word for "demon" is *daimon*, and it can be rendered as a "knowing one." There are demonized intelligences sent forth to harass the elect. But we have been clothed upon with a higher intelligence—we have the mind of Christ (1 Cor. 2:16)!

Why do you believe what you believe? Have you personally researched its history? Can it be found in the Law, the Psalms, and the Prophets of the Old Testament? Did Jesus teach it? Is it part of the apostles' doctrine in the Book of Acts? Most importantly, can you exegetically establish your theology or eschatology with the Pauline, Johannine, and general Epistles of the New Testament?

Those who preach and teach the Word of God are particularly morally responsible to answer these questions.

I beseech every preacher not to give your listeners cute little sayings and outdated, hand-me-down ideas backed up by a few sparsely scattered half-quoted proof texts, but rather solid biblical exegesis from the New Testament Epistles.

1 Jn. 4:1, KJV

> *Beloved, believe not every spirit, but try the spirits whether they are of God: because many false prophets are gone out into the world.*

1 Jn. 4:1, TLB

> *Dearly loved friends, don't always believe everything you hear just because someone says it is a message from God: test it first....*

Chapters Two and Three set forth several Biblical examples describing Jesus' total and complete victory over our adversary. Chapters Four and Five clearly showed that the earth belongs to Jesus and His Church, not the devil. The warfare is accomplished, but His Bride still experiences the good fight of faith (1 Tim. 6:12). We stand complete in our victorious Captain, warding off any thought or vain imagination that tries to rise above that understanding (2 Cor. 10:3-6; 2 Thess. 2:4).

But the devil, like Goliath of old, still strides up and down the earth mouthing his obscenities (Job 1:7; 2:2). The dragon still has a mouth. He is like the chained lion in Bunyan's *Pilgrim's Progress* who is still able to roar. Men have given him incredible influence, but satan is a spiritual terrorist, a tyrannical bully. His taunts and intimidations are aimed to handcuff the saints, keeping them in a defeated, defensive posture. The adversary wants to hold back every believer in the dark (2 Cor. 4:3-4), spiritually blind and deaf to his true identity in Christ as the seed of Abraham and David.

2 Cor. 2:11, KJV

> *Lest Satan should get an advantage of us: for we are not ignorant of his devices.*

Satan operates his ministry by the spirit of fear. The god of this world has religiously concocted an entire system of error and deception that irresponsibly gives this planet over to the kingdom of darkness. His devilish invention keeps the Church so heavenly minded, it's no earthly good. But Christians have been called to be the salt of the earth and the light of the world (Mt. 5:13-16). Wanting to rid the globe of our influence, satan desires to subtly evacuate our witness, to shrewdly remove us from history. The devil makes his pitch easy to swallow by only requiring men to be born again, to reign without suffering.

He hatched this baby at a critical time in British and American history, the early 1800s, and he named this futurist view of eschatology "dispensationalism."

Dispensationalism is taken from the word *dispense* which means "to weigh or meter out." This school of thought sees God working in different ways in different periods of time. The term "dispensation" can be found in the King James Version in First Corinthians 9:17, Ephesians 1:10; 3:2, and Colossians 1:25. This, along with "stewardship," is the translation of the Greek word *oikonomia* (Strong's #3622), which means "the administration (of a household or estate); specifically, a (religious) economy." Dispensationalism is the view that there is much variety in the divine "economy," that God has dealt differently with men during distinct eras of biblical history.

C.I. Scofield's classical definition states that a dispensation is "a period of time during which man is tested in respect of obedience to some *specific* revelation of the will of God." Scofield's (or J.R. Graves'?—see Chapter Seven, page 146) scheme of seven dispensations has been widely assumed and rehearsed:

1. Innocence (before the Fall of man).

2. Conscience (from the Fall of man to Noah).

3. Human Government (from Noah to Abraham).

4. Promise (from Abraham to Moses).

5. Law (from Moses to Christ).

6. Grace (the Church age).

7. Kingdom (the Millennium).

Scofield's understanding of a "dispensation" undercuts the biblical doctrine of grace in any age. His dispensational distinction between national Israel and the Church denies grace completely, maintaining as it does that there is more than one way of salvation.

Mild dispensationalism teaches the difference between law and grace, the old covenant and the new covenant. Extreme or "hyper-dispensationalism" relegates the miraculous, supernatural gifts of the Holy Spirit to the first century church, and the prophetic promises of the Old and New Testaments to the future state of natural Israel as a separate kingdom from the Church.

The dragon is defeated, but he still has a mouth. He wants men to believe that all Bible prophecy has been fulfilled, that Jesus may return at "any minute," and that the Bride has made herself ready to meet the Lord.

This present flood out of the dragon's mouth—the contemporary stronghold of Scofield's dispensationalism—constitutes the major obstacle keeping the Church from discovering her rightful covenantal inheritance in Christ, the one "whose right it is." It paralyzes and kills vision in young men and robs our children and grandchildren of their rightful destiny in Him.

The basic weakness of classical diespensationalism is that it interprets the New Testament on the basis of the Old Testament, rather than viewing the Old Testament in the light of the New Testament. Essentially based on a difference between the Church and national Israel, this popular eschatological view declares: "The second coming of Christ is in two stages. Before the tribulation period, He comes *for* the saints. Seven years later, He will come back *with* the saints. The day of Christ, the 'rapture,' is the first stage—Jesus comes secretly like a thief in the night for His Bride, the Church. The second stage is called 'the revelation' or the Day of the Lord, when He returns in judgment to destroy the antichrist and set up His Kingdom."

Men are quick to exclaim that the trumpet may sound before they finish preaching, or before the saints wake up in the morning. They tell of cemeteries bursting open and the dead rising, and living Christians zooming off into space to meet the Lord in the rapture. Prophecy teachers excitedly prognosticate the rebuilding of the

Jewish temple, and some (like Scofield's original notes) even predict the reinstitution of animal sacrifices.

Nationwide, preachers unabashedly recite the appearing of a future secular world leader—the antichrist—and the beginning of the tribulation period. Their sad implication is that the Church is too weak to survive such demonic fury (although the whole armor of Eph. 6:10-18 mentions none for the back). We are told that while the saints enjoy the marriage supper of the Lamb up in Heaven and receive the rewards of their earthly labors (at the judgment seat of Christ), their unsaved loved ones and untaught millions of heathen will suffer untold agonies on earth.

1 Jn. 4:8, KJV

...God is love.

There is a great gulf between the love of God and the fear in man. The opposite of love (God) is not hate, but fear (2 Tim. 1:7). Fear is of the devil. Any system of belief that is gendered and maintained by the spirit of fear is not of the Lord.

Man's Terminology

Unfortunately, aforementioned terms such as "rapture," "antichrist," or "tribulation period" are assumed. To facilitate the understanding of every reader, brief definitions of key eschatological perspectives with their attending vocabulary are included here.

Eschatology is taken from the Greek word *eschatos* (Strong's #2078), which means "farthest, final (of place or time)." *Vine's* adds, "utmost or extreme." Eschatology is commonly understood to constitute the "Doctrine of Last Things," that branch of theology that focuses upon prophetic events—the endtimes and the Second Coming of the Lord Jesus Christ.

Men have coined and created words to describe certain prophetic views. Each has its own set of religious baggage. Quite frankly, I hesitate to point them out, lest I possibly obstruct the purpose of this writing. First, I don't want to feed the universal frenzy of religious people. Any open-hearted person who reads this book along with his Bible can see that the Scriptures do not support the views of Darby, Scofield, and Larkin. "So if dispensationalism with its charts is incomplete information, then tell us the whole truth with regard to end-time events," men cry. The problem is, school isn't out—we are all still learning. I have exasperated more than one young inquiring preacher by honestly replying, "I don't know the answers to some of these things."

Second, it must be made clear that each of these eschatological perspectives contain beliefs and ideas that may or may not be true to the Word of God. Each has become a camp or stream. You may reference this in my book *The Issues of Life* (Shippensburg, PA: Destiny Image Publishers, Inc., 1992, p. 37), where I dared to ask these questions:

Will there be a "rapture"?
If so, will it be pre-trib, mid-trib, or post-trib?
Is there a tribulation?
Which is right: pre-millennialism or
   amillennialism?
Is the thousand-year millennium literal or
   figurative?

See what I mean? While aspects of some of these sentiments may be scripturally sound, we don't want to get locked into all the residuals—the assumptions or speculations of men—that come with a given school of thought.

All these views are limited. Nonetheless, for the sake of being acquainted with man's definitions of leading eschatological opinion, we note that there are three primary millennial schools of interpretation. *Millennium* comes from the Latin *mille* ("a thousand") and *annum* ("one year"). It is used by most to refer to a literal, future thousand-year reign of Christ (Rev. 20). With regard to prophetic events, one may be amillennial, post-millenial, or pre-millennial.

"A" means "without." An amillennialist generally does not believe in a literal, future millennium, but that the present age is the time of Christ's reign. Some see no future tribulation, while others anticipate a future time of unparalleled trouble. This person generally holds to a post-tribulation rapture.

Post means "after." A post-millennialist is similar to the amillennialist, except he believes that Christ will come at the end of the millennium. He foresees the world becoming better and better, with the Church ushering in a time of universal peace. However he would define the tribulation, he would necessarily be post-tribulational with regards to the rapture.

Pre means "before." Pre-millenialism is the arena of the greatest debate over the time of the rapture and the Church's relationship to the tribulation. All premillennialists look for Christ's return before the millennium, and they generally hold that it will be preceded by certain signs—the preaching of the gospel to all nations, a great apostasy, wars, famines, earthquakes, the appearance of a universal dictator known as the antichrist, and a great tribulation.

With regards to the rapture, there are four pre-millennial ideas: the pre-tribulation rapture, the mid-tribulation rapture, the post-tribulation rapture, and the partial rapture.

All four views assume a future rapture and time of unparalleled trouble (the tribulation period). Before defining these four eschatological perspectives, one must ask two obvious questions: What is the "rapture"? What is the "tribulation"?

First, the word *rapture* is not found in the Bible. According to Webster, "rapture" (compare the English word *rape*) is taken from the Latin *rapius* or *rapere* ("to seize, to carry away"). It means:

1. A seizing by violence (obsolete).
2. The state of being carried away with joy, love, etc.: ecstasy.
3. An expression of great joy, pleasure, etc.
4. A carrying away in body or spirit (rare).
5. An attack of intense excitement; delirium; hysterics; fit or spasm (obsolete).

The word *rapture* (in a body-lifting sense) was used for centuries by Medieval mystics to describe their own levitation a few inches (or even several feet) above the floor or ground. Such "raptures" were often condemned by Roman Catholic leaders.

Most Christians have been taught that the "rapture" is the imminent or "any moment" catching away, or translation, of the saints—Jesus coming secretly as a thief "for" the Church. Accordingly, in this literal removal of the Church from the earth, all born-again believers, living and dead, will experience the redemption of their bodies. They will be resurrected and changed from a state of mortality to a state of immortality.

Now that we have defined the "rapture," what is the "tribulation"? Scofield's dispensationalism holds to a futuristic view of Matthew 24 and Revelation 4–19, calling this period of time the "tribulation." Accordingly, this time corresponds to the seventieth week (or last seven years) of Daniel's famous prophecy (Dan. 9:24-27).

The word "tribulation" is taken from the Latin *tribulare* ("to press or afflict") or *tribulum* ("a threshing sledge"). The Greek word for "afflicted" and "tribulation" in Matthew 24:9, 21, 29 is *thlipsis* (Strong's #2347), and it means "pressure." It is translated in the King James Version as "afflicted, affliction, anguish, burdened, persecution, tribulation, trouble." It comes from *thlibo* ("to crowd") and the root *tribos* ("to rub").

Vine's adds that *thlipsis* means "a pressing," anything that burdens the spirit. This word denotes the pain of childbirth in John 16:21, and reminisces Egypt's famine in Acts 7:11. It is used especially in Second Corinthians to describe the weighty portion of genuine apostolic ministry (see 2 Cor. 1:4,8; 2:4; 4:17; 6:4; 7:4; 8:2,13). Interestingly, *thlipsis*, or "tribulation," is mentioned in First Thessalonians 1:6; 3:3, 7, Second Thessalonians 1:4, 6, and these verses:

Mt. 13:21, KJV

*Yet hath he not root in himself, but dureth for a while: for when **tribulation** or persecution ariseth because of the word, by and by he is offended.*

Jn. 16:33, KJV

*These things I have spoken unto you, that in Me ye might have peace. In the world ye shall have **tribulation**: but be of good cheer; I have overcome the world.*

Acts 14:22, KJV

*Confirming the souls of the disciples, and exhorting them to continue in the faith, and that we must through much **tribulation** enter into the kingdom of God.*

Rom. 8:35, KJV

*Who shall separate us from the love of Christ? shall **tribulation**…?*

Rev. 7:14, KJV

*…These are they which came out of great **tribulation**, and have washed their robes, and made them white in the blood of the Lamb.*

Dispensationalists constantly reference a future seven-year tribulation period, also termed the "time of Jacob's 'trouble.' " (Compare the notes on Genesis 32:24-32 in Chapter Four.)

Jer. 30:7, KJV

*Alas! for that day is great, so that none is like it: it is even the time of Jacob's **trouble**; but he shall be saved out of it.*

Dan. 12:1, KJV

*And at that time shall Michael stand up, the great
prince which standeth for the children of thy people: and
there shall be a time of **trouble**, such as never was since
there was a nation even to that same time: and at that
time thy people shall be delivered, every one that shall
be found written in the book.*

The Hebrew word for "trouble" in these verses is
tsarah (Strong's #6869), meaning "tightness." It is used
frequently throughout the Book of Psalms. For a fuller
treatment of this word, see Chapter Nine of my book *Rest
in the Day of Trouble* (Shippensburg, PA: Destiny Image
Publishers, Inc., 1993, pp. 235-236).

To summarize, the tribulation period is seen by dispensationalists to be a future time of great distress, suffering, and persecution, called by some the "time of
Jacob's trouble."

Based on Daniel's prophecy of seventy weeks
(exegeted in Chapter Ten), some interpret this to be a
time of three-and-a-half years. Most see a seven-year
tribulation, and further delineate the latter half of
Daniel's seventieth week as the time of "great tribulation"(Mt. 24:21), or the outpouring of the "wrath" of God
(citing Zeph. 1:15; Rom. 2:5; Eph. 5:6; 1 Thess. 1:10; 5:9;
Rev. 6:17; 14:19; 15:7; 19:15).

The pre-tribulation pre-millennial view (the most
popular) foresees the rapture—Jesus coming "for" the
Church—taking place before the tribulation.

Post-tribulationists believe that the Church will go
through the tribulation and that Jesus will come at the

end of the tribulation. They see the Church being empowered by the Spirit to survive the worst onslaughts of satan. This is an admirable attitude, and it is much closer to the truth than the pre-trib view, born out of fear and selfishness.

Others prefer a safer, more compromising, "middle of the road" position called mid-tribulationism, because of the many Scriptures that show that God will keep His own. This view holds that the catching away of the Church takes place in the middle of the tribulation.

The partial rapturist believes that there are more than one rapture, or a series of raptures taking place at different times.

All four pre-millennial ideas embrace a post-tribulational coming of Jesus Christ as King of kings (the revelation) when He comes to judge the world. But all except the post-tribulation view see Him coming first as a "thief" in a secret rapture (the translation), referencing First Thessalonians 4:13-18; 5:1-9. This is the historic posture of John Darby and the Plymouth Brethren—the now popular two-stage, two-phase, or split coming of the Lord.

As noted, even these simple definitions need further explanation and clarification. All assume a literal three-and-a-half or seven-year period known as the "tribulation" (solely based on Dan. 9:24-27), not to mention the biggest buzzword of all—the "rapture"!

Are we to be a-mill, pre-mill, or post-mill? We don't want to be "wind-mill," going round and round on these issues. Maybe we should all hold the "pan-trib" view—be ready for anything, knowing that it will all "pan out" in the end!

Even apostles and prophets have tried to put present truth into the old dispensational framework, new wine into old bottles. That's why we must focus on *who* we know, not *what* we know.

This volume was not written to assail dispensationalism. It is an apostolic cry that all men refocus on *Him* "whose right it is." Eschatology is not the issue. We do not preach a message. We proclaim a Person!

Jesus Is Coming

Jesus is coming! These exciting words carry different meaning and weight with a myriad of camps in the Body of Christ. There are devout, God-fearing men and women in every one of these aforementioned groups.

Let me go on record to say that I do believe in the coming of the Lord, literally and spiritually. Jesus is coming— bodily, physically, corporeally. Before that, He will appear in the saints to be glorified.

Because I have dared (in the last 25 years) to re-examine the historical and biblical roots of pre-tribulation Darbyism, some folks say, "Varner doesn't believe in the rapture." I have cautioned our own local church not to use that terminology, else people will think that we do not believe in the literal return of King Jesus—and we do!

But the "any minute" rapture theory has become a "sacred cow" in America. For one to question this teaching or expose its historical or biblical roots is risky business, paramount to attacking the blood of Jesus, or the virgin birth, or motherhood. Good men almost become violent when Scofieldian dispensationalism is challenged (perhaps a hint of its spiritual source). Reading this book may prove dangerous to your reputation. But a true prophet cares more about the truth of God than being recognized by people, even his ministerial colleagues.

The Bible focuses on His coming, not our going. It emphasizes the appearing of the Lord, not the disappearance of the saints!

Before we take a fresh look at dispensational proof texts (Chapters Eight and Nine), especially Daniel's prophecy of seventy weeks (Dan. 9:24-27), the foundational Bible base of futurism (Chapter Ten), we must briefly investigate the historical roots of classical dispensationalism.

Mt. 24:36, KJV

But of that day and hour knoweth no man, no, not the angels of heaven, but My Father only.

Acts 1:7, NIV

He said to them: "It is not for you to know the times or dates the Father has set by His own authority."

The Father has purposefully allowed end-time events to remain veiled within His own jurisdiction. No one has a complete handle on these matters. God is breaking apart every pre-packaged theological and eschatological box. The Day of the Lord has dawned.

The real issue and controversy lies not within the field of eschatology, but government: Who's in charge—sectarian tradition or apostolic, biblical orthodoxy? Men don't like the idea of having to walk by faith when it comes to understanding the Scriptures. They are too familiar and comfortable with Larkin's charts, priding themselves in being able to expound "God's Plan for the Ages." Where did it all begin?

Chapter Seven

A Fresh Historical Look at Dispensationalism

"...try the spirits...."

First John 4:1

Chapter Six introduced us to the various views and familiar semantics of eschatology. Words like "rapture," "tribulation," "antichrist," and others are common to the ear of most Christians. Yet we have assumed spiritual hand-me-downs. When Pentecost fell at the turn of the twentieth century, the eschatology formulated in the British Isles from 1830-1850 and carried to America from 1850-1900 was passed on without question. Classical Darbyism was not to be challenged until the late 1940s and the Latter Rain outpouring.

Christianity is essentially historical. The Bible is full of history. The Scriptures cannot be understood without a foundational knowledge and grasp of historical events. Without this weapon, we are most vulnerable (Hos. 4:6). In the study of eschatology, are we historically armed?

God has given us history for our minds and His Word for our hearts or spirits. Prove all things, and hold fast to that which is good (1 Thess. 5:21). The next two chapters will provide answers from the Bible. For now, what is the witness of history? To limit our space concerning dispensationalism's historical perspective, I have included a short bibliography of resource materials (for Chapters Six through Ten) as an appendix at the end of this volume. I especially recommend reading *The Incredible Cover-up* by Dave MacPherson and *Seventy Weeks: The Historical Alternative* by Robert Caringola.

There is little point in closely surveying early Church history for anticipations of dispensationalism proper. Futurists themselves claim novelty for their system. They recognize that it was mainly a nineteenth-century phenomenon (from 1830 to the present).

More significantly, dispensational teachings have been handed down by men who were not baptized with the Holy Ghost. When the Pentecostal revival came to Azuza St. in Los Angeles (1906), William Seymour and other Spirit-filled forefathers assumed Darby's and Scofield's eschatology. The only new historical distinctive was *glossalalia*, or speaking with other tongues (Acts 2:4).

During the sixteenth century Protestant Reformation, most reformers were historicists concerning the interpretation of the prophetic books of the Bible, especially the Book of Revelation. They believed that its fulfillment had been taking place throughout the church age. This contrasts the dispensational or futurist view, which waits for these Scriptures (especially Rev. 4–19) to be fulfilled. The latter sentiment became more pronounced in the early nineteenth century.

The general view of Bible students for 1800 years was that the approaching coming, or advent, of Jesus Christ would be *visible, personal, and glorious*. The simplicity of this conviction stated that His arrival would be accompanied by a variety of phenomena and various judgments bearing upon the world and the Church. Terms such as "coming," "appearing," "day," and "revelation" all signified one entrance in glory. For example, the Apostles' Creed simply says of our Lord, "...and sitteth on the right hand of God, the Father Almighty. From thence He shall come to judge the quick and the dead..."—in *one* coming.

Specifically, during the first three centuries of the Christian era, pre-millennialism appears to be have been the dominant eschatological interpretation. Among its adherents were Irenaeus, Justin Martyr, and Tertullian. However, it is worth noting that dispensational premillennialism represents quite an innovation over against historic pre-millennialism and traditional Christian eschatology in general.

The amillennial view arose later in the fourth century when Emperor Constantine gave favor to the Church. The eminent theologian Augustine articulated this position, and it become the favored interpretation during medieval times. Even though official Roman Catholic Church doctrine was amillennial, pre-millennialism continued during the Middle Ages among certain groups of believers.

The Protestant Reformers largely stayed with Augustinian amillennialism and identified the papacy as the antichrist, the Pauline "man of sin" (2 Thess. 2:3-4). To counter this, in A.D. 1585, Francisco Ribera, a Jesuit priest, began an intensive study of Bible prophecy. He later published a 500-page prophetic commentary concerning Babylon and the antichrist. Ribera's futuristic treatment of Daniel 9:24-27, the foundation stone of dispensationalism, was furthered by the work of another Jesuit, Cardinal Robert Bellarmine.

Ribera put the first three chapters of the Book of Revelation in the first century, and the rest of the Apocalypse (Rev. 4–19) in the distant future. He taught that the Jewish temple would be rebuilt and that a future antichrist would abolish Christianity, deny Christ, pretend to be God, and conquer the world. Sound familiar? This sixteenth-century Roman Catholic priest put the first "rubber band" on Daniel's seventieth week and stretched it out to the end of time. Like that of Lacunza's in 1812, Ribera's sole purpose was to counter the protestant Reformation and to set aside the reformers' teaching of the time that the Roman papacy was the antichrist!

Ribera's views set the stage for a great renewal of pre-millenialism during the seventeenth century, led by the German Calvinistic theologian Johann Alsted and his book *The Beloved City* (1627). The pre-millennial school began to wane, and the 1700s saw the rise of post-millennialism, led by men like Daniel Whitby. These historicists believed that the 1,260 days (3 1/2 years), the "time, times, and a half" of Daniel 12:7 represented 1,260 years. Men used this year-for-a-day theory to set the time of Christ's return. Some calculated that the tribulation period started in A.D. 533 with the edict of Justinian (ruler of the Byzantine empire from A.D. 527-565 and formulator of the Justinian code of law).

The French Revolution of 1793 (A.D. 533 plus 1,260 years brought us to A.D. 1793) caused many to believe that Napoleon was the antichrist, the first of many such guesses in the last 200 years (including world figures such as Hitler, Mussolini, Stalin, Kruschchev, Gorbachev, Hussein, *ad nauseum*). This sense of the revolutionary destruction of world order caused many Christians to believe that their world had reached "the endtimes"—that the return of the Lord was very near.

Moreover, the year 1823 was marked with great prophetic significance. Based on the 1,290 days of Daniel 12:11, A.D. 1793 plus 30 more years brought us to 1823. All date setting proves futile, as shown later with the Adventist Millerites in 1843-44, and, more recently, with Edgar Whisenant's books, *88 Reasons Why the Rapture Is in 1988* and *The Final Shout: Rapture Report 1989*. Many South Korean believers were convinced that Jesus was coming in October of 1992. Consider as well the predictions of John Hinkle and Harold Camping in June and September of 1994, respectively. Piled on top of all this humanistic prognostication is the unceasing sensationalizing of the "signs of the times." Do you remember the "Jupiter Effect" (or non-effect?), the aligning of the planets, in 1982?

In the early nineteenth century, this kind of speculation paved the way for a "new" view. This strong reaction to post-millennialism set the stage for the futurist, or dispensational, school of thought, including its future antichrist. Then in 1826 Samuel Maitland, librarian to the Archbishop of Canterbury, discovered Francisco Ribera's manuscript and published it for the sake of public interest. His consequent prophetic pamphlets were read and received by John Darby and the Plymouth Brethren.

Thus tremendous interest in prophetic events continued to rise with regard to the second coming of Christ. British newspapers and journals openly discussed prophecy. Prophetic Bible conferences abounded, emphasizing the imminent ("any moment") return of Jesus Christ. One of the earliest and most important of these prophetic gatherings was held annually from 1826-1830 outside of London, at Albury Manor, the stately home of banker Henry Drummond. Another key location, just south of Dublin, Ireland, was the palatial residence belonging to Lady Theodosa Powerscourt. Historians have associated two men—Edward Irving and John Darby—with these early conferences and the futurist development of this period.

Edward Irving

Edward Irving was born in Scotland in 1792. A brilliant young romanticist with a particular taste for literature (including *Don Quixote* and *Tales from the Arabian Nights*), he received his M.A. at Edinburgh when only 16, and he was ordained as a Presbyterian minister at 22. Irving possessed extraordinary qualities of person and character. He was exceptionally tall and elegantly handsome; his mind was that of a genius, though tending toward eccentricity; his spirit was almost childlike in its simplicity, yet at the same time mightily masculine. He was full of courage and unflinching in conviction, and as a preacher was dubbed by some as "the greatest orator of the age" (though he was not an expository preacher).

In 1822 Irving went to the Caledonian Chapel, London, which proved so inadequate for the hundreds who wanted to hear him that a new church was built in Regent Square in 1827. In 1828 his open air meetings in Scotland drew crowds of up to 10,000 people. His church in London seated 1,000 people and was packed week after week. Irving's early ministry attracted many of London's aristocracy, including the acclaimed English poet and philosopher Samuel Taylor Coleridge (a former disciple of Unitarianism, which denies the deity of Christ). Coleridge impacted Irving's mind and ministry, especially his views concerning the Person of Jesus Christ.

Called "the father of modern Pentecostalism," Irving believed that the spiritual gifts of the early Church were a present reality and a sign of Christ's imminent return. Ironically, Irving himself never spoke in tongues or prophesied. While addressing the London Missionary Society in 1825, Irving first mentioned his views about an end-time outpouring of the Holy Spirit, which he called "the latter rain." He was later influenced in 1828 by A.J. Scott, who believed that the *charismata* (spiritual gifts) were still available to the Church. One of first instances of *glossalalia* among the Irvingites took place in March of 1830 when Mary Campbell of the Gare Loch area of Scotland began to speak in tongues. The Campbells were also friends with the Macdonald family of nearby Port Glasglow, themselves influenced by the ministries of Scott and Irving himself.

Irving met Henry Drummond in 1824 and later participated in the Albury conferences, which began two years later. It is most significant that the Albury conference of December, 1928, decided to publish (with Drummond's wealth) a quarterly journal of prophecy called *The Morning Watch.*

Irving's interest in eschatology was further sparked by the views of notable Hatley Frere (who based his studies on the Books of Daniel and Revelation). In 1824 Frere felt that the biblical prophecies had been fulfilled and that the coming of Christ was only a few years away. Irving also translated Jesuit Manuel de Lacunza's work, *The Coming of Messiah in Glory and Majesty* (1812), from Spanish to English in 1826 (the same year that Maitland "discovered" Ribera's writings). Lacunza had written about a future antichrist, an indication of Irving's changing views. Dispensationalists need to understand that Lacunza's primary literary purpose (like Ribera's in 1585) was to counter Protestant thinking by setting aside the then current teaching that the pope was the antichrist! The charismatic Irvingites were teaching the pretribulation rapture as early as 1830, according to their prophetic journal, *The Morning Watch.*

By September of 1831, Irving's church was divided over the practice of spiritual gifts. Seven months later, he was excommunicated by the London presbytery for his excessive charismatic views and practices. Some 700 of his faithful followers left with him to form an independent group that came to be known as the Catholic

Apostolic Church. Edward Irving was eventually condemned in March of 1833 by the Church of Scotland for teaching the sinfulness of Christ's humanity. His arraignment was primarily based on his 1830 writing, *The Orthodox and Catholic Doctrine of our Lord's Human Nature.*

Though believing God to heal his deteriorating physical condition, this colorful charismatic dispensationalist died December 7, 1934, in Glasglow at the age of 42. Some said he died of tuberculosis and a broken heart.

Irving published many works on prophecy and helped to organize the Albury Park prophecy conferences. These meetings set the pattern for similar gatherings throughout the nineteenth and twentieth centuries. The prophetic enthusiasm of Edward Irving spread to other groups and found firm support among the Plymouth Brethren, led by John Darby.

John Darby and the Plymouth Brethren

John Nelson Darby was born on November 18, 1800, in London, England. Following his father's wishes, he studied law at Westminster College and received his B.A. degree from Trinity College, Dublin. A change in career plans led him to prepare for the ministry, and he was ordained to the Anglican priesthood around 1825. From 1826-27, Darby and those who stood with him formed the Plymouth Brethren movement (which began in Dublin)—the eventual ardent advocates of the "any moment" doctrine. During this interval, Darby began to formulate his dispensational ideas. Some historians say that the Brethren were teaching a two-stage coming as early as 1831. Others contend that Darby introduced the secret rapture theory at the Powerscourt meetings in 1833. Interestingly, some of the outstanding Brethren, such as George Muller, were in open opposition to this new theory because of its lack of Scriptural soundness!

In the 1860s and 1870s, the Brethren's two-phase coming of the Lord with its "secret rapture" made its way to America with several visits by Darby himself. (He also traveled to the West Indies and New Zealand.) Darby's first visit to the United States seems to have been around 1864, and his influence was greatest among Presbyterians and Baptists. Darby also translated the Bible into German and French. Eventually, his futurist views found their way into the notes of the famous *Scofield Reference Bible* (1909).

This purported "father of dispensationalism" died on April 29, 1882, in Bournemouth, England, at the age of 81. He was buried there with 8,000-10,000 persons present at the service. It has been estimated that John Darby left 40 volumes of writings and some 1,500 assemblies around the world. The editor of Darby's works was William Kelly (1820-1906), who attempted to credit Darby as the originator of dispensationalism. Through these books, which include four volumes on prophecy, the futurist system was carried throughout the English-speaking world. A line of continuity from Darby to the present can be traced from his contemporaries and followers (C.H. Mackintosh, William Kelly, F.W. Grant) through the interceding scholars (W.E. Blackstone, G. Campbell Morgan, H.A. Ironside, A.C. Gaebelein, C.I. Scofield) directly to the current adherents of his views.

The extent of Darby's influence has been so vast that dispensationalism prevails in most evangelical circles today. It escalated in popularity in the United States after the Civil War (1861-1865), especially when William E. Blackstone wrote *Jesus Is Coming* in 1878. Then Henry Moorhouse persuaded the great preacher D.L. Moody to this view. Most important of all was Darby's impact on C.I. Scofield, who made dispensationalism an integral part of his Bible study notes.

C.I. Scofield

Cyrus Ingerson Scofield was born in Michigan in August of 1843, and was raised in Tennessee. After a stint in the Confederate Army, he studied law. Ambiguous historical sources say that he was converted in 1879 in St. Louis under the ministry of D.L. Moody. In July of 1880 Scofield joined the Pilgrim Congregational Church of St. Louis. Pastor D.C. Goodell was a good friend of James Brookes (see below) and agreed with Brookes' views on prophecy. This church licensed Scofield to preach and pastor a church in Dallas, Texas, even though Scofield had been converted less than three years, had no theological training, and had limited formal schooling (some purport that the Dr. in front of his name was self-given).

At about the same time, his Roman Catholic wife Leontine (whom he had married in 1866) drew up divorce papers July 28, 1881. She charged that Cyrus had absented himself, abandoned the family, neglected his duty, failed to support or contribute thereto, and made no provision for food, clothing, or home. Scofield denied each allegation. The court issued a decree for Leontine, but somehow the case was dismissed (March, 1882). On October 1, 1883, Leontine filed a second divorce petition. On December 8, 1883, the divorce was granted, stating that the young pastor was not a fit person to have custody of the children. Three months later, in March of 1884, Scofield married Hettie VanWark, a member of his Dallas congregation.

Nevertheless, Presbyterian minister James Brookes, who had worked with John Darby, helped to sponsor Scofield's ministerial endeavors and shaped the young preacher's eschatological views. Scofield was also influenced by the writings of J.R. Graves (*The Work of Christ Consummated in Seven Dispensations*, 1883), John Darby, and William Kelly. He began the "Scofield Bible Correspondence Course" on dispensationalism in 1890 (later taken over in 1914-15 by the Moody Bible Institute).

In the early 1890s Scofield was also the head of Southwestern School of the Bible in Dallas, forerunner of Dallas Theological Seminary, which was founded in 1924 by Lewis S. Chafer (1871-1952). Until his death, Chafer served as Dallas Theological Seminary's president, professor of theology, and editor of the journal *Bibliotheca Sacra*. He is best known for his eight-volume *Systematic Theology* (1947), perhaps the fullest theological expression of dispensationalism. The major line of dispensational orthodoxy is clear and unbroken from Darby to Scofield to Chafer. Today, Dallas Theological Seminary remains the final great bastion for classical Scofieldism.

The Scofield Reference Bible (whose seven consulting editors included A.C. Gaebelein and A.T. Pierson) was officially published by the Oxford University Press on

January 15, 1909 (then revised in 1917 and 1967). This dispensational, pre-millennial Bible was edited by Scofield with the financial assistance of prominent Brethren businessmen. Within 50 years, over three million copies were printed in the United States. Similarly, Finis Jennings Dake furthered the propagation of Scofield's dispensationalism with his *Dake's Annotated Reference Bible* (1961).

C.I. Scofield died July 24, 1921, and was buried in Flushing, New York. However, his Bible with its Darbyism lives on. Bible teachers swear by his notes with the same fervor as others do with Dake's.

The Lassie From Fort Glasgow

Neither Edward Irving nor John Darby took credit for the origin of the pre-tribulation rapture theory, yet both proclaimed it. Still, no significant body of Christians ever taught about a secret rapture before 1830.

Where did this thinking originate? Did Irving or Darby have a mysterious mentor? The key resource that answers this important historical question is a book (now out of print) called *The Restoration of Apostles and Prophets; In the Catholic Apostolic Church* by Robert M. Norton (1861).

Born in London, Robert Norton received his M.D. in 1829 from Edinburgh's University's Faculty of Medicine, only to later enter the Anglican ministry in the 1840s. When news of the charismatic revival in western Scotland broke in 1830, Norton, like Darby and others, went there as an observer. He published these initial findings in 1839, referencing the twin brothers James and George

Macdonald as principal leaders. Norton published their memoirs a year later.

From 1857 to 1862, Robert Norton lived at Albury, previously noted for its famous prophetic conferences. His 1861 history of the Irvingites mentions key leaders of the nineteenth century "Latter Rain" movement such as James Stewart and John Campbell. In *The Restoration of Apostles and Prophets* he tells about the Macdonald family in Port Glasglow, a small shipbuilding town in western Scotland, and especially notes Margaret, the youngest (born January 14, 1815). Norton's Irvingite chronicle states that in the spring of 1830, Margaret, a semi-invalid, confined to a sick bed, was given the gift of prophecy. Her subsequent healing caused no small stir. It was during this season (February-April of 1830) that this young lassie (at age 15) had a vision about the Church being caught away before a time of tribulation. On page 15 of his writing Norton says,

> "...the power of the Holy Ghost rested upon her for several successive hours, in mingled prophecy and vision...here we see the distinction between that final stage of the Lord's coming, when every eye shall see Him, and His prior appearing in glory to them that look for Him."

Although the Irvingites experienced charismatic manifestations of the Spirit, including tongues and the gift of prophecy, it has been documented that Margaret was not baptized with the Spirit at the time of her "revelation." The pre-tribulation rapture teaching did not originate with an utterance of tongues. It is doubtful that the Macdonalds ever visited the charismatic revival taking place in Irving's London congregation; however, Margaret privately sent handwritten copies of her Scripture-riddled "revelation" to some leading clergymen, including Irving.

Margaret's father, Captain James Macdonald, had died earlier (as had her mother). The Macdonald clan included three sisters (Margaret, Mary, and Jane, of which Margaret was the youngest) and two brothers (James and George). The boys had tried their hand at business. When their venture failed, they turned to spiritual matters. The Macdonalds maintained and continued the practice of holding prayer meetings in their home for years, eventually adding church ordinances to their Sunday and Wednesday services. Uneducated, clannish emotionalism took precedence over serious Bible study.

Margaret's eschatological views, the central theme of her spiritual manifestations, were well-known to those who visited her home, among them John Darby of the Plymouth Brethren. Copies of her vision were circulated as men began to preach this rapture idea as gospel. Her "two-stage" vision of the Lord's coming was parroted in a prophecy by Mrs. J.D. Cardale (whose husband was leader of the Albury delegation to Scotland) on April 30, 1831, in a house meeting. The Cardales soon after joined Edward Irving's church. Irving himself began to teach these "revelations" at Powerscourt house in prophetic meetings. These sessions were attended by some of the Plymouth Brethren, including John Darby and C.H. Mackintosh.

Clarence Larkin

As noted, C.I. Scofield was largely responsible for popularizing the "any minute" teaching, detailing it in the notes of his still-famous study Bible. The charts that soon followed were the handiwork of men like Clarence Larkin of Philadelphia, Pennsylvania, a mechanical engineer and architect, whose classic *Dispensational Truth* was copyrighted in 1918.

Larkin entered the ministry directly from business and without any theological training at the age of 34. He was not a pre-millennialist at the time of his ordination, but later adopted the futurist view. On page 5 of *Dispensational Truth*, Larkin admitted that the material he got for his prophetic charts and the futurist view of dispensationalism "in its present form...originated at the end of the sixteenth century with the Jesuit Ribera" (previously mentioned)! Thousands of sincere Protestant ministers have used these charts.

When the Latter Rain revival broke out in February of 1948, Pentecostal men and women began to question the traditional approach of Darby, Scofield, and Larkin. The latter likened those who spoke with other tongues and believed in the miracle-working power of the Holy Ghost to be demonically inspired. On page 102 of *Dispensational Truth*, concluding his chapter on "Spiritism," Larkin said,

> "Another of the 'signs of the time' is the revival of what is called the 'gift of tongues,' in which the recipient claims he is taken possession of by the 'Spirit of God' and empowered to speak in an

'unknown' or 'foreign tongue.' But the conduct of those possessed, in which they fall to the ground and writhe in contortions, causing disarrangements of the clothing and disgraceful scenes, is more a characteristic of 'demon possession,' than a work of the Holy Spirit, for the Holy Spirit does not lend Himself to such vile impersonations. From what has been said we see that we are living in 'perilous times,' and that all about us are 'seducing spirits,' and that they will become more active as the dispensation draws to its close, and that we must exert the greatest care lest we be led astray by them."

The same man who has indirectly (through his charts) taught thousands of Spirit-filled people about Bible prophecy and end-time events ignorantly made light of the realities of the Feast of Pentecost! This stunning information caused men in the late 1940s to begin to reevaluate Scofield's pre-tribulation rapture. From 1948 to the present, God has answered the prayers of that courageous generation, raising up prophets and teachers who began to expound what the Bible had to say about prophetic events by inspiration and enlightenment as revealed by their Teacher, the Holy Ghost.

Prior to 1830, the majority of ecclesiastical history and the Church fathers saw the Church enduring unto the end as an overcoming, glorious people. All that changed with the "revelation" of a 15-year-old girl not baptized with the Holy Ghost, not covered by a local church, and perhaps delirious with fever!

The dragon is defeated, but he still has a mouth. His purpose is to abort the Seed of Abraham and David, to keep the Church in the dark as to her true covenantal identity in Christ. To this end, the god of this world invented dispensationalism in all its forms. Interestingly, every major false religion in America began to evolve and develop at the *same time*!

1. Mormonism—Joseph Smith organized the "Church of Jesus Christ of Latter-Day Saints" in 1830.

2. Seventh-Day Adventism—Following William Miller's false predictions of 1843-44, the S.D.A. Church was organized in 1860. It was later led by Ellen G. White.

3. Spiritism—Beginning with the Fox sisters in 1847, the "National Spiritualist Association of the U.S. of A." was formed in 1863.

4. Christian Science—Mary Baker Eddy published her bible, *Science and Health*, in 1875.

5. Jehovah's Witnesses—Charles Taze Russell published the first issue of *The Watchtower* in 1879.

To distract men from the genuine Pentecostal outpouring of the Spirit (1900-1910), the devil attempted to counterfeit and prostitute New Testament realities. One of his most powerful tools was the futurism found in the notes of Scofield's Bible (1909).

Extreme dispensationalism butchers the past by relegating and confining the *charismata* (spiritual gifts) to the early Church and the Book of Acts. It destroys destiny by robbing the Church of her true identity in Christ as the seed of Abraham and David.

Did satan allow all these "obvious" false teachings to come about as a smokescreen for his most effective tool—dispensationalism?

2 Cor. 11:12-15, NIV

And I will keep on doing what I am doing in order to cut the ground from under those who want an opportunity to be considered equal with us in the things they boast about.

For such men are false apostles, deceitful workmen, masquerading as apostles of Christ.

And no wonder, for Satan himself masquerades as an angel of light.

It is not surprising, then, if his servants masquerade as servants of righteousness. Their end will be what their actions deserve.

Having tapped the historical roots of dispensationalism, we now turn to the Bible to take another look at the Scriptures men use to substantiate it. The false-faced angel of light always comes wrapped up in the Word of God.

(Recommended reading for additional information on the historical and biblical analysis of dispensationalism can be found in the Appendix at the end of this book.)

Chapter Eight

A Fresh Biblical Look at Dispensationalism

"…what saith the scripture?"

Galatians 4:30

The preceding chapter examined the historical roots of dispensationalism. We met some very interesting people, among them Francisco Ribera, Edward Irving, John Darby, Margaret Macdonald, Robert Norton, C.I. Scofield, and Clarence Larkin. In only 165 years (1830-1995), the "any minute" rapture has become sacrosanct to many in America. Why is it so appealing?

Dispensationalism's whole prophetic scheme, historically and conceptually, rests on one premise—a distinction between national Israel and the Church. The most important underlying "truth" that led to the evolution of the pre-tribulation rapture theory was the separation or dichotomy of "Jew and Greek."

Chapter Four established from the doctrinal epistles of the New Testament that Jesus and His Church are the

Seed of Abraham. Furthermore, if the foundation of Ribera's and Scofield's house (essentially based on Daniel's prophecy of seventy weeks, exegeted in Chapter Ten) will not stand the scrutiny of unbiased scriptural investigation, the whole structure will crumble.

After two years in college as a music major, I went to a small Pentecostal Bible school (where I also met my dear wife Joann). One of our first classes was *Dispensational Truths*. As a young Christian, my spirit could not accept that God's total redemptive plan could fit inside a chart three feet long and one foot high, although Larkin's precision was quite intimidating at the time. Then in 1969, the Lord Himself opened my eyes to the truth that the *Church* is the Seed of Abraham (Gal. 3:29)! Chapters Four and Five established that the Abrahamic and Davidic Covenants are amplified, clarified, and brought to fulfillment in the New Covenant, the New Testament in the blood of Jesus Christ. My Christian friend, the Jew is you.

In review, the apostle Paul taught that the law, not the Church, was "added" or parenthetical, and did not disannul the Abrahamic Covenant (Gal. 3:13-19). Jesus confirmed or secured the promises made to the fathers—Abraham, Isaac, and Jacob (Acts 3:13; Rom. 15:8). The Abrahamic Covenant gave Jesus the *promises* as Heir of all things (Heb. 1:2). The Davidic oath gave Jesus the *throne*, the legal authority to appropriate, activate, and administer those promises. By extension, Jesus now shares these covenantal blessings and responsibilities with His Church, joint-heirs with Him of the grace of life (see Rom. 8:17; Gal. 3:7; Col. 1:27; 1 Pet. 3:7).

Mk. 7:13, KJV

Making the word of God of none effect through your tradition....

The Church today allows the power of man's tradition to hinder the power of God. These cherished hand-me-downs have taken the Kingdom of God and given it to another time (the future) and another people (the natural Jew).

I am pro-Jesus. God loves all the races of the earth (Jn. 3:16; Acts 10:34-35). He laid the axe to the Old Testament plant and established a new, true, genuine Vine (Mt. 3:7-12; Jn. 15:1-7). Men and women from all nations are the branches of that planting! In Christ, we are not gentiles (Eph. 2:11-12). To be a new creature is to be an Israelite indeed (Jn. 1:47; Rom. 2:28-29)!

Nonetheless, Scofield's classical dispensationalism made a distinction between "the Kingdom of God" (for the Church) and "the Kingdom of Heaven" (for millennial Jews). But what the Gospel of Matthew says about the "Kingdom of Heaven" (see Mt. 4:17; 5:3; 10:7-8; 13:31; 19:14,23-24), Mark and Luke say about "the Kingdom of God" (see Mk. 1:14-15; 4:30-31; 10:14; Lk. 6:20; 9:2; 18:24-25). Simply stated, the phrase "Kingdom of Heaven" shows us where it is from, and the phrase "Kingdom of God" tells us who runs it! More recent dispensational theologians are moving away from Scofield's early thinking.

What some have called "rapture fever" is like an addicting drug. Men incessantly focus on an imminent return of Christ that will remove them from history. Daily headlines are continually used to prove their latest sign of the times ("newspaper exegesis") as "the clock of prophecy" ticks on. The basic problem with this natural-mindedness is that everything in God begins in the heavens and then manifests in the earth. True prophets gaze into the unseen realm of the Spirit and then declare what will happen in the visible realm. Men without the Holy Ghost can only read the morning paper and guess.

Ironically, the ticking-clock mentality contradicts itself! If *any* prophecies are to be fulfilled today, that would mean that there are events in the Church Age that must take place prior to the rapture! Such a view of signs being fulfilled in our day actually denies an "any moment" coming.

Despite the embarrassing setbacks of the 1980s, prophecy teachers geared up their machines again during the Gulf War (1990). Book sales soared, but then crashed with Iraq's defeat. Real problems soon began for these prognosticators. The defeat of the Communist coup in the Soviet Union (August, 1991) ended any immediate threat to the state of Israel from Russia (the "magog" of Ezek. 38–39). To compensate, extremists are inventing more and more fringe rapture scenarios that become wilder and wilder, mixed with pyramidology, UFO's, black holes in outer space, and other strange suppositions. These assumptions only confuse God's people.

Staunch dispensationalists self-consciously reject the idea of any visible, institutional, social progress. They do not really believe that the Church and the gospel can change the world. What some call realism is little more than pessimism. Wake up, brethren. This is exactly what the devil wants Christians to think: *Let the world go to hell...just give me my mansion!* Such escapism is the root of cultural irrelevance and spiritual irresponsibility (Mt. 5:13-16).

Let the truth of the Word of God renew your mind. Jesus Christ is the Seed of Abraham and David, the one "whose right it is." The Spirit of the Son who lives within is greater than he who is in the world!

"Any Minute" or "Until"?

To repeat, I believe and teach the literal, physical, bodily return of Jesus Christ to this planet. But His coming is not "any minute"—as to its timing; the key word is "until."

Tit. 2:13, KJV

> *Looking for that blessed hope, and the glorious appearing of the great God and our Saviour Jesus Christ.*

1 Jn. 3:2-3, KJV

> *Beloved, now are we the sons of God, and it doth not yet appear what we shall be: but we know that, when He shall appear, we shall be like Him; for we shall see Him as He is.*

> *And every man that hath this hope in him purifieth himself, even as He is pure.*

The dragon is defeated, but continues to mouth his ideas through mass media, video, and audio cassettes. Men must understand that the "any minute" rapture is not the second coming. They have been taught that the pre-tribulation rapture is the "blessed hope" of the Church.

The coming of the Lord is not a blessed hope—it is a blessed fact (Acts 1:11). My expectation is not that He will come again, but rather that I will be like Him when He does!

The coming of the Lord is not "any minute." It is, according to the Word of God, "until"—a word denoting time. No man knows the day nor the hour (Mt. 24:36; Acts 1:7).

Acts 2:1, KJV

And when the day of Pentecost was fully come....

Gal. 3:19, KJV

*Wherefore then serveth the law? It was added because of transgressions, **till** the seed should come to whom the promise was made....*

Gal. 4:1-4, KJV

Now I say, That the heir, as long as he is a child, differeth nothing from a servant, though he be lord of all;

*But is under tutors and governors **until** the time appointed of the father.*

Even so we, when we were children, were in bondage under the elements of the world:

But when the fulness of the time was come, God sent forth His Son, made of a woman, made under the law.

Jesus' first coming, naturally (in Bethlehem's manger) and spiritually (in the upper room), was not "until" the fullness of time! Our root text corroborates this: "...until He come whose right it is" (Ezek. 21:27).

As detailed later in this study, His first coming is a seed form and pattern of His second coming. Jesus is coming again, but He cannot come *until*:

1. His enemies are made His footstool in the earth (Mk. 12:36; Acts 7:49). His foes are defined by the curse of the Law: sin, sickness, poverty, and death (Deut. 28).

Ps. 110:1, KJV

> *The Lord said unto my Lord, Sit thou at My right hand, **until** I make thine enemies thy footstool.*

Heb. 10:12-13, NIV

> *But when this priest had offered for all time one sacrifice for sins, He sat down at the right hand of God.*
>
> *Since that time He waits for His enemies to be made His footstool.*

2. The times of the restitution (restoration) of all things of which the prophets have spoken.

Acts 3:19-21, NIV

> *Repent, then, and turn to God, so that your sins may be wiped out, that times of refreshing may come from the Lord,*
> *and that He may send the Christ, who has been appointed for you—even Jesus.*
> *He must remain in heaven **until** the time comes for God to restore everything, as He promised long ago through His holy prophets.*

3. The Church comes into the unity of the faith, the full and accurate knowledge of the Son of God, and attains to the measure of the full stature of Christ.

Eph. 4:13, NIV

> **Until** we all reach unity in the faith and in the knowledge of the Son of God and become mature, attaining to the whole measure of the fullness of Christ.

4. The heavenly Husbandman receives the early and latter rains of Joel 2:23-32.

Jas. 5:7, KJV

> Be patient therefore, brethren, unto the coming of the Lord. Behold, the husbandman waiteth for the precious fruit of the earth, and hath long patience for it, **until** he receive the early and latter rain.

Psalm 110 reveals the purpose of God's Kingdom—the extension of His rule and dominion in the earth and universe. The Church is called to be the instrument of the Kingdom, to rule in the midst of its enemies.

Note especially Ephesians 4:11-16. Many who cherish the imminent return of the Lord do not acknowledge the contemporary ministries of apostles and prophets—the foundational ministries given by Jesus to the Church to equip and mature the saints (Lk. 11:49; Eph. 2:20; 3:1-5). Everybody wants to go up, but nobody wants to grow up. In Galatians, the apostle Paul emphasized this theme of maturity with regard to the seed, in particular, the Seed of Abraham.

Gal. 4:1-2, NIV

> What I am saying is that as long as the heir is a child, he is no different from a slave, although he owns the whole estate.

*He is subject to guardians and trustees **until** the time set by his father.*

The heir is under the authority of "tutors and governors" (KJV) until the time appointed by the Father. Again, these guardians of the seed are the five ascension-gift ministries (the Greek word is *doma*) of Ephesians 4:11!

Salvation is progressive as well as "once and for all" (2 Cor. 1:10; Eph. 2:1-3). The pre-trib rapture belief is popular because in it men can reign without suffering. We are told that all we need to experience is the new birth and we're "out of here on the first load." But once a person has been delivered by the blood, he needs to be baptized in water in the name of the Lord, and then be filled with the Holy Ghost (Acts 2:38; 1 Cor. 10:1-11). These three witnesses (1 Jn. 5:8) inaugurate the New Covenant in a man's life, covering his past and making him a candidate, or pupil, to learn the ways of the Lord (Mt. 28:18-20).

Lk. 19:13, KJV

*...Occupy **till** I come.*

Lk. 19:13, NKJ

*..."Do business **till** I come."*

Jesus' second coming is not "any minute" but "until...." Nothing could be plainer than His own words. The word for "occupy" (used only in this passage) is *pragmateumai* (Strong's #4231). It means "to busy oneself with, to trade." Compare the English word *pragmatic*.

The gospel is practical and relevant to everyday living. Stay busy till He comes. Keep doing what God told you to do; Jesus cannot come "until"….

Kept During the Hour of Trial

The false hope of an "any minute" rapture must be replaced with a true expectation (1 Jn. 3:2-3). King Jeroboam I devised and ordained a false Feast of Tabernacles "like unto the feast" of the Lord (1 Kings 12:25-33). This idolatrous leader said to his followers, "It is too much for you to go up to Jerusalem…"—the place that God had chosen (Deut. 16:16). Like the pastors of some "seeker sensitive" churches in America, Jeroboam wanted to make it easy for the people so as not to offend them.

As noted in the previous chapter, classical dispensationalism is less than 200 years old. How did it become so popular in a short time? What are some of the main Scriptures put together by Darby, Scofield, and Larkin to substantiate the futurist view? Let's begin our fresh biblical look at dispensationalism.

Rev. 3:9-10, KJV

Behold, I will make them of the synagogue of Satan, which say they are Jews, and are not, but do lie; behold, I will make them to come and worship before thy feet, and to know that I have loved thee.

Because thou hast kept the word of My patience, I also will keep thee from the hour of temptation, which shall come upon all the world, to try them that dwell upon the earth.

In its primary application, this promise would have pertained to the Church of Philadelphia in the first century. Furthermore, this text is conditional—those who keep the Word of God (not men's traditions) with endurance will be kept. Besides, Revelation 3:9 says the opposite of the dispensational view—God will bring the enemy down before our feet (we have to be here for that to happen). The word for "keep" in Revelation 3:10 is *tereo* and means "preserve, attend to, take care of, guard." Even though the Greek word for "from" is *ek* and means "out of," it does not necessarily denote geographical removal. Compare this verse with other words of Scripture, including those of Jesus Himself.

Ps. 125:1, KJV

They that trust in the Lord shall be as mount Zion, which cannot be removed....

Prov. 10:30, KJV

The righteous shall never be removed....

Prov. 2:21-22, KJV

For the upright shall dwell in the land, and the perfect shall remain in it.

But the wicked shall be cut off from the earth, and the transgressors shall be rooted out of it.

Jn. 17:15, NIV

My prayer is not that You take them out of the world but that You protect them from the evil one.

Throughout the Bible, God keeps His own during the hour of trial. Consider Noah and the ark, Joseph in the pit, Israel in Goshen, the three Hebrew children in the fiery furnace, Daniel in the lions' den, Paul in his journeys, and even Jesus in His earthly trials.

Lk. 4:29-30, KJV

And rose up, and thrust Him out of the city, and led Him unto the brow of the hill whereon their city was built, that they might cast Him down headlong.

But He passing through the midst of them went His way.

The preservation of the saints is emphasized in Chapter Three of my book *Prevail: A Handbook for the Overcomer* (Shippensburg, PA: Destiny Image Publishers, 1982). That chapter is entitled, "Pressing Through Tribulation." If there is a literal three-and-a-half or seven-year tribulation period, the Church will be here *during* it, not *for* it (Is. 26:20-21). Read and study Psalms 37 and 91. The whole armor of God is for the evil day, that believers might stand against the enemy, not fly away (Eph. 6:11-13). We have died, and our lives are hidden, safe and secure, with Christ in God (1 Cor. 10:13; Col. 3:1-3).

Rev. 4:1-2, KJV

After this I looked, and, behold, a door was opened in heaven: and the first voice which I heard was as it were of a trumpet talking with me; which said, Come up hither, and I will show thee things which must be hereafter.

And immediately I was in the spirit: and, behold, a
throne was set in heaven, and one sat on the throne.

Following Jesuit Francisco Ribera's original segment-
ing of the Book of Revelation, early dispensationalists
pinpointed Revelation 4:1 as the rapture of the Church.
Darby, Scofield, and Larkin later popularized this notion.
But what about the trumpet that blows in Revelation 1:10
(John was "in the Spirit" at that time)? If the Church isn't
mentioned after chapter 3, what about the "saints" of
Revelation 5:13; 7:3; 11:13; 12:17; 14:1-5; 15:2? Paul made
it clear that the "saints," the "Body of Christ," and the
"Church" are the same (Eph. 4:11-12; 5:27).

This open door in Revelation 4:1 is the rent veil. Walk
through it and behold the Most Holy Place, the throne
room of Revelation 4–5, the destiny of our high calling.
This realm of the Spirit has nothing to do with natural
location or geography. As noted in Chapter Five, His
throne is the place of His authority and rule.

The Olivet Discourse

The Olivet Discourse is the New Testament center-
piece of futurism. King Jesus' powerful prophecy is
found in Matthew 24, Mark 13, and Luke 21. In order to
get the full picture, the careful student will read and
compare all three accounts. This part of our study is crucial and is to be tied to the discussion of Daniel's prophecy of seventy weeks in Chapter Ten.

Remember that the purpose for discussing these passages throughout Chapters Eight and Nine is to deliver
the Church from giving place to the devil by accepting

the bad news of the futurist view. We are to proclaim the good news of Him "whose right it is."

Matthew 24, along with Daniel's seventieth week and Revelation 4–19, constitutes the seven-year "tribulation period" (after the rapture) for many Bible students. Accordingly, futurists apply these verses about deceivers, wars, earthquakes, famines, and pestilences to our time. The abomination of desolation is regarded as an idol of the antichrist (or the antichrist himself), a future world leader, to be set up in the holy of holies of a rebuilt Jewish temple at Jerusalem. When this happens, the Jews will flee into the mountains, for then shall be great tribulation.

But we shall see that these events that Jesus said would *soon* happen took place before the destruction of the temple in A.D. 70. The abomination of desolation was the Roman army that surrounded Jerusalem to cause its desolation (Mt. 24:15-21; Lk. 21:20-22). Upon heeding the warning of Jesus, His disciples fled from Jerusalem and Judea. The "great tribulation" that Jesus predicted fell upon the Jewish nation (A.D. 67-70), resulting in the destruction of their city and sanctuary (Dan. 9:26-27).

To understand Matthew 24:1-34, one must begin with the eight "woes" pronounced upon the Pharisees by Jesus in Matthew 23. He ended His denunciation by announcing that their "house" would be left desolate (Mt. 23:38).

Mt. 24:1-3, KJV

And Jesus went out, and departed from the temple: and His disciples came to Him for to show Him the buildings of the temple.

> *And Jesus said unto them, See ye not all these things? verily I say unto you, There shall not be left here one stone upon another, that shall not be thrown down.*
>
> *And as He sat upon the mount of Olives, the disciples came unto Him privately, saying, Tell us, when shall these things be? and what shall be the sign of Thy coming, and of the end of the world?*

Another key that unlocks Matthew 24 is to see that Jesus was asked and then answered *three* questions:

1. When shall these things (Mt. 24:2) be?

2. What shall be the sign of Thy coming?

3. And of the end of the world (age)?

Mt. 23:36, KJV

> *Verily I say unto you, All these things shall come upon this generation.*

"This generation" (Mt. 24:34) refers to the contemporary generation, the generation alive at the hearing of Jesus' words (compare the same phrase in Mt. 11:16; Mk. 8:12,38; 13:30; Lk. 7:31; 11:29-32,50-51; 17:25; 21:32).

As shown in connection with Daniel's prophecy of seventy weeks (Chapter Ten), Matthew 24:1-34 was historically fulfilled in A.D. 70 with the overthrow of Jerusalem by the Roman prince Titus and his army, yet this passage has future prophetic overtones.

Mt. 24:4-12, KJV

> *And Jesus answered and said unto them, Take heed that no man deceive you.*

For many shall come in My name, saying, I am Christ; and shall deceive many.

And ye shall hear of wars and rumours of wars: see that ye be not troubled: for all these things must come to pass, but the end is not yet.

For nation shall rise against nation, and kingdom against kingdom: and there shall be famines, and pestilences, and earthquakes, in divers places.

All these are the beginning of sorrows.

Then shall they deliver you up to be afflicted, and shall kill you: and ye shall be hated of all nations for My name's sake.

And then shall many be offended, and shall betray one another, and shall hate one another.

And many false prophets shall rise, and shall deceive many.

And because iniquity shall abound, the love of many shall wax cold.

While dispensationalists make much over the "signs of the times" and that these things are happening in our day, they also occurred in the first century:

1. False Christs (Acts 5:36-37; 8:9-11; 13:6).

2. Wars (corroborated by history; see Chapter Ten).

3. Famines (Acts 11:27-29; Rom. 15:25-28; 1 Cor. 16:1-5).

4. Earthquakes (Acts 16:26).

5. False prophets (2 Cor. 11:13; 2 Pet. 2:1-3; 1 Jn. 4:1).

6. Apostasy (see 1 Cor. 5:1-2; Gal. 1:6-10; 2 Tim. 1:15; 4:16).

Mt. 24:13, KJV

But he that shall endure unto the end, the same shall be saved.

Mt. 24:21-24, KJV

For then shall be great tribulation, such as was not since the beginning of the world to this time, no, nor ever shall be.

And except those days should be shortened, there should no flesh be saved: but for the elect's sake those days shall be shortened.

Then if any man shall say unto you, Lo, here is Christ, or there; believe it not.

For there shall arise false Christs, and false prophets, and shall show great signs and wonders; insomuch that, if it were possible, they shall deceive the very elect.

Mt. 24:29, KJV

Immediately after the tribulation of those days shall the sun be darkened, and the moon shall not give her light, and the stars shall fall from heaven, and the powers of the heavens shall be shaken.

These verses describe God's people enduring a time of tribulation and pressure. The tribulation prophesied by Jesus in Matthew 24:29 marked the end of Judaism

(A.D. 67-70). The twelve tribes of Israel are described as the sun and moon (Gen. 37:9-10). The cosmic imagery describing the judgment and vindication of God meant "lights out" for the old order (Mt. 21:42-43; 1 Pet. 2:9-10). Consider the parallel language of the Old Testament describing the end of Babylon (Is. 13:9-10), Edom (Is. 34:4-5), and Israel (Amos 5:18-22; 8:9).

Mt. 24:30, KJV

> *And then shall appear the sign of the Son of man in heaven: and then shall all the tribes of the earth mourn, and they shall see the Son of man coming in the clouds of heaven with power and great glory.*

Mt. 24:30, NIV

> *...They will see the Son of Man coming on the clouds of the sky, with power and great glory.*

The Son of man coming "on" or "upon" the clouds is an Old Testament portrayal of God riding on a swift cloud, revealing His sovereignty over the nations as their Judge (Ps. 104:3). Daniel's picture of this (Dan. 7:13-14) predicts Messiah coming onstage, on the scene. It beautifully describes Jesus, "the Son of man," ascending and coming to the Father, "the Ancient of days," to receive all power and dominion (Mt. 28:18). Accordingly, Stephen saw Jesus standing in Heaven (Acts 7:56). Jesus had told the high priest of this (Mt. 26:64). Israel's leader "saw" that at Pentecost and Stephen's stoning. With the destruction of Jerusalem in A.D. 70, the truth of their true Messiah's exaltation sank in for the whole nation.

Mt. 24:31, KJV

And He shall send His angels with a great sound of a trumpet, and they shall gather together His elect from the four winds, from one end of heaven to the other.

While Matthew 24:31 could be compared to First Thessalonians 4:13-18, it also pictures the trumpeting of the gospel in obedience to the Great Commission (Mk. 16:15-20), sounding forth the message of the good news to gather the harvest from every nation. The word for "gather together" is *episunago.* The true "synagogue" of God—the Church—is made up of believing Jews and Greeks.

Mt. 24:32-33, KJV

Now learn a parable of the fig tree; When his branch is yet tender, and putteth forth leaves, ye know that summer is nigh:

So likewise ye, when ye shall see all these things, know that it is near, even at the doors.

Dispensationalists say that these two verses predict the Jews becoming a nation again and returning to their homeland, a sign of the last days. But Luke 21:29 mentions "all the trees." What was "near"? The promise that Jesus Christ made about the destruction of their temple and city within a generation!

Israel did become a nation again on May 14, 1948. Many prophecy teachers feel that this was the most important "sign" in Matthew 24, making much of a "generation" being 40 years. Adding 40 years to 1948 brought us to 1988, when dispensationalism rose to new heights. The major problem facing this prediction was that a pre-tribulation view would have to subtract seven years from 1988, putting the "rapture" in 1981. That was fourteen years ago. Even though these predictions fell through, men have yet to apologize. Paperback prophecy books still sell.

Mt. 24:34, KJV

> *Verily I say unto you, This generation shall not pass, till all these things be fulfilled.*

This verse brings the Olivet Discourse full circle (from Mt. 23:36). Notwithstanding, a primary question is: Who are the "elect" in Matthew 24? The Greek word *eklektos* means "selected, picked out, chosen." It is used 23 times in the New Testament, and is translated, sixteen times as "elect" (see Mt. 24:22,24,31; Mk. 13:20,22,27; Lk. 18:7; Rom. 8:33; Col. 3:12; 1 Tim. 5:21; 2 Tim. 2:10; Tit. 1:1; 1 Pet. 1:2; 2:6; and 2 Jn. 1:1,13), and seven times as "chosen" (see Mt. 20:16; 22:14; Lk. 23:35; Rom. 16:13; 1 Pet. 2:4,9; and Rev. 17:14).

Compare *eklektos* with *ekklesia*, the Greek word for "church." These verses and others (see Acts 10:34-35; Gal. 3:28-29; Eph. 1:4; 1 Thess. 1:4) make it clear that the "elect" mentioned in Matthew 24 are Christians, "elect" Jews (Rom. 11:1-5) who accepted their Messiah (see the notes on Dan. 9:27 in Chapter Ten)!

Extreme dispensationalists teach Matthew 24 in a non-Christian context. Scofield and other early futurists did this with most of the Book of Matthew, even relegating the Sermon on the Mount, the constitution of the Kingdom of God (Mt. 5–7), solely to the Jew. Don't be spoiled by men's reasonings (Col. 2:8).

One Shall Be Taken

Mt. 24:37-41, KJV

But as the days of Noe were, so shall also the coming of the Son of man be.

For as in the days that were before the flood they were eating and drinking, marrying and giving in marriage, until the day that Noe entered into the ark,

And knew not until the flood came, and took them all away; so shall also the coming of the Son of man be.

Then shall two be in the field; the one shall be taken, and the other left.

Two women shall be grinding at the mill; the one shall be taken, and the other left.

Lk. 17:27, KJV

They did eat, they drank, they married wives, they were given in marriage, until the day that Noe entered into the ark, and the flood came, and destroyed them all.

Some like to point to Enoch (Gen. 5:18-24; Heb. 11:5-6), who was translated, and say that he is a type of those who are raptured before tribulation. But Enoch did not live during the time that judgment was being poured out on the earth in the form of a flood. Enoch was translated 669 years before the Flood, and he never met Noah. In other words, his translation was not for the purpose of escaping the Flood. Noah went *through* the Flood, protected by the Ark he had prepared.

The *Pentecostal Evangel* (the official voice of the Assemblies of God) dated January 1, 1967, boldly showed the obvious truth of this passage—the wicked were "taken" in judgment, and the righteous (Noah and his sons) stepped out of the ark and inherited the earth (see Ps. 2:8; Mt. 5:5; Rev. 1:6; 5:10)! No one else was "left" to dispute Noah's claim. Those who read and understand the words of the prophet Jesus don't want to be "taken"…they want to be "left"!

Eph. 6:13, KJV

Wherefore take unto you the whole armour of God, that ye may be able to withstand in the evil day, and having done all, to stand.

Not fly away, but stand! Paul never preached a message of fear. He never told the saints that they would escape the battle. God's complaint against the false prophets in Ezekiel's day (Ezek. 13:1-5) was that they did not prepare the people for what was coming in the Day of the Lord.

Ezek. 13:10, KJV

Because, even because they have seduced My people, saying, Peace; and there was no peace; and one built up a wall, and, lo, others daubed it with untempered mortar.

Ezek. 13:10, NIV

Because they lead My people astray, saying, "Peace," when there is no peace, and because, when a flimsy wall is built, they cover it with whitewash.

1 Thess. 5:3, KJV

For when they shall say, Peace and safety; then sudden destruction cometh upon them...and they shall not escape.

Margaret Macdonald and Edward Irving built the wall, while Darby, Scofield, and Larkin daubed at it. But the one "whose right it is" is about to ride through the Church and blow down every whitewashed wall (Mt. 23:37; Acts 23:3) by the wind of His Spirit. Contrary to popular opinion and soothing reassurances, men "shall not escape" when the Messenger of the covenant comes suddenly to cleanse His temple (Mal. 3:1; Mt. 3:12).

What About Armageddon?

A sidelight of the futurist interpretation of Matthew 24 and an integral part of dispensationalism's future "great tribulation" (Mt. 24:21) is the much-heralded Battle of Armageddon. "Armageddon" is synonymous with mass destruction, carnage, and unprecedented bloodshed. Interestingly (although Rev. 14:20 is used as a cross-reference), this term is not used in the Old Testament and is mentioned but once in the New Testament.

Rev. 14:20, KJV

And the winepress was trodden without the city, and blood came out of the winepress, even unto the

> horse bridles, by the space of a thousand and six hundred furlongs.

Rev. 16:16, KJV

> *And he gathered them together into a place called in the Hebrew tongue Armageddon.*

Dispensationalists teach that there are no prophetic events to take place prior to the rapture. That means that current events ("newspaper exegesis") are irrelevant when used to speculate when the rapture may occur. However, if evidence can be produced to show that Armageddon might be near, then (as taught) the rapture must be imminent. Men shamelessly declare that blood will flow 6 feet deep for 200 miles (a furlong is an eighth of a mile).

To literally accomplish this, the blood would have to encompass the whole valley from Mount Carmel on the Mediterranean Sea along the Kishon River through the valley of Megiddo and Jezreel to the river Jordan, then south through the plain of the river Jordan to and through the Dead Sea, and onward south through the valley of the wilderness of Zin and past Kadesh-Barnea into the Sinai Peninsula! This is absurd, not to mention impossible! There's not that much blood in the entire global population. Megiddo and Revelation 14:20; 16:16 is *symbolic*.

Armageddon is transliterated from the Greek *Armageddon* (Strong's #717) and means "Armageddon (or *Har-Meggiddon*), a symbolic name." It is taken from two Hebrew words: *Har*, meaning "mountain," and *Megiddown*, meaning "rendezvous; Megiddon or Megiddo, a place in Palestine." It is derived from *gagad* ("to crowd; to gash") and *guwd* ("to crowd, to attack"). In the King James Version, the former is translated as "assemble (selves by troops)" and the latter as "invade, overcome."

Megiddo, or "place of troops," was a walled city on a plain. There never will be a literal "Battle of Armageddon," for there is no such place, no "mountain of Megiddo," on this planet!

The city (not the mountain) of Megiddo was located about 70 miles north of Jerusalem in the Carmel mountain range. Situated on the main road that linked Egypt and Syria, it was the site of many Old Testament battles. Overlooking the Valley of Jezreel (Plain of Esdraelon), Megiddo was the most strategic city in Palestine as a military stronghold.

Megiddo is mentioned 11 times in the Old Testament (see Josh. 12:21; 17:11; Judg. 1:27; 5:19; 1 Kings 4:12; 9:15; 2 Kings 9:27; 23:29-30; 1 Chron. 7:29; 2 Chron. 35:22). Two notable events took place there—Deborah and Barak's defeat of Sisera, and the slaying of King Josiah of Judah by the pharaoh of Egypt.

Judg. 5:19, KJV

> *The kings came and fought, then fought the kings of Canaan in Taanach by the waters of Megiddo; they took no gain of money.*

2 Chron. 35:22, KJV

> *Nevertheless Josiah would not turn his face from him, but disguised himself, that he might fight with him, and hearkened not unto the words of Necho from*

the mouth of God, and came to fight in the valley of Megiddo.

Megiddo is a symbol of war between rival kings and kingdoms. In the examples given, Israel was both a winner and a loser. Revelation 16:16 references the latter, where Josiah would not listen to God's warning (2 Chron. 35:20-25).

Dispensationalists have combined these and all the Megiddo battles into one great "great tribulation" conflict where the future antichrist will bring all the nations of the world into a final war against Israel.

There are two contextual applications necessary for properly understanding the Battle of Armageddon. As with Matthew 24 and Daniel's prophecy of seventy weeks, the passage has been historically fulfilled, yet it has spiritual implications.

First, Israel remembered Megiddo as a place where God vented His divine wrath against rebellion, whether exhibited by Israel or a foreign power. God brought the nations of the world (through the empire of Rome) against first-century Jerusalem as Jesus had promised (Mt. 24:34; Lk. 21:20). There were those who actually attempted to fight against this world empire and, like King Josiah, met their "Waterloo" (see Josephus' account of this in Chapter Ten).

Mt. 22:7, KJV

But when the king heard thereof, he was wroth: and he sent forth his armies, and destroyed those murderers, and burned up their city.

Mt. 27:25, KJV

Then answered all the people, and said, His blood be on us, and on our children.

Many in Israel had disowned Jesus and asked for the murderer Barabbas. The armies of Rome came in A.D. 70 and set their city on fire at the symbolic battlefield of "Megiddo."

Second, Armageddon is a spiritual battle, an ongoing campaign between the forces of salvation and the forces of sin. It is right against wrong, righteousness against unrighteousness, light against darkness, the Kingdom of God against the kingdom of evil. We are assured of the outcomes, for the Captain of our salvation has prevailed. Satan is defeated and Jesus is Lord!

This "battle of that great day of God Almighty" (Rev. 16:14) is between the sons of God and the powers of darkness. For now, the battleground is our homes, schools, and churches. As God judges nations, denominations, and imaginations, the true Church will emerge triumphant in her God, strong through the one "whose right it is"!

Joel 3:12-14

Let the heathen be wakened, and come up to the valley of Jehoshaphat: for there will I sit to judge all the heathen round about.

Put ye in the sickle, for the harvest is ripe: come, get you down; for the press is full, the vats overflow; for their wickedness is great.

Multitudes, multitudes in the valley of decision: for the day of the Lord is near in the valley of decision.

God and Magog

Woven in and out of dispensationalism's Armageddon scenario is a mixture of thought concerning Gog and Magog, and a future invasion of the nation of Israel by Russia.

Ezek. 38:2, KJV

> *Son of man, set thy face against Gog, the land of Magog, the chief prince of Meshech and Tubal....*

Rev. 20:8, KJV

> *And shall go out to deceive the nations which are in the four quarters of the earth, Gog and Magog, to gather them together to battle: the number of whom is as the sand of the sea.*

Before we note the etymologies of the key words in these verses, we perceive serious problems for the dispensationalists who insist on the principle of literal interpretation. First, *all* of the soldiers are riding horses, and brandishing ancient weapons—swords, bows and arrows, war clubs, and spears (Ezek. 38:15; 39:9). More importantly, there is no mention of Gog, Magog, Meshech, or Tubal in Revelation 4–19, when Darby and Scofield tell us the battle is to take place. John's battle of Gog and Magog is *after* the millennium!

"Gog" is from the Hebrew *Gowg* (Strong's #1463) and means "some northern nation." It has an uncertain derivation, and has been translated as "golden ornament" by some and "elastic, stretched out, extended" by others. "Gog" is mentioned 10 times in the Old Testament (see 1 Chron. 5:4; Ezek. 38:2-3,14,16,18; 39:1,11) and in Revelation 20:8. He is said to be the leader of a confederacy of armies, the "chief prince of Meshech and Tubal."

"Magog" is from the Hebrew *Magowg* (Strong's #4031) and means "a barbarous northern region." It has been translated as "region or land of God, from the upper (north)." "Magog" is mentioned four times in the Old Testament (see Gen. 10:2; 1 Chron. 1:5; Ezek. 38:2; 39:6), in addition to its use in Revelation 20:8.

Gog is the "chief prince" of Meshech and Tubal. This is the Hebrew word *ro'sh* (Strong's 7218) and means "head" (so translated over 30 times in the Book of Ezekiel). *Vine's* adds that *ro'sh* also means "top, first, sum."

Incredibly, Scofield translated *ro'sh* as if it were a nation—Russia! In addition, *Meshech* sounds like Moscow, and *Tubal* like Tobolsk, one of the prominent Asiatic provinces of Russia. *Meshech* was a son of Japheth, and is mentioned nine times in the Old Testament (see Gen. 10:2; 1 Chron. 1:5,17; Ps. 120:5; Ezek. 27:13; 32:26; 38:2-3; 39:1). *Tubal*, also a descendant of Japheth, is mentioned in many of the same verses.

This hermeneutic is like that of the Worldwide Church of God (Armstrongism) who teach that the ten lost tribes, the Israel of God, are Anglo-Saxon peoples. "Saxon" sounds like "Isaac's sons" and *berith* (the Hebrew word for covenant) sounds like "Britain." As seen in Chapter Four, the true Israel of God has always been a spiritual people—race or skin color has nothing to do with it. British-Israelism is heresy. Its racial bigotry has also given rise to its counterpart among blacks. Today is not the day of the white man or the black man—it's the day of the new man, the day of the Church, the day of the Lord! So much for *ro'sh*, or Russia!

Some historians assume that Ezekiel 38–39 was fulfilled in the Seleucids and Antiochus Epiphanes IV (175-164 B.C.). Regardless, it is not a picture of Russia invading Israel. For a fuller discussion of Gog and Magog (including notes from Bill Britton), see my *Principles of Present Truth From Ezekiel* (Richlands, N.C.: Tabernacle Press, 1987).

The Mark of the Beast Is a Present Reality

Prophecy teachers have stated and restated their conviction that a political world leader, the "antichrist" or "beast" of Revelation 13, is alive today somewhere in the earth.

Rev. 13:16-18, KJV

And he causeth all, both small and great, rich and poor, free and bond, to receive a mark in their right hand, or in their foreheads:

And that no man might buy or sell, save he that had the mark, or the name of the beast, or the number of his name.

Here is wisdom. Let him that hath understanding count the number of the beast: for it is the number of a man; and his number is Six hundred threescore and six.

Dispensationalists say that the antichrist will come to prominence as part of a ten-nation confederation (the

United States of Europe) approximating the land area of the old Roman Empire (Dan. 7:7-8, 19-26; Rev. 13:1-10).

The Bible term "antichrist" was explained in an earlier chapter. To review, the word appears only in John's epistles. How does the definition of popular eschatology stack up to the biblical meaning? According to the apostle John, the antichrist is...

1. Someone who denies that Jesus is the Christ (1 Jn. 2:22).

2. Someone who denies the Father and the Son (1 Jn. 2:23).

3. Every spirit that does not confess Jesus (1 Jn. 4:3).

4. Those who do not acknowledge Jesus Christ as coming in the flesh (2 Jn. 7).

An "antichrist" is anything or anyone that fits John's explanation. Simply stated, *antichrist* aptly describes any system of apostasy or individual apostates (the carnal mind). Moreover, an *antichrist* is a religious apostate from true Christianity, not some secular political figure.

1 Jn. 2:18, KJV

> ...*even now are there many antichrists*....

Darby, Scofield, and Larkin heavily emphasized the coming of this one called the antichrist, the "beast" of Revelation 13. As noted, they were seduced by the efforts of the Jesuits Ribera and Lacunza to counter Protestantism by the invention of a future antichrist. But the mark of the beast is a present reality, as is the mark of the Lord mentioned in Revelation 7:3; 14:1-5; 22:4 (see Chapter Seven of my book *The More Excellent Ministry* [Shippensburg, PA: Destiny Image Publishers, 1988, pp. 227-235]). This beastly tattoo is not referring to one's credit cards or a giant computer somewhere in the world.

The Greek word for "mark" is *charagma* (English *character*), and it means "a stamp or impress." The forehead and right hand speaks of the *wisdom* and *strength* of man (666), respectively. There are only two types of men on the planet: Christ and Adam—beauty and the beast. The word for "beast" in Revelation 13 is *therion*, and means "a wild beast"—the old man, the Jacob nature, the Ishmael nature (Gen. 16; 32). Ishmael was a good idea, the product of Sarah's head and Abraham's loins. The man of flesh will always persecute the Christ, the man of the Spirit, the son of promise (Gal. 4:21-31; 5:17).

Acts 17:29, KJV

Forasmuch then as we are the offspring of God, we ought not to think that the Godhead is like unto gold, or silver, or stone, graven by art and man's device.

When Paul went to Athens, the whole city was given to worshipping idols, fashioned by the *mind* and *hand* of man. The word for "graven" is *charagma*, translated as "mark" in Revelation 13:16! The word for "art" is *techne* and describes things made by hand. The word for "device" refers to man's inner reasonings.

Ironically, dispensationalism proudly boasts that we won't have to worry about the mark of the beast, all the while bearing the humanistic image of the thing it seeks to escape! The mouthy dragon has used the minds of men to invent tradition, and denominational technology and financial backing have pushed it. But God has a mind and a "hand" (Eph. 4:11)! What His divine intellect has envisioned for a glorious Church, His holy apostles and prophets will fashion by the spoken, living Word.

The Man of Sin

Ribera, Lacunza, Darby, Scofield, and Larkin emphasized a future world leader called the antichrist. The first two men wanted to take the heat off the pope. The other three parrots made a name for themselves. The previous section and the remainder of this chapter reveal what the Bible has to say about this "beast" and the "man of sin"—"the son of perdition." The primary Scripture before us is Second Thessalonians 2:1-12.

From antiquity, men have attempted to identify the antichrist. For centuries, the papacy was the unanimous candidate, as "the vicar of Christ" took the place of Christ. Accordingly, the "restrainer" of Second Thessalonians 2:6-7 was the Roman Empire under pagan rule, taken out of the way by the Gothic invasions. Pagan Rome vanished in the West (A.D. 476), only to be replaced by papal Rome. The Reformers taught that the pope, like Judas, the "son of perdition" (Jn. 17:12; 2 Thess. 2:3), was a false bishop, a false apostle (Acts 1:20).

Other choices for the identity of "the beast" in the last 200 years have included world figures such as Napoleon, Hitler, Mussolini, Stalin, Kruschchev, Kissinger, Gorbachev, Hussein, and even Ronald Wilson Reagan (because of the number of letters in his name). I'm somewhat relieved; were it not for the "Jr." after my name, somebody would be after Kelley Howard Varner! It seems that a person is the antichrist until he's not the antichrist. Then "adjustment theology" brings forward a new candidate.

Enough nonsense. What does Second Thessalonians really say?

After delivering Paul's first epistle to the Christians at Thessalonica, Timothy returned to the apostle with the news that the Thessalonians were suffering severe persecution for their Christian faith. Moreover, false teachers had led them to believe that the Day of the Lord was at hand and that Christ's second coming would occur at any time. As a result, many had left their employment and were idling their time away awaiting the return of the Lord.

Paul's second epistle to the Thessalonians was then written to correct these errors in understanding and attitude, to adjust the "any minute" escapist mind-set in the early Church!

In the first chapter the apostle assures them of their deliverance from tribulation at the coming of Christ, and in the second chapter he warns that there were certain events that had to transpire *before* Christ could come. The third chapter is an exhortation for the Thessalonians to return to their normal employment while awaiting the coming of the Lord.

2 Thess. 2:1, KJV

Now we beseech you, brethren, by the coming of our Lord Jesus Christ, and by our gathering together unto Him.

2 Thess. 2:1, AMP

...and our gathering together to [meet] Him....

The word for "coming" is *parousia*. The phrase "gathering together" parallels our being caught up together (1 Thess. 4:17); the Greek word is *episunagoge* (Strong's #1997), meaning "a complete collection; to collect upon the same place" (Mt. 24:31; Heb. 10:25). Some see this as the "rapture" of the saints. If that is true, the following verses indicate that certain things have to happen *before* the coming of the Lord. Accordingly, the apostle goes on to warn about "dispen-sensationalism."

2 Thess. 2:2, KJV

That ye be not soon shaken in mind, or be troubled, neither by spirit, nor by word, nor by letter as from us, as that the day of Christ is at hand.

2 Thess. 2:2, TLB

Please don't be upset and excited, dear brothers...If you hear of people having visions and special messages from God about this, or letters that are supposed to have come from me, don't believe them.

Despite this wise apostolic counsel, thousands were quickly duped in 1988, and again in 1992 and 1994. Christian bookstores have been filled for 25 years with the suppositions of Darby's and Scofield's disciples.

Paul told the Church not to be agitated or disturbed (Mt. 11:7; Heb. 12:26-27). The word for "trumpet" (a symbol for the prophetic word) is derived from this word for "shaken"—don't be moved by what some are prophesying. Don't let these things trouble or frighten you (Mt. 24:6). Don't allow any spirit or discourse of men, especially those contained in man-made writings, confuse you (1 Thess. 5:27; 2 Thess. 2:15; 3:14,17).

Some dispensationalists differentiate between the "Day of Christ" (first stage, the rapture) and the "Day of the Lord" (second stage, the revelation)—the Bible keeps it simple (Lk. 2:11; Acts 2:36). The following terms are used interchangeably to reference the same "day":

1. The Day of Christ (Phil. 1:10).

2. The Day of Jesus Christ (Phil. 1:6).

3. The Day of our Lord Jesus Christ (1 Cor. 1:8).

4. The Day of the Lord Jesus (2 Cor. 1:4).

5. The Day of the Lord (1 Thess. 5:2).

2 Thess. 2:3-4, KJV

Let no man deceive you by any means: for that day shall not come, except there come a falling away first, and that man of sin be revealed, the son of perdition;

Who opposeth and exalteth himself above all that is called God, or that is worshipped; so that he as God sitteth in the temple of God, showing himself that he is God.

2 Thess. 2:3-4, NIV

Don't let anyone deceive you in any way, for that day will not come until the rebellion occurs and the man of lawlessness is revealed, the man doomed to destruction.

He will oppose and will exalt himself over everything that is called God or is worshiped, so that he sets himself up in God's temple, proclaiming himself to be God.

2 Thess. 2:3-4, AMP

...that day will not come except the apostasy comes first...

Who opposes and exalts himself so proudly and insolently against and over all that is called God....

2 Thess. 2:3-4, TLB

...and then the man of rebellion will come—the son of hell.

He will defy every god there is, and tear down every other object of adoration and worship....

Paul warns us not to allow any man to deceive or seduce us (Rom. 7:11; 16:18; 1 Cor. 3:18). The serpent wants to "beguile" men from the simplicity that is in Christ (2 Cor. 11:3). Tradition is a thief, spoiling us through vain deceit. We are not to be ripped off by the various "means" or "modes and styles" (the high-tech glitz of

Madison Avenue flash and splash) that men use to traffic their wares.

The coming of the Lord will not happen except or unless there is "the falling away" first (there is a definite article used; *he apostasia*). What is "the" falling away in Second Thessalonians 2:3?

Historically, I believe it was the rise of the Roman Catholic Church. Pragmatically, this present falling away is from right Church order, from sound doctrine, holy living, and the manifest presence of God. While John indicated that the "spirit" of antichrist was already present, the endtimes will be marked by this spirit becoming more pronounced and personal, even among God's people.

2 Thess. 2:3, KJV

> *...a falling away first....*

Used only here and in Acts 21:21 (translated as "forsake" in the King James Version), this Greek word is *apostasia* (Strong's #646). It means "defection from truth." *Vine's* adds, "revolt, apostasy." Dispensationalists grasp at this word, interpreting it as the "departure" of the Church from the earth in the rapture. Historically, the medieval Roman church did depart from the apostles' doctrine.

After the apostasy, the "man of (the) sin" will be "revealed." "Sin" is from *hamartia*, which means "the missing of the mark." The Greek word for "revealed," also used in verses 6 and 8 of Second Thessalonians 2, is *apokalupto* (Strong's #601), meaning "to take off the cover, to disclose; to unveil."

This one is also called the mature son (*huios*) of "perdition," or damnation and destruction. Peter in his second epistle (2 Pet. 2:1-3; 3:7,16) and John in the Book of Revelation use the same word to describe the destiny of the "beast" (Rev. 17:8,11). It could be translated here as "the son of waste, corruption, or ruin."

The man of sin lies opposite to and is adverse to God the Word (Jn. 1:1). He sets himself as an repugnant opponent against truth, replacing it with tradition (1 Cor. 16:9; Gal. 5:17; Phil. 1:28). Paul told Timothy that this attitude is contrary to sound doctrine (1 Tim. 1:10). This impudent, contemptuous one arrogantly and haughtily raises himself up above all that is called God, all that is adored or revered (Acts 17:11). This one seats or enthrones himself as God "in" (or "unto, into") the temple of God, showing himself that he is God.

"He as God" is the essence of "the mystery of iniquity." This word for "showing" in Second Thessalonians 2:4 is *apodeiknumi* (Strong's #584). It means "to show off, exhibit; figuratively, to demonstrate, accredit" (Acts 2:22; 25:7; 1 Cor. 4:9).

2 Thess. 2:4, NIV

> ...*so that he sets himself up in God's temple, proclaiming himself to be God.*

Dispensationalists use these verses to predict their future antichrist in a rebuilt Jewish temple. However, the key to understanding Second Thessalonians 2:3-4 is the Greek word for "temple," treated in depth in the second chapter of my book *Unshakeable Peace* (Shippensburg, PA: Destiny Image Publishers, Inc., 1994, pp. 25-27). There we learn that there are two Greek words for "temple": *heiron*, the physical temple in Jerusalem, and *naos*, the spiritual temple, Jesus and His Church.

Heiron is used throughout the Gospels, the Book of Acts, and First Corinthians 9:13 to describe the literal building, the natural temple at Jerusalem. This word is #2411 in *Strong's Exhaustive Concordance*. It means "a sacred place (the entire precincts) of the temple (at Jerusalem or elsewhere)."

Naos, the spiritual building, the real temple, pertains to the Lord Jesus Christ and His Body, the Church. It is #3485 in Strong's, meaning "a fane, shrine, or temple." The *naos* of God is "the inner sanctuary," taken from the primary word *naio* (to dwell). The word *fane* is from the Latin *fanum* (a sanctuary or temple) and *fari* (to speak, consecrate) and means "a temple or church."

First, *naos* pertains to the temple of God in Christ Jesus, the one who came from the heart or bosom of the Father (Mk. 14:58; Jn. 2:19-21).

Rev. 21:22, KJV

> *And I saw no temple therein: for the Lord God Almighty and the Lamb are the temple of it.*

Second, *naos* refers to the temple of God, the Church—individually, locally, and universally (see 1 Cor. 6:19; 2 Cor. 6:16; Eph. 2:21; and especially 2 Thess. 2:4). This word is used in all 16 references for "temple" found in the Book of Revelation. This is the house, the people, the spiritual family that Father God desires to assemble, restore, and fill with His glory and unending peace. *Naos*, the "inner sanctuary, the most holy place" is the true temple, the Most Holy Place, the spirit of man—his heart.

1 Cor. 3:16-17, NIV

> *Don't you know that you yourselves are God's temple and that God's Spirit lives in you?*
>
> *If anyone destroys God's temple, God will destroy him; for God's temple is sacred, and you are that temple.*

There is a historical and spiritual application of these truths. First, it is my opinion that Second Thessalonians 2:3-4 is a direct historical reference to the rise of Roman Catholicism with its papacy (once the pagan Roman Empire under the rule of Caesar moved out of the way). But Jesus Christ alone is the one "whose right it is." Jesus is the Head of the Church!

Some notables of Church history who believed and taught that the papacy was the Pauline "man of sin" included John Foxe (*Foxe's Book of Martyrs*), John Wycliffe, John Huss, Martin Luther, Philipp Melanchthon, John Knox, Ulrich Zwingli, William Tyndale, Thomas Cranmer, John Wesley, Roger Williams, Cotton Mather, Samuel Cooper, and Jonathan Edwards. These men were some of the reasons why Francisco Ribera and Manuel de Lacunza invented their future antichrist.

Notwithstanding, we must focus upon the *spirit* that energizes *all* religious tradition—systematic *and* personal. The "temple" of Second Thessalonians 2:4 and the Book of Revelation is spiritual, not natural. The "man of (the) sin" is sinful man with his carnal mind—man in fullness (666).

Incredibly, some futurists use Second Thessalonians 2:4 to substantiate the reinstitution of *animal* sacrifices in their anticipated natural, restored temple! Even if offered as a memorial (a revision of the classical Scofield view of 1909), this teaching frustrates the grace of God and fails to acknowledge the Epistle to the Hebrews with its revelation of Jesus Christ's once-and-for-all final blood sacrifice (Heb. 7:27; 9:12,26-28; 10:10). If a temple is rebuilt in Jerusalem, it would only prove to be a "strong delusion" that men might "believe a lie" (2 Thess. 2:11).

For a full treatment of Ezekiel 40–48, used to substantiate a rebuilding of the temple, see my book, *Principles of Present Truth From Ezekiel* (Richlands, NC: Praise Tabernacle, 1987). There we note that Ezekiel's vision had an ideal character, with laws and ordinances differing from the Law of Moses. The dimensions he offers are much greater than Mount Moriah! Ezekiel's temple is larger than Jerusalem and Ezekiel's Jerusalem is larger than Canaan. Most importantly, Scofield's prediction of restoring animal sacrifices is a direct insult to the words of Jesus in John 4:19-24 and the clear teaching of Hebrews that His sacrifice was perfect, never to be repeated!

Until He Come in the Midst

2 Thess. 2:5-6, KJV

Remember ye not, that, when I was yet with you, I told you these things?

And now ye know what withholdeth that he might be revealed in his time.

2 Thess. 2:5-6, NIV

Don't you remember that when I was with you I used to tell you these things?

And now you know what is holding him back, so that he may be revealed at the proper time.

2 Thess. 2:6, AMP

And now you know what is restraining him....

2 Thess. 2:6, WMS

...the power that is holding him back....

The apostle had already systematically related these things to the Thessalonians. Paul wants men today to "know," or "fully see" this mystery.

The Greek word for "withholdeth" is *katecho* (Strong's #2722). It means "to hold down (fast)." (See Romans 1:18; 7:6; First Thessalonians 5:21.) Some ascribe this restraining force to be Michael and the angels (Dan. 10:13,21). Dispensationalists say that this "restrainer" is the Holy Spirit in the Church who is taken out of the way in the pretribulation rapture, but consider these three applications:

1. A careful study of the Word of God, especially the prophets, shows that God has indeed placed a divine "restraining order" upon the spirit of antichrist (in any form).

2. Historically, the restrainer was the pagan Roman empire (as previously discussed). Once the imperial government was removed, papal Rome was unveiled with all its trappings.

3. The man of sin, the carnal mind, is the problem—the hinderer, the restrainer—until he is unveiled. His discovery is his undoing (compare the exegesis of Second Thessalonians 2:7-8).

The word for "revealed" in Second Thessalonians 2:6 is the same as that found in verses 3 and 8. The man of sin will be unveiled, plainly and distinctly disclosed in his own set or proper time. *Vine's* says that this is a fixed or definite period, a season having a marked characteristic.

2 Thess. 2:7, KJV

For the mystery of iniquity doth already work: only he who now letteth will let, until he be taken out of the way.

2 Thess. 2:7, NIV

For the secret power of lawlessness is already at work; but the one who now holds it back will continue to do so till he is taken out of the way.

2 Thess. 2:7, AMP

For the mystery of lawlessness (that hidden principle of rebellion against constituted authority) is already at work in the world....

The Greek word for "mystery" is *musterion* (Strong's #3466), a derivative of *muo* (to shut the mouth). It means "a secret or mystery." It describes a concealed principle or power that cannot be known until it is revealed. For a fuller exegesis of this word, compare the notes in the next chapter on First Corinthians 15:51.

This pivotal verse dealing with the mystery of (the) iniquity or lawlessness is corroborated by John, who declared that the "spirit of antichrist" was already (1,900 years ago) in the world (1 Jn. 4:3). This spirit was and is at "work." This word, *energeo*, means "to communicate energy and activity," and shows lawlessness actively operating "in" man (*en* and *ergon*).

The word for "letteth" and "let" here in Second Thessalonians 2:7 is the same as "withholdeth" in verse 6. "Only" (but) he who now "restrains" will "restrain" until... Until what? "Until he be taken out of the way."

As noted, dispensationalists use this strange expression of Second Thessalonians 2:7 to say that the "restrainer" is the Holy Spirit (in all believers), who shall be "taken" out of the way when the Church is raptured from the earth (also citing Mt. 24:37-41). The major problem with that supposition is that no man can be saved (during a future tribulation period or any other time) without the Holy Spirit (Jn. 6:44)!

It is puzzling that few Bible students have paid any attention to the original language Paul used by the Spirit. "Taken" is the word *ginomai* (Strong's #1096). Occurring over 600 times in the Greek New Testament, *ginomai* is translated "is taken" only here. This middle voice form of a primary verb means "to cause to be, to become (come into being)." Greek lexicons indicate latitude with *ginomai* and note that it can mean "to come into existence, to be created, to exist by creation, to be born, produced, to grow, to arise, to come on, to occur." The essence of *ginomai* reveals something was started, has matured, and now comes forth.

"Out of the way" is *ek mesos*—"out of, or from, the midst." "Way" is the word *mesos* (Strong's #3319), and it means "middle." It is translated as "among, between, midst" in the King James Version.

Second Thessalonians 2:7-8 translates from Greek to English, "Until he come into the midst, and then shall that wicked be revealed," or "Until out of the midst it comes, and then shall that wicked be revealed...."

The main point is this: The man of sin is not some future antichrist. The real mystery of iniquity revealed is that man himself is the culprit. This awareness or understanding must come into the "middle" of man—his soul or mind.

The *discovery* of the "man of sin" is his undoing! The mystery of lawlessness is solved. Once this awareness comes into our "middle"—our soul, our minds, our understanding—then the brightness of the inward Son, the new Man—the Daystar—will swallow up the man of sin! The bright "coming" (*parousia*), or "presence," of the Lord does away with the spirit of antichrist (2 Thess. 2:8). Once a man's heart turns to Jesus' Lordship, the veil of the mystery of iniquity is removed, and the glory of the good news of the Christ shines forth (2 Cor. 3:12–4:4). This is the revelation of the man of sin from God's perspective, from within the rent veil of the finished work of the Most Holy Place.

2 Pet. 1:19, NIV

And we have the word of the prophets made more certain, and you will do well to pay attention to it, as

*to a light shining in a dark place, until the day dawns
and the morning star rises in your hearts.*

Although the contextual evidence points to a negative
application of Second Thessalonians 2:7, some teachers
interpret this verse to describe the birthing of an overcoming people, the "manchild"—the mature sons of
God—from (*ek mesos* in 2 Thess. 2:7) the sun-clothed
woman (Rev. 2:26-28; 12:1-5; 21:7). Compare God's restraint upon the four winds of Revelation 7:1-3 until His
servants are sealed. They translate this verse "out of the
midst" (as a point of origin and character), or "until he
be birthed out…"

Regardless, one is hard pressed to find any future antichrist here.

2 Thess. 2:8-10, KJV

*And then shall that Wicked be revealed, whom the
Lord shall consume with the spirit of His mouth, and
shall destroy with the brightness of His coming:*

*Even him, whose coming is after the working of Sa-
tan with all power and signs and lying wonders,*

*And with all deceivableness of unrighteousness in
them that perish; because they received not the love of
the truth, that they might be saved.*

2 Thess. 2:8-10, NIV

*And then the lawless one will be revealed, whom the
Lord Jesus will overthrow with the breath of His mouth
and destroy by the splendor of His coming.*

The coming of the lawless one will be in accordance with the work of Satan displayed in all kinds of counterfeit miracles, signs and wonders,

and in every sort of evil that deceives those who are perishing. They perish because they refused to love the truth and so be saved.

2 Thess. 2:8, RHM

...And paralyse with the forthshining of His Presence....

2 Thess. 2:8, WMS

...and put a stop to his operations by His appearance and coming.

2 Thess. 2:9-10, AMP

...with all sorts of [pretended] miracles and signs and delusive marvels...

And by unlimited seduction to evil...because they did not welcome the Truth....

2 Thess. 2:10, NEB

...because they did not open their minds to love the truth....

Appearing in the midst, the lawless one shall be "revealed" (2 Thess. 2:3,6). The Lord, the one "whose right it is," shall consume or destroy him with the "breath or spirit" of His mouth. This consuming fire is the living Word of God in the mouth of His servants the prophets (Jer. 23:29; Jn. 1:1; Heb. 12:29). The spirit of truth sets fire to the traditions of men.

The carnal mind—the lawless one (Rom. 8:5-8)—is "destroyed." This word is *katargeo*. It means "to render entirely useless; to reduce to inactivity" (2 Tim. 1:10; Heb. 2:14). This destruction of the lawless one comes about by the sudden bright shining of His presence, like a burst of light (1 Tim. 6:14; 2 Tim. 4:1,8; Tit. 2:13).

This manifestation of lawlessness will operate with the dynamic of satanic power or ability accompanied by signs and lying wonders. In the arena of the supernatural, we will see a ongoing, intensified confrontation between the corporate son of satan and the corporate Son of God. This is pictured in the Old Testament by Moses and the magicians of Egypt (Ex. 7:1-13), and in the New Testament with Peter's and Paul's encounters with the sorcerers Simon and Elymas, respectively(Acts 8:9; 13:8).

These false miracles will be with complete delusion of unrighteousness in them that are perishing (Eph. 4:22; Col. 2:8; Heb. 3:13), those who have hardened their hearts. Because of their ignorance of history and the Bible, too many Christians in America are gullible, swimming on in a sea of deception. They love their traditions more than they unconditionally love the truth of the Word of God. Salvation and deliverance is available in Christ, but they stubbornly reject reality, and embrace "the" lie.

"The" Lie

2 Thess. 2:11-12, KJV

> *And for this cause God shall send them strong delusion, that they should believe a lie:*

> *That they all might be damned who believed not the truth, but had pleasure in unrighteousness.*

2 Thess. 2:11-12, NIV

> *For this reason God sends them a powerful delusion so that they will believe the lie*
>
> *and so that all will be condemned who have not believed the truth but have delighted in wickedness.*

2 Thess. 2:11, AMP

> *Therefore God sends upon them a misleading influence, a working of error and a strong delusion to make them believe what is false.*

2 Thess. 2:11, WEY

> *...a fatal delusion....*

2 Thess. 2:11, NEB

> *...the lie....*

"A lie" in Second Thessalonians 2:11 is *ho psuedos* in the Greek. With the definite article, it reads, "*the* lie." Since Adam's transgression, three forces of evil have passed to his descendants—sin, deception, and death. Paul in his writings declared these to be:

1. *he hamartia*—"the sin"

2. *ho pseudos*—"the lie"

3. *ho thanatos*—"the death."

The only remedy for these ruling principles is the one who came to destroy the works of the devil (1 Jn. 3:8)— He is "the way, the truth, and the life" (Jn. 14:6)!

To those who reject His Word, God will dispatch a working of error. The Greek word for "delusion" is *plane*, and means "a straying from orthodoxy or piety; roving (as a tramp); an impostor or misleader." *Vine's* adds that *plane* means "a wandering," whereby those who are led astray roam hither and thither. These persons, like a planet out of orbit, are marked by mental straying, wrong opinion, and error in morals (Eph. 4:14; 1 Jn. 4:6).

Men and women are roaming the countryside and the convention circuits looking for goose bumps. Their feet, family, and finances need to land and establish roots. They have believed "the" lie, putting their faith, trust and confidence in tradition rather than the Bible.

The devil speaks "the" lie (Jn. 8:44). Men change or exchange "the" truth for "the" lie (Rom. 1:25). We are commanded by God to put away "the" lie (Eph. 4:25). Those who believe "the" lie are sent strong delusion (2 Thess. 2:11).

"The" lie is that satan is alive and well on planet earth and that the old man is still alive.

"The" truth is that satan has been defeated and the old man has been crucified with its affections and lusts. This was accomplished in the finished work of the Lord Jesus Christ, the Messiah the Prince (Dan. 9:25). On an old rugged cross just outside the old city of Jerusalem, over 1,900 years ago, three men were crucified. We have discovered that the man in the middle was God in the flesh. The thief on the right who repented, was remembered (put back together) and entered paradise was Adam in the flesh. The thief who returned that day to be crucified was satan in the flesh (Lk. 4:3,9,13; 23:39)!

Darby, Scofield, and Larkin have uttered things that are not true. Their greatest atrocity was to replace the seventieth week of Daniel—the days of Christ the Prince, the Word made flesh (A.D. 27-34)—with their infamous future antichrist, satan made flesh (see Chapter Ten)!

The Lord alone is the one "whose right it is." The coming years will afford men and women the grace to exchange "the" lie for "the" truth!

We have examined many favorite dispensational proof texts. But what about *the* passages—First Thessalonians 4:13–5:9 and First Corinthians 15:51-58? Is there going to be a meeting in the air?

Chapter Nine

The Meeting in the Air

"...the dead in Christ shall rise first...."

First Thessalonians 4:16

The warfare is accomplished, and the earth is the Lord's. The dragon is defeated, but he still has a mouth. From 1830 until now, he has attempted to abort the seed of God. One of the greatest hindrances to the present move of God and the ripening of the harvest—the maturity of the saints—is the false hope of Scofield's "any minute" pre-tribulation rapture theory.

The preceding chapter highlighted most of the outstanding proof texts for dispensationalism, especially Matthew 24:1-34 and Second Thessalonians 2:1-12.

Yet the literal, physical coming of King Jesus back to this planet is a glorious reality. There will be a meeting in the air! The exegesis of First Thessalonians 4:13-18, taken in the context of the whole Epistle, provides great comfort and strength to the saints.

1 Thess. 3:4, KJV

For verily, when we were with you, we told you before that we should suffer tribulation; even as it came to pass, and ye know.

1 Thess. 3:13, KJV

To the end He may stablish your hearts unblameable in holiness before God, even our Father, at the coming of our Lord Jesus Christ with all His saints.

Them Which Are Asleep

1 Thess. 4:13, KJV

But I would not have you to be ignorant, brethren, concerning them which are asleep, that ye sorrow not, even as others which have no hope.

1 Thess. 4:13, AMP

...as the rest do who have no hope [beyond the grave].

1 Thess. 4:13, TLB

...I want you to know what happens to a Christian when he dies....

First, get Paul's context. To comfort the saints at Thessalonica, the apostle asked a simple question: What happens to the dead in Christ? His answer is plain enough—Jesus will bring them with Him when He comes again! Revelation 22:12 adds that He will bring His reward with Him. Somebody says, "I want to go over yonder and see Grandma." According to Paul, if Grandma died in Christ, He will bring her to see you! From Genesis (Gen. 1–3) to Revelation (Rev. 21–22), the pattern is clear: God comes to dwell with man (Jn. 1:14). In Revelation 21, the "city"—the Bride, the Lamb's wife—comes down, out of the realm of the invisible to the visible.

Jesus' Ascension was not geographical, but spiritual— He was caught up into the heavenly realm of Spirit. He will come again "in like manner" (Acts 1:11). At His coming, He descends from the invisible to the visible. As we shall see, the living saints will welcome and escort their returning, glorified Lord back into our visible realm.

2 Cor. 5:6, KJV

> *Therefore we are always confident, knowing that, whilst we are at home in the body, we are absent from the Lord.*

Paul tells us in Second Corinthians 5:1-6 that at death a man's body goes to one place and his spirit goes to another. That part of us that has eternal life is still living and conscious when we go into His presence. Our dead bodies sleep in the grave. Whether it is put into a tomb, cremated, or eaten by lions makes no difference. When the spirit leaves the body, the body immediately "descends" (Eph. 4:9) into that state of death while the spirit "ascends" into His presence.

At the resurrection, the order will be reversed. The physical body rises from the state of death (whether bones, dust, or ashes) into a glorified state and is "fashioned like unto His glorious body" (Phil. 3:21). So Paul is comforting the hearts of the Thessalonian saints about the fate of their loved ones who have gone on to be with the Lord. He makes it plain that the departed saints are coming back with Jesus.

Paul uses this Greek word for "ignorant" often in his writings, with regard to covenantal theology (1 Cor. 10:1) and spiritual gifts (1 Cor. 12:1; 14:38). Doctor Luke used it concerning worship (Acts 17:23). *Agnoeo* (compare the English *agnostic*) means "not to know (through lack of information of intelligence); by inclination, to ignore (through disinclination)." Make sure your information is complete. Above all, don't ignore the truth.

"Others which have no hope" (1 Thess. 5:13) could refer to the Sadducees, who did not believe in the resurrection (Acts 23:8). The Greek word for "sorrow" indicates that the Thessalonian saints were distressed and saddened. The apostle wanted to restore their anticipation and expectation (see 1 Thess. 1:3; 2:19; 5:8; 2 Thess. 2:16).

1 Thess. 4:14, KJV

For if we believe that Jesus died and rose again, even so them also which sleep in Jesus will God bring with Him.

1 Thess. 4:14, AMP

...those who have fallen asleep [in death].

1 Thess. 4:14, TLB

...when Jesus returns, God will bring back with Him all the Christians who have died.

Conybeare's translation says that God will "bring back those who sleep." The word for "bring" is *ago* (Strong's #71), meaning "to lead." *Vine's* adds, "to lead along to bring." It is used in Romans 8:14, Galatians 5:18, and Hebrews 2:10.

1 Thess. 4:15, KJV

> *For this we say unto you by the word of the Lord, that we which are alive and remain unto the coming of the Lord shall not prevent them which are asleep.*

1 Thess. 4:15, AMP

> *For this we declare to you by the Lord's [own] word....*

1 Thess. 4:15, TLB

> *...we who are still living when the Lord returns will not rise to meet Him ahead of those who are in their graves.*

1 Thess. 4:15, RHM

> *...unto the Presence of the Lord....*

The word for "remain," used only here and in verse 17, is *perileipo* (Strong's #4035). It means "to leave all around, survive." *Vine's* adds, "to leave over." The Revised Standard Version mentions those "who are alive, and left" (as in Mt. 24:40-41). A righteous remnant will survive any future shakings (Is. 26:20-21; Heb. 12:25-29).

The word for "coming" is *parousia* (Strong's #3952) and means "a being near, advent." *Vine's* adds "a presence," denoting both an "arrival" and a consequent "presence with." Nothing in this word conveys the idea of secrecy. *Parousia* is a compound of two words: *para*, meaning "with, near, beside," and *ousia*, meaning "being" (from *eimi*, "to be").

In an eschatological sense, *parousia* is used in Matthew 24:3, 27, 37, 39, First Corinthians 15:23, First Thessalonians 2:19; 3:13; 4:15; 5:23, Second Thessalonians 2:1, 8-9, James 5:7-8, Second Peter 3:4, 12, and First John 2:28.

Dispensationalists attempt to prove Darby's two-stage theory with Greek words, saying that the *parousia* is His coming "for" the saints and that the *apokalupsis* (revealing, unveiling) is His coming "with" the saints. But these and other Greek words for "coming" are used interchangeably!

1. *Parousia*—"the personal presence of one who comes and arrives."

Jas. 5:7, KJV

Be patient therefore, brethren, unto the coming of the Lord....

2. *Apokalupsis*—"appearing, revelation."

2 Thess. 1:7, KJV

And to you who are troubled rest with us, when the Lord Jesus shall be revealed from heaven with His mighty angels.

3. *Epiphaneia*—"manifestation, glory."

1 Tim. 6:14, KJV

> ...*until the appearing of our Lord Jesus Christ.*

4.   *Phaneroo*—"to render apparent."

1 Jn. 3:2, KJV

> ...*when He shall appear, we shall be like Him; for we shall see Him as He is.*

5.   *Erchomai*—"the act of coming, to come from one place to another."

Lk. 19:13, KJV

> ...*Occupy till I come.*

6.   *Heko*—"the point of arrival."

Rev. 2:25, KJV

> ...*hold fast till I come.*

All these Greek words are used interchangeably, presenting various shades of meaning. Jesus did not go to Heaven in two ascensions. He will come again "in like manner" (Acts 1:11).

1 Thess. 4:15, KJV

> ...*we which are alive and remain unto the coming of the Lord shall not prevent them which are asleep.*

The word for "prevent" in First Thessalonians 4:15 is *phthano* (Strong's #5348). It means "to be beforehand, anticipate or precede; to have arrived at." *Vine's* adds, "to anticipate, to come sooner." Paul comforts the bereaved by declaring that the dead in Christ shall rise first.

1 Thess. 4:16, KJV

> *For the Lord Himself shall descend from heaven with a shout, with the voice of the archangel, and with the trump of God: and the dead in Christ shall rise first.*

1 Thess. 4:16, NIV

> *For the Lord Himself will come down from heaven, with a loud command....*

1 Thess. 4:16, TLB

> *...with the soul-stirring shout of the archangel and the great trumpet-call of God....*

Again, the Lord Jesus went directly from earth to Heaven, and He shall return "in like manner" (Acts 1:11)—directly from Heaven to earth. There will be no rapture back to Heaven for a later third coming! Moreover, if this verse is used to say that Jesus is coming secretly as a "thief," He's sure making a lot of noise! There's a shout, a voice, and a trumpet!

The word for "Lord" is *kurios* (Strong's 2962). Taken from *kuros*, it means "supreme in authority, controller." This is the Master, the Lord Jesus "Himself"! Follow Him through the four Gospels, and you'll usually find a noisy crowd. He will "descend" or go down (Rev. 21:2,10) from Heaven (Mt. 24:29-31; 1 Thess. 1:10; 2 Thess. 1:7). The Greek word for "shout" (used only here) is *keleuma* (Strong's #2752) and means "a cry of incitement." *Vine's* adds that *keleuma* means "a call, summons, shout of command." All who are in the graves shall hear His voice (Jn. 5:28).

The word for "voice" in First Thessalonians 4:16 is *phone*. In the King James Version, it is translated as "noise, sound, voice." Interestingly, *phone* is a derivative of *phaino* ("to lighten, show") and *phos* ("to shine or make manifest, especially by rays; luminousness"). The latter is translated in the King James Version as "fire, light."

"Archangel," the transliteration of *archaggelos* (Strong's #743), means "a chief angel" and is taken from *archo*, meaning "to be first (in political rank or power)," and *aggelos*, meaning "messenger."

Archaggelos is not found in the Greek Old Testament. It is used in the New Testament only here and in Jude 9 (referring to Michael). Daniel calls Michael "one of the chief princes" and "the great prince" (or "the great angel," according to the Septuagint) (Dan. 10:13,21; 12:1). Because Michael (Rev. 12:7) is "one of the chief princes," many believe that there is more than one archangel (like Gabriel, mentioned in Dan. 8:16; 9:21; Lk. 1:1,26).

The word for "trump" in First Thessalonians 4:16 is *salpigx* (Strong's #4536). It is perhaps taken from *salos* (Strong's #4535), which means "vibration, (specifically, billow)" and is translated as "wave" in the King James Version. Compare *saino* ("to shake, disturb") and *seio* ("to rock, agitate, cause to tremble, throw into a tremor"). Throughout the Scriptures, trumpets symbolize a clear word from God—the voice of the Lord. *Salpigx* is also used in First Corinthians 14:8, Hebrews 12:19, Revelation 1:10; 4:1; 8:2, 6, 13; 9:14, and in these key cross-references:

Mt. 24:31, KJV

And He shall send His angels with a great sound of a trumpet, and they shall gather together His elect from the four winds, from one end of heaven to the other.

1 Cor. 15:52

In a moment, in the twinkling of an eye, at the last trump: for the trumpet shall sound, and the dead shall be raised incorruptible, and we shall be changed.

Paul closes First Thessalonians 4:16 by declaring that the dead in Christ shall "rise" first. This is the Greek word *anistemi* (Strong's #450), which means "to stand up (again)." It is used in First Thessalonians 4:14 concerning Jesus' resurrection and in other key passages (see Mt. 17:9; 20:19; Jn. 20:9; Acts 2:24; Rom. 14:9). Paul assures the Thessalonian saints that their dead loved ones would rise "first," or "firstly (in time, place, order, or importance)."

Caught Up Together

1 Thess. 4:17, KJV

Then we which are alive and remain shall be caught up together with them in the clouds, to meet the Lord in the air: and so shall we ever be with the Lord.

1 Cor. 15:51, KJV

Behold, I show you a mystery; We shall not all sleep....

Those who are living at the time of the Lord's coming will be "caught up" together with the resurrected dead. When the Bible speaks of being "caught up," it is not speaking in terms of being taken miles or light-years away. This Greek word *harpazo* (Strong's #726) means "to seize," and it is translated in the King James Version as "catch (away, up), pluck, pull, take (by force)." It is derived from *haireomia* ("to take for oneself, prefer") and *airo* ("to lift up"). *Vine's* adds that *harpazo* means "to snatch or catch away." It is used in Matthew 11:12; 13:19, John 6:15; 10:12, 28-29, Acts 23:10, Jude 1:23, and these verses:

Acts 8:39, KJV

*And when they were come up out of the water, the Spirit of the Lord **caught away** Philip, that the eunuch saw him no more: and he went on his way rejoicing.*

Acts 8:39, NIV

*When they came up out of the water, the Spirit of the Lord suddenly **took** Philip **away**....*

2 Cor. 12:2, KJV

*I knew a man in Christ above fourteen years ago, (whether in the body, I cannot tell; or whether out of the body, I cannot tell: God knoweth;) such an one **caught up** to the third heaven.*

2 Cor. 12:4, KJV

*How that he was **caught up** into paradise, and heard unspeakable words, which it is not lawful for a man to utter.*

Rev. 12:5, KJV

*And she brought forth a man child, who was to rule all nations with a rod of iron: and her child was **caught up** unto God, and to His throne.*

Rev. 12:5, NIV

> *She gave birth to a son, a male child, who will rule*
> *all the nations with an iron scepter. And her child was*
> ***snatched up*** *to God and to His throne.*

Philip the evangelist and Paul the apostle were "seized" by the Spirit and never left the planet. Where did Paul go? Physically, his body went nowhere. Moffatt's translation says that the apostle "heard sacred secrets which no human lips can repeat." Fourteen years later, he was still suffering the afflictions of a mortal body. But he had been into that third heaven.

The manchild of Revelation 12:5 is either Jesus or a company of overcoming sons (Rev. 2:26-28; 21:7), or both. Regardless, in connection with the "throne," geography is not the primary issue (as shown in Chapter Five). Throughout the universe, there is no such direction as "up." If the American and Australian saints were simultaneously caught "up" (vertically), the Church would go flying off the planet in all directions! But the saints, living and dead, are caught up "together." This word is *hama* (Strong's #260), and means "at the same time, denoting close association." *Vine's* adds, "at once" and compares its use in Romans 3:12 and First Thessalonians 5:10.

1 Thess. 4:17, NIV

> *...caught up together with them in the clouds....*

The word for "clouds" is *nephele* (Strong's #3507). It means "cloudiness, a cloud," and is mostly used in a metaphorical or spiritual sense in the New Testament. It is evident from the applications given below, including the mention of "cloud" or "clouds" in the Book of Revelation (see Rev. 1:7; 10:1; 11:12; 14:14-16) that the "clouds" of First Thessalonians 4:17 are not literal:

1. The cloud at Jesus' transfiguration (Mt. 17:5; Mk. 9:7; Lk. 9:34-35).

2. The Son of man coming in the clouds of Heaven (see Mt. 24:30; 26:64; Mk. 13:26; 14:62; Lk. 21:27).

3. The cloud out of the west bringing showers (Lk. 12:54).

4. The cloud that received Jesus at His ascension (Acts 1:9).

5. The glory cloud of the old Testament (1 Cor. 10:1-2).

6. The cloud of witnesses who died in faith (Heb. 12:1).

7. Clouds of wicked men (2 Pet. 2:17; Jude 1:12).

Acts 1:9-11, KJV

And when he had spoken these things, while they beheld, He was taken up; and a cloud received Him out of their sight.

And while they looked stedfastly toward heaven as He went up, behold, two men stood by them in white apparel;

Which also said, Ye men of Galilee, why stand ye gazing up into heaven? this same Jesus, which is taken up from you into heaven, shall so come in like manner as ye have seen Him go into heaven.

"In like manner..." Men teach that Jesus will come out of the sky and stop on a cloud to meet the saints. But Jesus started from the apostles' visible presence, then disappeared from view in a cloud, ascending by that means into Heaven. Reverse the order, and we see Him appearing out of a cloud and descending back into our visible presence where we can see Him and be with Him.

Moreover, stratocumulus clouds range from ground level to 6,500 feet high, a little over a mile. Altocumulus clouds go from 6,500 feet up to 23,000 feet high (over 4 miles). The cirrus and cirrocumulus clouds (the highest), range from 16,500 to 45,000 feet high (less than 9 miles). That's not in outer space, or "beyond the Milky Way." While flying above the clouds on more than one occasion, I have thought, *If there is a rapture like most folks believe, I will have to be "caught down."*

1 Thess. 4:17, KJV

> *...to meet the Lord....*

There will be a "meeting" in the air! The Greek word for "meet" is *apantesis* (Strong's #529), and it means "a friendly encounter." It is a derivative of *apanteo* ("to meet away") and *apo* ("off, away from"). The latter can be used literally or figuratively. *Vine's* says that *apantesis* was used with regard to a newly arriving magistrate. The special idea of the word was the official welcome of a newly arrived dignitary.

Kittel's *Theological Dictionary of the New Testament* adds that *apantesis* was used for the public welcome accorded to important visitors, and that Christians will welcome Christ through acclaiming Him as Lord (abridged, Gherhard Kittel, ed., Grand Rapids, MI: Eerdman's, 1985). It means "returning with" the welcoming party, not "remaining at" the place of meeting. Again, we are not going. Jesus is coming! The "meeting" in the air is to welcome Him back to this planet. *Apantesis* is used only here and in:

Mt. 25:1, KJV

*Then shall the kingdom of heaven be likened unto ten virgins, which took their lamps, and went forth to **meet** the bridegroom.*

Mt. 25:6, KJV

*And at midnight there was a cry made, Behold, the bridegroom cometh; go ye out to **meet** him.*

Acts 28:15, KJV

*And from thence, when the brethren heard of us, they came to **meet** us as far as Appii forum, and The three taverns: whom when Paul saw, he thanked God, and took courage.*

In these Scriptures, *apantesis* means "to meet as an escort, to meet and return with." In the first instance, the bride went out to welcome her bridegroom and return to the wedding feast. In the closing chapter of the Book of Acts, the Roman Christians walked 43 miles to meet and welcome Paul, then escorted the apostle back into the city (compare 2 Sam. 19:12). Compare the similar usage of *apanteo* (see Mt. 28:9; Mk. 5:2; 14:13; Lk. 14:31; 17:12; Jn. 4:51; Acts 16:16).

1 Thess. 4:17, KJV

…in the air.

We will meet the Lord in the "air," the stuff we breathe—the higher you go, the thinner it gets. It's all around us, and there is none in outer space. One preacher said that we will be caught high enough to be out of the jaws of the snapping dragon. The Greek word for "sky" is *ouranos* (also translated as "heaven, air" in the King James Version), but it is not used here.

In this verse "air" is the transliteration of *aer* (Strong's #109), and it means "to breathe unconsciously, respire; air (as naturally circumambient)." *Vine's* adds that *aer* signifies "the atmosphere." Certainly this is true in five of the seven occurrences (see Acts 22:23; 1 Cor. 9:26; 14:9; Rev. 9:2; 16:11), and almost certainly in the other two (Eph. 2:2; 1 Thess. 4:17).

1 Thess. 4:17, KJV

…and so shall we ever be with the Lord.

So shall we "ever or always, at all times" be with the Lord—on the earth (Ps. 2:8; Mt. 5:5; Rev. 5:10).

Besides this fresh exegesis, it doesn't matter whether one believes that he will "fly away" any minute, be gone for seven years, three-and-a-half years, seven seconds, or not leave the ground at all. He will return to this *earth*—so what's the big deal?

1 Thess. 4:18, KJV

Wherefore comfort one another with these words.

1 Thess. 4:18, NIV

Therefore encourage each other with these words.

Paul closes this passage with his purpose for writing it—to "comfort" the saints (see 1 Thess. 3:2,7; 4:1,10; 5:11,14; 2 Thess. 2:17; 3:12).

It is noteworthy that the apostle provides no definitive information in this entire passage (1 Thess. 4:13-18) as to the *time* of this catching away. That, like most dispensational concepts, is assumed.

A Thief in the Night

Chapter divisions are not inspired. Keep reading the context of First Thessalonians 4:13–5:9.

1 Thess. 5:1-5, KJV

But of the times and the seasons, brethren, ye have no need that I write unto you.

For yourselves know perfectly that the day of the Lord so cometh as a thief in the night.

For when they shall say, Peace and safety; then sudden destruction cometh upon them, as travail upon a woman with child; and they shall not escape.

But ye, brethren, are not in darkness, that day should overtake you as a thief.

Ye are all the children of light, and the children of the day: we are not of the night, nor of darkness.

First Thessalonians 5:1-9 shows that the Lord is *not* coming as a "thief" to those who are sons of light. Only the wicked will be surprised. As noted, the Old Testament prophets reveal the Day of the Lord to be both great and terrible—day and night, light and darkness—at the *same time* (Is. 60:1-5; Joel 2:1-2; Mal. 4:1-2). To those who are walking after the flesh, it will get darker and darker— hell on earth. To those who are walking after the Spirit and the Word of God, it is getting brighter and brighter— Heaven on earth (Prov. 4:18). The same flood that destroyed the wicked lifted righteous Noah. The same plagues that judged Pharaoh and Egypt delivered Moses and the children of Israel from bondage. The same furnace that destroyed the mighty men of Babylon brought the three Hebrews into a place of rulership. The same stormy wind (Ps. 148:8) that destroyed the ship made Paul the captain instead of a prisoner.

Jesus' coming as a "thief" is to surprise the wicked, not the righteous. The term "thief" is used in the Bible to illustrate *suddenness* (see Mt. 24:43; Lk. 12:39; 2 Pet. 3:10; Rev. 3:3; 16:15). As a thief springs suddenly on his unsuspecting victim, the Day of the Lord bursts with a startling appearing on the unexpectant ungodly world. As throughout Psalm 37, the first eight verses of First Thessalonians 5 reveal two groups of people:

1. The *righteous*—"ye," "you," "yourselves," "us," "brethren," "children of light," "children of the day."

2. The *wicked*—"they," "them," "of the night," "of darkness," "others."

The wicked shall not "escape" (1 Thess. 5:3). This same word is used in Luke 21:36. For its meaning, see the exegesis of Daniel 9:26 in Chapter Ten.

1 Thess. 5:6-8, KJV

Therefore let us not sleep, as do others; but let us watch and be sober.

For they that sleep sleep in the night; and they that be drunken are drunken in the night.

But let us, who are of the day, be sober, putting on the breastplate of faith and love; and for an helmet, the hope of salvation.

The righteous are to watch in prayer and be "sober." This word in First Thessalonians 5:6, 8 means "to be free from the influence of intoxicants" (compare 2 Tim. 4:5; 1 Pet. 1:13; 4:7; 5:8). The wicked, by contrast, are asleep and drunk. Christians throughout America stay drunk on the latest dose of dispensationalism's "signs of the times." Enamored by the latest developments in the Middle East, even preachers stay numb to the truth. Metaphorically, the word "sleep" reveals a carnal indifference to spiritual things. As noted, Paul did not teach an "any minute" rapture. The "escape" that the Bible does teach was written by the same apostle.

1 Cor. 10:13, KJV

There hath no temptation taken you but such as is common to man: but God is faithful, who will not suffer you to be tempted above that ye are able; but will with the temptation also make a way to escape, that ye may be able to bear it.

Our hiding place is in Christ (Col. 3:1-3). Some are seeking refuge in some natural place—a farm, a desert, a foreign country, a wilderness area. That is only another form of "self-rapture." Some extreme survivalists who want to run to the wilderness have stored "tribulation food" or even guns. Real protection is found only in Christ, in absolute obedience to the Spirit of God. Whether it be on a farm or in the city, in the wilderness or some metropolitan center—a man's safety is in his obedience.

1 Thess. 5:9, KJV

> *For God hath not appointed us to wrath, but to obtain salvation by our Lord Jesus Christ,*

1 Thess. 5:9, TLB

> *For God has not chosen to pour out His anger upon us, but to save us through our Lord Jesus Christ.*

This is a true promise of divine protection (compare the thoughts in Chapter Eight regarding Rev. 3:10). The Greek word for "obtain" is *peripoieomai*. It means "to make around oneself, acquire (buy)" (see Eph. 1:14; 2 Thess. 2:14; Heb. 10:39; 1 Pet. 2:9). To "obtain" is to get possession of by trying, to procure, to prevail—to be victorious, having won the victory! We do not obtain salvation by escaping. God brings us through. The Day of the Lord is day and night at the *same time*—the "wrath" of God destroys the wicked, while "tribulation" perfects the saints.

In a Moment

When Jesus returns, those saints who come back with Him shall receive their bodies again, ascending or rising out of that state of death into a blessed state like His body of glory. Then those who are still dwelling in these mortal bodies shall be "caught up" into that same place. This mortal shall put on immortality. Death shall be swallowed up in victory!

So reads the fifteenth chapter of First Corinthians, the *resurrection* chapter. Unlike First Thessalonians 4:13-18, it does reveal a time frame for the coming of the Lord.

1 Cor. 15:51, KJV

> *Behold, I show you a mystery; We shall not all sleep, but we shall all be changed.*

1 Cor. 15:51, MOF

> *...not all of us are to die....*

1 Cor. 15:51, TLB

> *...we shall not all die, but we all shall be given new bodies!*

The apostle wants us to see and know the truth concerning the resurrection. He wants to "show" or "lay forth" in systematic discourse this "mystery." Noted in our earlier exegesis of Second Thessalonians 2:4, this latter word is *musterion* (Strong's #3466), a derivative of *muo* ("to shut the mouth"), and it means "a secret or mystery." *Vine's* adds that *musterion* is that which is known by the *mustes* ("the initiated"). It denotes that which is outside the range of unassisted natural apprehension, known only by divine revelation, made known in a time and manner appointed by God—only to those who are illumined by the Spirit (Rom. 11:25; 1 Cor. 2:7; Eph. 3:3-9).

Besides the mystery of the resurrection, the New Testament reveals other "sacred secrets":

1. The mystery of the Kingdom of God (Mk. 4:11).

2. The mystery of His will (Eph. 1:9).

3. The mystery of Christ and His Church (Eph. 5:32).

4. The mystery of the gospel (Eph. 6:19).

5. The mystery of Christ in you (Col. 1:26-27; 4:3).

6. The mystery of God (Col. 2:2; Rev. 10:7).

7. The mystery of iniquity (2 Thess. 2:7).

8. The mystery of the faith (1 Tim. 3:9).

9. The mystery of godliness (1 Tim. 3:16).

10. The mystery of the seven stars (Rev. 1:20).

11. The mystery of Babylon the great (Rev. 17:5-7).

We shall not all "sleep," or "repose, decease" (Jn. 11:13; 1 Cor. 11:30; 1 Thess. 4:14), but shall be "changed." The latter is the Greek word *allasso* (Strong's #236). It means "to make different." *Vine's* adds, "to make other than it is (from *allos*, 'another'); to transform, change" (Acts 6:14; Rom. 1:23; Heb. 1:12).

1 Cor. 15:52, KJV

In a moment, in the twinkling of an eye, at the last trump: for the trumpet shall sound, and the dead shall be raised incorruptible, and we shall be changed.

1 Cor. 15:52, NIV

in a flash...the dead will be raised imperishable....

1 Cor. 15:52, AMP

...(free and immune from decay), and we shall be changed (transformed).

1 Cor. 15:52, PHIL

...beyond the reach of corruption....

1 Cor. 15:52, TLB

...all the Christians who have died will suddenly become alive, with new bodies that will never, never die; and then we who are still alive shall suddenly have new bodies too.

The phrase "in a moment" is the Greek *en atomos*—our change (Job 14:14) will take place in the atoms! The Coming of the Lord will consummate and finalize a change in us that has been ongoing, day-by-day (see Ps. 84:7; Rom. 1:17; 2 Cor. 3:18; Phil. 3:21). *Atomos* (Strong's #823) means "uncut, indivisible (an 'atom' of time)."

This change will take place in the "twinkling" of an eye. This is the Greek word *rhipe* (Strong's #4493), and it means "a jerk (of the eye), an instant." It is a derivative of *rhipto* ("to fling with sudden motion, a quick toss") and *rhapizo* ("to let fall, rap, slap"). *Vine's* adds that *rhipe* is akin to *rhipto* ("to hurl") and was used of any rapid movement. This transition will be in the twinkling of an "eye." (Compare First Samuel 14:24-27, Matthew 6:22-24, and Ephesians 1:18.) Only the Word of God can give us the understanding to perceive these things with a single eye. We are being changed until we see Him "eye to eye" (Is. 52:8) and "face to face" (see Gen. 32:30; Ex. 33:11; Deut. 34:10; 1 Cor. 13:12).

This change takes place "at" the last trump. This is the Greek preposition *en*, which means "in" or "during." As we shall see, the "last" trump is the seventh trump—the message of perfection for the maturity of the Church (Eph. 4:13). This Greek word is *eschatos* (English *eschatology*). It means "farthest, final, last, utmost, extreme." The "last" trumpet in the Book of Revelation is the seventh one. It begins to sound in Revelation 10:7 and blows until Revelation 11:15 (1 Thess. 4:16)—right in the middle of Scofield's anticipated "tribulation period" (Rev. 4–19)! There won't be any trumpets after the last one. If the "last trump" is the rapture trumpet, pre-tribbers have a problem.

Rev. 10:7, KJV

But in the days of the voice of the seventh angel, when he shall begin to sound....

Rev. 11:15, KJV

And the seventh angel sounded; and there were great voices in heaven, saying, The kingdoms of this world are become the kingdoms of our Lord, and of His Christ; and He shall reign for ever and ever.

In the Old Testament, trumpets were used as an instrument that related God's voice and authority to His people. They represented the "call to attention" to a word or command from the Lord. The people heard it as a noise, but Moses heard it as God's voice (Ex. 20:19).

Concerning trumpets, see also Exodus 19:13-19, Leviticus 23:24; 25:9, Numbers 10:1-10; 29:1, First Chronicles 15:28, Ezra 3:10, Psalms 47:5; 81:3, Jeremiah 51:27, Ezekiel 33:3-6, Hosea 5:8, and Zechariah 9:14.

In the New Testament, Jesus Christ, the Word and Truth of God by the Spirit, is the Trumpet of God (Jn. 1:1; 14:6; 1 Tim. 4:11).

Jn. 5:28-29, KJV

Marvel not at this: for the hour is coming, in the which all that are in the graves shall hear His voice,

And shall come forth; they that have done good, unto the resurrection of life; and they that have done evil, unto the resurrection of damnation.

Rev. 20:4-6, KJV

And I saw thrones, and they sat upon them, and judgment was given unto them: and I saw the souls of them that were beheaded for the witness of Jesus, and for the word of God, and which had not worshipped the beast, neither his image, neither had received his mark upon their foreheads, or in their hands; and they lived and reigned with Christ a thousand years.

But the rest of the dead lived not again until the thousand years were finished. This is the first resurrection.

Blessed and holy is he that hath part in the first resurrection: on such the second death hath no power, but they shall be priests of God and of Christ, and shall reign with Him a thousand years.

As noted, there will be no trumpet after the "last trump," and there will be no resurrection before the "first resurrection" (compare 1 Cor. 15:23)!

The trumpet will sound a blast (1 Cor. 15:52), and the dead shall be "raised." Used 20 times in this same chapter, this word is *egeiro* (Strong's #1453). It means "to waken, rouse (from sleep, from sitting or lying, from disease, from death; or figuratively, from obscurity, inactivity, ruins, nonexistence)." The word translated as "incorruptible" means "not liable to corruption or decay," and it is used in Romans 1:23, First Corinthians 9:25, First Timothy 1:17, and First Peter 1:4, 23; 3:4. The word for "changed" is the same as that found in First Corinthians 15:51.

1 Cor. 15:53-54, KJV

For this corruptible must put on incorruption, and this mortal must put on immortality.

So when this corruptible shall have put on incorruption, and this mortal shall have put on immortality, then shall be brought to pass the saying that is written, Death is swallowed up in victory.

1 Cor. 15:53-54, NIV

For the perishable must clothe itself with the imperishable, and the mortal with immortality.

When the perishable has been clothed with the imperishable....

1 Cor. 15:53, WMS

For this decaying part of us must put on the body that can never decay, and this part capable of dying must put on the body that can never die.

1 Cor. 15:54 GDSD

...Death has been triumphantly destroyed....

Compare these verses with Paul's words in his second Epistle to the Church at Corinth.

2 Cor. 5:1-5, KJV

For we know that if our earthly house of this tabernacle were dissolved, we have a building of God, an house not made with hands, eternal in the heavens.

For in this we groan, earnestly desiring to be clothed upon with our house which is from heaven:

If so be that being clothed we shall not be found naked.

For we that are in this tabernacle do groan, being burdened: not for that we would be unclothed, but clothed upon, that mortality might be swallowed up of life.

Now He that hath wrought us for the selfsame thing is God, who also hath given unto us the earnest of the Spirit.

2 Cor. 5:5, NIV

Now it is God who has made us for this very purpose and has given us the Spirit as a deposit, guaranteeing what is to come.

2 Cor. 5:5, AMP

Now He Who has fashioned us [preparing and mak-ing us fit] for this very thing is God, Who also has given us the [Holy] Spirit as a guarantee [of the fulfillment of His promise].

It is awesome to consider that the apostle declared that incorruption and immortality "must" be put on! This word means "it is necessary," and is traced to the Greek root *deo* ("to bind"), a covenantal word (see Jn. 3:7; 4:24; Acts 3:21; 1 Cor. 15:25). The word for "put on" is *en-duo* (Strong's #1746). It means "to sink into a garment; to invest with clothing." Compare the English *endued* (Lk. 24:49). The mystery of resurrection life has to do with God's people putting on:

1. The wedding garment (Mt. 22:11).

2. The best robe, the ring, the shoes (Lk. 15:22).

3. Christ (Rom. 13:11-14; Gal. 3:27).

4. The new man (Eph. 4:24; Col. 3:10).

5. The whole armor of God (Eph. 6:11; 1 Thess. 5:8).

6. Mercy and kindness (Col. 3:12).

7. Fine linen, white and clean (Rev. 19:14).

The word for "incorruption" in First Corinthians 15:53 is *aphthrsia*, and means "unending existence; fig-uratively, genuineness" (1 Cor. 15:42,50,54). It is trans-lated as "immortality" in Romans 2:7 and Second Timothy 1:10, and as "sincerity" in Titus 2:7. The word for "mortal" is *thnetos*. It means "liable to die; subject to death" (Rom. 6:12; 8:11; 2 Cor. 4:11). "Immortality" is *athanasia* (Strong's #110), meaning "deathlessness" (1 Tim. 6:16).

First Corinthians 15:54 quotes Isaiah 25:8. The word for "swallow" means "to drink down, devour" (2 Cor. 5:4; Rev. 12:16). The word for "victory" means "conquest, triumph" (Mt. 12:20).

1 Cor. 15:55-57, KJV

O death, where is thy sting? O grave, where is thy victory?

The sting of death is sin; and the strength of sin is the law.

But thanks be to God, which giveth us the victory through our Lord Jesus Christ.

1 Cor. 15:56, PHIL

It is sin which gives death its sting, and it is the Law which gives sin its power.

The exegesis of First Corinthians 15:51-57 closes out Paul's revelation of the resurrection of the dead and this section of our study. These proof texts for dispensationalism were not noted to show the weakness of that view; they were given to facilitate the reader and student as a resource when he prays and rethinks these important matters.

In and With the Saints

The Lord *has* come, *is* ever coming, and *shall* come. He has already had several "comings" in the Old Testament (see Ex. 19:9,18,20; 25:22; 2 Kings 19:15; 1 Cor. 10:4).

Earlier, we briefly examined the various words translated as "come" or "coming" in the New Testament. Of all these meanings, it is noteworthy that *parousia* (compare the previous notes on 1 Thess. 4:15) in many places simply refers to the "presence" of the Lord. When Messiah came the first time, He came in two forms:

1. In *flesh*—in Bethlehem's manger (Jn. 1:14).

2. In *spirit*—on the day of Pentecost (see Jn. 14:17-18; Acts 2:1-4; Rom. 5:5; 2 Cor. 1:22; 5:5; Gal. 4:6).

His first comings in the New Testament are a seed form of His comings (more than just a "second" coming) at the end of the age. The cycle of restoration reverses the order. Jesus will come:

1. In *spirit*—manifesting Himself in the fullness of the Feast of Tabernacles through His Church, His people (Jn. 3:34; 1 Cor. 13:8-13; Eph. 4:13).

2. In *flesh*—literally, bodily, corporeally as the King of kings and Lord of lords (Acts 1:11; Rev. 19:11-16).

Jude 1:14-15, KJV

And Enoch also, the seventh from Adam, prophesied of these, saying, Behold, the Lord cometh with ten thousands of His saints,

To execute judgment....

Not one place in the entire Bible does it say that Jesus will come *for* the saints. It does say:

1. He will come *in* the saints.

2. He will come *with* the saints.

One could do a parallel study on His coming *in* the clouds (see Mt. 24:30; 26:64; Mk. 13:26; 14:62; 1 Thess. 4:17) and *with* the clouds (Dan. 7:13; Rev. 1:7).

2 Thess. 1:10-12

> *When he shall come to be glorified **in** His saints, and to be admired **in** all them that believe (because our testimony among you was believed) in that day.*
>
> *Wherefore also we pray always for you, that our God would count you worthy of this calling, and fulfil all the good pleasure of His goodness, and the work of faith with power:*
>
> *That the name of our Lord Jesus Christ may be glorified **in** you, and ye in Him, according to the grace of our God and the Lord Jesus Christ.*

Christ is coming *in* His saints! This will happen *before* we meet Him in the air (see Rom. 8:9; 2 Cor. 3:17-18; Gal. 4:4-6; Col. 1:25-29). Christ is *in* and among all of us. His incorruptible seed is being formed in a people (Gal. 4:19). There will be a future coming *in* the saints that will complete, fulfill, and bring to fullness all that He *began* to do (Phil. 1:6).

His first coming in the *spiritual* dimension is the Feast of Pentecost, the Holy Ghost Baptism, the earnest of our inheritance (Eph. 1:13-14). The firstfruits (Rom. 8:23) of Pentecost will give way to the fullness of the Feast of Tabernacles. He must come *in* the saints. It is probably agreed by most if not all that the second coming of the

Lord is associated with the final realization of our full inheritance, which includes the redemption and change of our mortal bodies into immortal bodies (Rom. 8:19-23).

Most assume that it is His personal coming that will activate this change. We shall experience a change in connection with the time of His second coming, but what will energize it? The Lord Jesus, the Pattern Son, was resurrected and quickened from *within* (see Jn. 3:34; 5:26; 10:17-18; 1 Pet. 3:18). The Spirit of God *in* Him produced the springing forth of life. We shall be brought into immortality by being *changed* from *within*. Resurrection is past and presently progressive as well as future (Eph. 2:1; Rom. 8:11).

Phil. 3:10-11, AMP

> *[For my determined purpose is] that I may know Him [that I may progressively become more deeply and intimately acquainted with Him, perceiving and recognizing and understanding the wonders of His Person more strongly and more clearly], and that I may in the same way come to know the power outflowing from His resurrection [which it exerts over believers], and that I may so share His sufferings as to be continually transformed [in spirit into His likeness even] to His death [in the hope]*

> *That if possible I may attain to the [spiritual and moral] resurrection [that lifts me] out from among the dead [even while in the body].*

Compare these thoughts with Paul's apostolic burden for the Church at Rome.

Rom. 12:1-2, NIV

Therefore, I urge you, brothers, in view of God's mercy, to offer your bodies as living sacrifices, holy and pleasing to God—this is your spiritual act of worship.

Do not conform any longer to the pattern of this world, but be transformed by the renewing of your mind. Then you will be able to test and approve what God's will is—His good, pleasing and perfect will.

The real issue is that God wants to *change* us, to renew our minds. The word for "renewing" in Romans 12:2 means "renovating." God is coming in and tearing up much of our theology and eschatology.

1 Cor. 15:52, KJV

In a moment, in the twinkling of an eye, at the last trump....

As noted, the Greek word for "at" is *en*, and means "in, or during." The last or final trump in the Book of Revelation is the *seventh* trump. It begins to sound in Revelation 10:7 and blows until Revelation 11:15, at which time the kingdoms of this world become the kingdoms of our Lord and of His Christ. Whether one interprets this seventh trump to be natural or spiritual (the oracle voice of the Lord trumpeted by His ministers), it remains that the last trump is a *continual* sound, typified by the "long blast" of Joshua 6:15.

Seven is the Bible number denoting perfection or completion. The "seventh" trumpet is the Third Day message of perfection calling the Church to maturity in the Feast of Tabernacles (Eph. 4:13). As noted, trumpets represent a *clear word* coming forth from the Lord in the mouth of His prophets (see Is. 58:1; Joel 2:1-2,15; Amos 3:6-8; 1 Cor. 14:8). The proclamation of the gospel of the Kingdom is going to destroy and bring down every wall! Are you hearing what He is saying? Have you experienced a personal Feast of Trumpets (Num. 10:1-10)?

The devil is defeated, but he still has a mouth. The gist of satan's strategy is to abort or dwarf the seed, to keep God's people immature and undeveloped, especially in view of the finished work of Jesus Christ. For over 150 years, he has tried to do this by peddling a system of error that robs the Church of her rightful identity as the seed of Abraham.

But he saves his best shot for last. No other book in the Bible and no other singular prophecy has stymied and intimidated the saints more than Daniel's prophecy of seventy weeks—the grandfather clause of classical dispensationalism and, from the standpoint of history and eschatology, the most precise Messianic prediction in the Old Testament.

The seventieth week of Daniel's prophecy (Dan. 9:24-27)—the most significant week in human history—is worthy of our investigation.

Chapter Ten

Daniel's Prophecy of Seventy Weeks

"Seventy weeks are determined...."

Daniel 9:24

The devil is defeated, but he still has a mouth. His deterrent to present truth is classical dispensationalism. Chapters Eight and Nine brought an adjusted view to the Scriptures and refocused our attention back upon Him "whose right it is." We have frustrated the wiles of the enemy. In this chapter, we will strip him bare!

Darby and Scofield's two-stage split coming of the Lord is primarily based on one portion of Scripture, Daniel's prophecy of seventy weeks (Dan. 9:24-27). Of all the chapters in the Word of God, our adversary has most greatly muddied the waters on this one. His strategy is to puzzle and intimidate the saints lest we understand the gospel of glory (2 Cor. 4:3-4). He began his scheme over 400 years ago.

As noted in Chapter Seven, the Jesuit priest, Francisco Ribera (1585), was the first to stretch Daniel's prophecy and separate the sixty-ninth and seventieth weeks by a "gap" or "parenthesis" of 2,000 years. Accordingly, he taught that during this seven-year period the events of Revelation 4–19 take place. Many Bible scholars are agreed that the first sixty-nine weeks of Daniel's prophecy take us up to the time of Jesus' public ministry and crucifixion, yet dispensationalists contend that the entire seventieth week is yet to be fulfilled. Without this futurized seventieth week, the pre-tribulation rapture formula falls apart. Whether one is pre-trib, mid-trib, or post-trib in his views, all is tied to a future "trib," to the assumption that Daniel's seventieth week is yet to come!

Daniel 2:40-44, KJV

And the fourth kingdom shall be strong as iron: forasmuch as iron breaketh in pieces and subdueth all [things]: and as iron that breaketh all these, shall it break in pieces and bruise.

And whereas thou sawest the feet and toes, part of potters' clay, and part of iron, the kingdom shall be divided; but there shall be in it of the strength of the iron, forasmuch as thou sawest the iron mixed with miry clay.

And as the toes of the feet were part of iron, and part of clay, so the kingdom shall be partly strong, and partly broken.

And whereas thou sawest iron mixed with miry clay, they shall mingle themselves with the seed of men: but they shall not cleave one to another, even as iron is not mixed with clay.

And in the days of these kings shall the God of heaven set up a kingdom, which shall never be destroyed: and the kingdom shall not be left to other people, but it shall break in pieces and consume all these kingdoms, and it shall stand for ever.

To work, classical Darbyism and Scofieldism requires a gap between the feet and ten toes of Nebuchadnezzar's statue (their revived Roman Empire, the "United States of Europe"), and between the sixty-ninth and seventieth weeks of Daniel's prophecy. But there is no exegetical reason to postpone the Kingdom set up "in the days of these kings" (Dan. 2:44). No gap is mentioned. The fifth kingdom, the stone-kingdom, follows the fourth kingdom with no interruption in time. There is one statue with four kingdoms, one following another, with God's Kingdom ultimately supplanting the kingdoms of men!

We have reexamined the historical roots and outstanding proof texts of traditional dispensationalism. Of the latter, Daniel's prophecy is the primary biblical text. Upon further scrutiny, if Darby's foundation proves faulty, his whole system crumbles.

The Bible mentions several instances of 40 years with *no gaps* in time (see Deut. 8:2; Judg. 3:11; 5:31; 8:28; 13:1; 1 Sam. 4:18; 2 Sam. 5:4; 1 Kings 11:42; 2 Chron. 24:1; Acts 7:23,30; 13:21). More importantly, because Israel refused to honor the Jubilee years—70 in all—God sent the nation into captivity for 70 years (Lev. 25).

Specifically, it was Jeremiah's prophecy that Daniel was contemplating when Gabriel brought God's explanation (2 Chron. 36:21-23; Jer. 25:12). There is *no* indication of a gap in this 70-year period! The near termination point of this 70-year period had provoked the prophet to prayer. Daniel based his supplication for restoration to the land on the certainty of the re-establishment promised by God when the seventy years were completed.

Jer. 29:10-11, KJV

For thus saith the Lord, That after seventy years be accomplished at Babylon I will visit you, and perform My good word toward you, in causing you to return to this place.

For I know the thoughts that I think toward you, saith the Lord, thoughts of peace, and not of evil, to give you an expected end.

Jer. 29:10, NIV

This is what the Lord says: "When seventy years are completed for Babylon, I will come to you and fulfill My gracious promise to bring you back to this place."

Seventy years meant 70 years...uninterrupted. Seventy weeks of years means 70 weeks of years...with no parenthesis. The continual 70-year period of captivity (606-536 B.C.) as declared by Jeremiah is the *pattern* for the seventy weeks of Daniel's prophecy (457 B.C.-A.D. 34)!

Dispensational or Christological?

Someone has said concerning Daniel's prophecy of seventy weeks, "These things lie beyond the range of natural sagacity...they demonstrate that this portion is from God." These verses, perhaps the greatest prophecy in the Old Testament, have produced a multitude of interpretations with many questions yet unanswered. Besides the dispensational view and the Messianic, Christological view of this writing, one might mention:

1. *The historical view.* Accordingly, the author of the Book of Daniel (dubbed psuedo-Daniel) lived in the second century B.C. The murder of the high priest Onias in 171 B.C., the desecration of the temple by Antiochus IV Epiphanes in 167 B.C. (the "abomination of desolation" mentioned in First Maccabees 1:54), and the restoration of the temple in 164 B.C. are said to be fulfillments of Daniel 9:24-27. This view relates the prophecy to its known history and avoids the danger of fanciful theory, but it also ignores New Testament realities and the witness of Jesus Himself to these verses (Mt. 24:15).

2. *The Jewish view.* Josephus' application of these verses to the fall of Jerusalem (Ant. X. xi. 7.) became standard Jewish teaching, and passed into early Christian exegesis. Concerning Daniel's prophecies and Titus' invasion, the historian said, "In the very same manner Daniel also wrote concerning the Roman government, and that our country should be made desolate by them" (*The Complete Works of Josephus,* Grand Rapids, MI: Kregel Publications, 1960).

There is a great difference between real Bible prophecy and humanistic eschatology. The vast majority of Old Testament predictions point to the coming and consequent death, burial, and resurrection of Jesus Christ the Messiah. Some prophecies in the New Testament point to the fall of Jerusalem by the Roman army in A.D. 70. Some scholars date the Book of Revelation much earlier than A.D. 96, placing its writing under Nero's persecution, sometime before or around A.D. 68.

The historical view believes that most Bible prophecies had been fulfilled by the time Jerusalem fell, or at least by the time the Roman Empire was "Christianized" by Constantine (the Edict of Milan in 313 A.D). Accordingly, the "last days" (different from the "endtimes") spoken of in the New Testament were the last days for Old Covenant national Israel and the early inaugural days of the New Testament Church (see the notes below on Dan. 9:27). This includes the "last days" of animal sacrifices in the temple (Heb. 9:22–10:6). Nonetheless, Scofield's notes on Ezekiel 43:19 snub the New Testament Epistles and call for the reinstitution of animal sacrifices in a millennial temple!

Heb. 9:26, NIV

> *Then Christ would have had to suffer many times since the creation of the world. But now He has appeared once for all at the end of the ages to do away with sin by the sacrifice of Himself.*

The key to the futurist's interpretation is that the seventieth week of Daniel's prophecy has been disconnected from the sixty-ninth week, and, is thus still future. Dispensationalism's two princes in Daniel's famous prophecy are Christ and antichrist. Darby taught that the first, the "Messiah the Prince" (Dan. 9:25), is Jesus Christ, the Prince of peace. He believed that the second is "the prince who shall come" (Dan. 9:26), the wicked antichrist who shall be revealed after the Church is raptured from the earth.

According to this interpretation, the last or seventieth week is a seven-year period of tribulation (Mt. 24; Rev. 4–19) in which the antichrist, the "beast" of Revelation 13, will make a covenant with the Jews for the first half of the week. He will then break that promise in the last half of the week, known by futurists as the time of "great tribulation" (compare Mt. 24:21 with the similar wording of Ex. 10:14; 11:6; Ezek. 5:9; Dan. 9:12; 12:1; Joel 2:2). Dispensationalists prophesy that antichrist will desecrate a newly rebuilt Jewish temple by proclaiming himself to be god, and then will set up a statue of himself for the world to worship (citing 2 Thess. 2:3-4; Rev. 13:13-18).

This idea of an indeterminable gap with its aforementioned trappings is one of the most unnatural and non-literal interpretations found in any eschatological system. Ironically, this interpretation is taught by those who insist on a *literal* hermeneutic!

How should Christians treat Daniel's prophecy? First, we must understand that the seventy weeks were determined "upon," or concerning, the "people" of Daniel and his "holy city." Obviously, the "holy city" is Jerusalem and Daniel's "people" are the Jews from which Messiah would come. Daniel is our brother in Christ as Abraham's seed, and the New Testament "city" is the Church, the heavenly Jerusalem (Mt. 5:14; Heb. 11:10; 12:22-24). However, Daniel's prophecy has to do with Jerusalem and the Jews, from whom came the Messiah the Prince.

The key to unlocking this powerful Christological passage is to recognize the sixfold prophetic purpose contained in its complete scope and fulfillment. Within the uninterrupted time frame of seventy weeks of years (490 years), historical events would take place among the Jews ("thy people") in Jerusalem ("thy holy city") that would:

1. Finish the transgression.

2. Make an end of sins.

3. Make reconciliation for iniquity.

4. Bring in everlasting righteousness.

5. Seal up the vision and prophecy ("prophet").

6. Anoint the most holy ("holy of holies").

Jer. 31:31-34, KJV

Behold, the days come, saith the Lord, that I will make a new covenant with the house of Israel, and with the house of Judah:

Not according to the covenant that I made with their fathers in the day that I took them by the hand to bring them out of the land of Egypt; which My covenant they brake, although I was an husband unto them, saith the Lord:

But this shall be the covenant that I will make with the house of Israel; After those days, saith the Lord, I will put My law in their inward parts, and write it in their hearts; and will be their God, and they shall be My people.

And they shall teach no more every man his neighbour, and every man his brother, saying, Know the Lord: for they shall all know Me, from the least of them unto

> *the greatest of them, saith the Lord: for I will forgive*
> *their iniquity, and I will remember their sin no more.*

Daniel had been studying the prophetic manuscripts of Jeremiah. The sixfold scope of Daniel's prophecy is summed up in Jeremiah's prediction of the "new" covenant. In spite of Jeremiah 31:31-34 being quoted in Hebrews 8:8-13 (following the truths of Hebrews 8:1-6 that declare Jesus' "more excellent" high priestly ministry after His resurrection), Scofield relegated these verses to national Judaism in the Millennium. Notwithstanding, the "new covenant" is the New Testament, a matter of the heart and not the letter (Rom. 2:28-29)!

Dan. 9:24, KJV

> *Seventy weeks are determined upon thy people and*
> *upon thy holy city, to finish the transgression, and to*
> *make an end of sins, and to make reconciliation for iniq-*
> *uity, and to bring in everlasting righteousness, and to*
> *seal up the vision and prophecy, and to anoint the most*
> *Holy.*

The prophecy of seventy weeks enlarges Jeremiah's predictions. It is wholly Christological and Messianic! Putting an end to the Old Covenant and inaugurating the New Covenant, Jesus Christ on the *cross*:

1. Finished the transgression (Is. 43:25; 53:5; Heb. 9:15).

Jn. 19:30, KJV

> *When Jesus therefore had received the vinegar, He*
> *said, It is finished: and He bowed His head, and gave up*
> *the ghost.*

2. Made an end of sins (Mt. 1:21; Heb. 8:12).

Jn. 1:29, KJV

The next day John seeth Jesus coming unto Him, and saith, Behold the Lamb of God, which taketh away the sin of the world.

Heb. 9:26, NIV

Then Christ would have had to suffer many times since the creation of the world. But now He has appeared once for all at the end of the ages to do away with sin by the sacrifice of Himself.

3. Made reconciliation for iniquity (Rom. 5:10; Eph. 2:16).

2 Cor. 5:19, KJV

To wit, that God was in Christ, reconciling the world unto Himself, not imputing their trespasses unto them; and hath committed unto us the word of reconciliation.

Col. 1:19-20, KJV

For it pleased the Father that in Him should all fulness dwell;

And, having made peace through the blood of His cross, by Him to reconcile all things unto Himself....

Heb. 2:17, KJV

Wherefore in all things it behoved Him to be made like unto His brethren, that He might be a merciful and faithful high priest in things pertaining to God, to make reconciliation for the sins of the people.

The first three promises of Daniel's seventy weeks were historically fulfilled at Calvary's cross! Compare Isaiah 53:12, Mark 15:28, John 4:34; 5:36; 17:4, Romans 10:4; 11:15, Second Corinthians 3:13; 5:17-21, Hebrews 2:17; 6:16, James 5:11, and Revelation 21:6. No wonder the devil, who met his demise at Golgotha, wants to obscure and confuse Daniel's words!

Before one can make any kind of eschatological or spiritual application of Daniel 9:24-27 (and related Scriptures), he must have the basic awareness that this significant Messianic prophecy was fulfilled in Jesus Christ, as evidenced in these three preceding points. What about the rest of this prophecy's range and purpose (Daniel 9:24)?

4. Jesus Christ brought in everlasting righteousness because He *is* everlasting righteousness (Rom. 10:3,10; 2 Cor. 5:21; Phil. 3:9).

1 Cor. 1:30, KJV

But of Him are ye in Christ Jesus, who of God is made unto us wisdom, and righteousness, and sanctification, and redemption.

Heb. 7:1-2, KJV

For this Melchisedec, king of Salem, priest of the most high God, who met Abraham returning from the slaughter of the kings, and blessed him;

To whom also Abraham gave a tenth part of all; first being by interpretation King of righteousness....

5. Jesus Christ sealed up the vision and the prophecy, to fulfill the law and the prophets, because He *is* the vision and the prophecy, or Prophet (see Is. 29:10-11; Mt. 5:17-20; 11:13; Jn. 5:39; 6:27; 19:28-37; Acts 3:18; 26:17-19).

Hab. 2:3, KJV

For the vision is yet for an appointed time, but at the end it shall speak, and not lie: though it tarry, wait for it; because it will surely come, it will not tarry.

Heb. 10:37, KJV

...He that shall come will come, and will not tarry.

Mt. 5:17, KJV

Think not that I am come to destroy the law, or the prophets: I am not come to destroy, but to fulfil.

Acts 3:22, KJV

For Moses truly said unto the fathers, A prophet shall the Lord your God raise up unto you of your brethren, like unto me....

Rev. 19:10, KJV

...for the testimony of Jesus is the spirit of prophecy.

6. Jesus Christ *is* the anointing and the most holy—the "holy thing" (Lk. 1:35) and the "holy One" (Acts 3:14; 1 Jn. 2:20). He ripped the veil from top to bottom, opening the way into the "holy of holies" (see Ps. 45:7; Is. 61:1; Lk. 4:16-21; Acts 2:27; 4:27; 10:38).

Jn. 14:6, KJV

Jesus saith unto him, I am the way, the truth, and the life: no man cometh unto the Father, but by Me.

1 Jn. 2:27, KJV

But the anointing which ye have received of Him abideth in you, and ye need not that any man teach you: but as the same anointing teacheth you of all things, and is truth....

Rom 1:4, KJV

And declared to be the Son of God with power, according to the spirit of holiness....

Heb. 10:14, KJV

For by one offering He hath perfected for ever them that are sanctified.

Heb. 10:19-20, KJV

Having therefore, brethren, boldness to enter into the holiest by the blood of Jesus,

By a new and living way, which He hath consecrated for us, through the veil, that is to say, His flesh....

Daniel 9:24-27 is all about Jesus. Whatever eschatological slant or speculative rabbit trail one derives from these verses, he must center them in the finished work of the Lamb of God!

As we shall see, none of Daniel 9:24 was accomplished in the first 69 weeks of his prophecy. All events in verse 24 occurred during the seven years after the sixty-ninth week—with no chronological break. Once the Messiah came, He was given one prophetic week of seven years to see it through.

Most teachers take either the historical or prophetic position when interpreting this passage. The full scope of truth includes both, with the latter revealing Jesus *and* His Church. Dispensationalists need an adjusted vision concerning Daniel 9:24-27. Their whole concept needs re-examination, which true Bereans won't mind (Acts 17:10-11).

Seventy Weeks Are Determined

Before one exegetes Daniel 9:24-27, he must review the context of the entire chapter. Daniel had discovered Jeremiah's prophecy (Jer. 25:8-11; 29:10) that Judah would be in captivity for 70 years (606-536 B.C.). The focus of his consequent fastings and prayers was the sinful condition of his people and the desolation of the national sanctuary (Dan. 9:1-19). While the prophet was confessing the sin of Israel and "the holy mountain of God" (Zion), the angel Gabriel appeared "at the time of the evening oblation" to give "skill and understanding" concerning the vision (Dan. 9:20-23).

God's perspective, as delivered by Gabriel, broadened Jeremiah's 70 years into 70 weeks of years. The angel's explanation prophesied the New Testament revelation of Jesus' finished work, the putting away of all sin, and the cessation of all sacrifice and oblation—the contextual emphasis of the entire chapter! The same archangel that announced the Messiah's birth to Mary (Lk. 1:26-31) prophesied His death to Daniel!

The time of the evening oblation was three o'clock in the afternoon—"the ninth hour"—the very hour of Jesus' crucifixion (Mt. 27:45-46; Jn. 19:30)! The Lamb of God didn't just die for the sins of the Jewish nation—He died for the sins of the world, for all men, Jew and Greek (Jn. 1:29; 3:16)!

As noted, the first coming of the Lord Jesus Christ is a seed form of His second coming. As we exegete each of these four important verses, we will note its:

1. *Historical* and *Messianic* application, for the time of Jesus' first coming.

2. *Prophetic* overtones, for the time of Jesus' second coming.

Dan. 9:24, KJV

Seventy weeks are determined upon thy people and upon thy holy city, to finish the transgression, and to make an end of sins, and to make reconciliation for iniquity, and to bring in everlasting righteousness, and to seal up the vision and prophecy, and to anoint the most Holy.

Dan. 9:24, NIV

Seventy "sevens" are decreed for your people and your holy city....

Dan. 9:24, AMP

Seventy weeks [of years, or 490 years] are decreed upon your people and upon your holy city [Jerusalem]....

Dan. 9:24, RHM

...and bring in the righteousness of ages....

Dan. 9:24 JB

...for introducing everlasting integrity...for setting the seal on vision and on prophecy....

Dan. 9:24, MOF

...to ratify the prophetic vision, and to consecrate a most sacred place.

Dan. 9:24, LAM

...to fulfill the vision of the prophets and to give the most holy to Messiah.

The Anchor Bible translates this verse. "...until crime is stopped, sins brought to full measure, guilt expiated, everlasting justice introduced, the prophetic vision confirmed, and the Holy of Holies anointed."

"Seventy weeks"...70 continual, consecutive weeks! "Seventy weeks" is 70 times 7, or 490 weeks, a total of 490 years ("weeks" could be translated as "sevens"). The word for "determined" here means "cut out or cut off"; that is, divided off from all the other years—decided, decreed, destined, appointed—set off by itself for a definite purpose.

Jesus knew the Father's plan, because 490 is the Bible number denoting *complete forgiveness* (Mt. 18:21-22)! The six truths of Daniel 9:24 reveal that God has "determined" in Christ to completely forgive His creation!

Notably, the term "seventy weeks" is plural, but "determined" is singular! From the Hebrew grammar, the seventy weeks are thus declared collectively to denote one period of time—with no gap.

The Hebrew word for "people" is *am* (Strong's #5971) and means "a people; tribe; troops; figuratively, a flock" (see Dan. 8:24; 9:6,15-20; 10:14; 11:14-15, 32-33; 12:1,7). It is also translated in the King James Version as "folk, men, nation."

The Hebrew margin of Daniel 9:24 ("to finish the transgression, and to make an end of sins") renders "finish" as "shut up, confine, restrain." For "transgression," compare Daniel 8:12-13, 23. "Make an end" means "to seal up" (Dan. 12:4,9), and "sins" is "sin offerings" (Lev. 4:3; Dan. 9:20). The offering of the Lamb of God was the consummate sin offering!

"Reconciliation" is the Hebrew word *kaphar* (Strong's #3722). It means "to cover; expiate, to placate or cancel." *Vine's* adds, "to ransom, atone, propitiate." It is also the Hebrew word for "atonement," to cover by blood sacrifice (see Lev. 17:11; Ps. 65:3; 78:38; 79:9; Prov. 16:6,14). For "iniquity," compare Daniel 9:13, 16. Thus everlasting righteousness would be brought in, literally "made to come" (Is. 45:17).

To "seal up" or "close up" the vision and prophet is to authenticate or confirm them, to make them sure (Dan. 12:4,9). Jesus fulfilled and confirmed the law and the prophets (Mt. 5:17; Rom. 15:8). Another interesting application of the seal (Dan. 6:17) is found by comparing Isaiah 29:10-11 with Second Corinthians 3:14-15.

Vision is also mentioned in Daniel 1:17; 8:1-2, 13, 15, 26; 9:21, 23; 10:14; 11:14. The word "prophecy" is actually *nabiy* (Strong's #5030), and it means "a prophet" (Deut. 18; Acts 3:19-24; compare Dan. 9:2,6,10). The word used for "anoint" means "to rub with oil; to consecrate" (Ps. 45:7; 89:20; Dan. 10:3) and "most holy" is "holy of holies." Jesus rent the veil and made a way to the Father. He is the Way, the Truth, and the Life (Jn. 14:6)!

The *historical* and *Messianic* fulfillment of Daniel 9:24 has been noted. Jesus Christ's finished work on the cross fulfilled all six prophetic points.

The *prophetic* overtone of Daniel 9:24 reveals the Church in His image, forgiven and delivered from sin by His finished work, accomplished in the Feast of Passover. There is a present, ongoing work of His cleansing the Church in the Feast Day of Atonement. Everlasting righteousness speaks of an everlasting Kingdom (Is. 9:6-7; Rom. 14:17) and an unchangeable priesthood after the order of Melchisedec (Heb. 5–7). The Head of the Church was sealed and anointed (Jn. 6:27; Acts 10:38; Heb. 2:9). There will be a many-membered prophetic Church (an "Elijah ministry") who will be sealed with the name or nature of God in the forehead, a Most Holy Place, Third Day people (see Ex. 28; Hos. 6:1-3; Rev. 7:3; 14:1-5; 22:4). The New Testament Epistles declare the ultimate fulfillment of Daniel 9:24.

1 Cor. 15:28, KJV

And when all things shall be subdued unto Him, then shall the Son also Himself be subject unto Him that put all things under Him, that God may be all in all.

Eph. 1:9-10, NIV

And He made known to us the mystery of His will according to His good pleasure, which He purposed in Christ, to be put into effect when the times will have reached their fulfillment—to bring all things in heaven and on earth together under one head, even Christ.

Unto the Messiah the Prince

Dan. 9:25, KJV

Know therefore and understand, that from the going forth of the commandment to restore and to build Jerusalem unto the Messiah the Prince shall be seven weeks, and threescore and two weeks: the street shall be built again, and the wall, even in troublous times.

Dan. 9:25, NIV

...until the Anointed One, the ruler, comes, there will be seven "sevens," and sixty-two "sevens"....

Dan. 9:25, TLB

Now listen! It will be forty-nine years plus 434 years from the time the command is given to rebuild Jerusalem until the Anointed One comes!...

Most interpretations of this verse carry us through a maze of numbers and historical information. Throughout Church history, commentators have tried to make this prophecy "fit" into ancient and as well as their own contemporary history. However, all these views are established on the Scriptural principle that a *day* can represent a *year* (Gen. 29:27; Lev. 25:8; Num. 14:34).

Ezek. 4:6, KJV

...I have appointed thee each day for a year.

There are four events that can be taken as answering to the commandment to "restore and build Jerusalem," the beginning point of Daniel's prophecy:

1. The decree of King Cyrus of Persia for the rebuilding of the temple only, 536 B.C. (2 Chron. 36:22-23; Ezra 1:1-4; Is. 44:28).

2. The decree of Darius I (Hystaspes) of Persia for Zerubbabel to continue and complete the temple, 520 B.C. (Ezra 4:24; 6:1-15).

3. The decree of Artaxerses (Longimanus) of Persia for Ezra to beautify the temple and restore its worship, and to rebuild the Jewish state, 457 B.C. (Ezra 7).

4. The decree of Artaxerses (Longimanus) of Persia for Nehemiah to rebuild the city's walls and gates, 445 B.C. (Neh. 2).

Dating from the first two of these decrees, the 70 prophetic weeks, or 490 years, would fall many years short of reaching the Christian era. Besides this, these edicts had reference principally to the restoration of the temple, not to the restoration of the Jewish civil state and polity, included in the phrase, "to *restore* and build Jerusalem."

So which of the other two decrees marks the beginning of Daniel's seventy weeks?

A mandate was granted to Ezra by the Persian emperor Artaxerses Longimanus to go up to Jerusalem with as many people as were like-minded. This commission granted him unlimited revenue to beautify the house of God, empowered him to ordain laws, set magistrates and judges, and execute government—in other words, to "restore" the Jewish state, civil and ecclesiastical, according to the law of God and the ancient customs of the Jewish people. This edict was a reaffirmation of the first two decrees of Cyrus and Darius.

Artaxerses made this decree in the seventh year of his reign (Ezra 7:8). Ezra arrived in Jerusalem on the first day of the fifth month (*Ab*) the same year (Ezra 7:9)—August 1, 457 B.C. According to ancient chronological records, Artaxerses' decree went into effect in Jerusalem in the fall of 457 B.C.

Thirteen years after this (444 B.C.), in the 20th year of the same king (Neh. 1:1), Nehemiah sought and obtained permission to go up to Jerusalem. Oral permission (not written) was given and pertained to him individually. When he arrived at Jerusalem, Nehemiah found rulers and priests, nobles and people, already engaged in the work of rebuilding Jerusalem (Neh. 2:16), acting under the decree given to Ezra 13 years before. Although there were "troublous times" (Neh. 2:8-17; 4:17, with Dan. 9:25), the wall was rebuilt. In 52 days, Nehemiah finished the work he came to accomplish (Neh. 6:15).

The starting point for Daniel's prophecy of seventy weeks was Artaxerses' decree to Ezra—457 B.C.!

It is noteworthy that some chronologists, such as Philip Mauro in his *The Wonders of Bible Chronology*, use a different system of dates (other than Ptolemy's history of the Persian kings) and believe that "the commandment to restore and to build Jerusalem" (Dan. 9:25) was the decree of Cyrus, which Mauro dates at 457 B.C. (still the same date) (Sterling, VA: Grace Abounding Ministries, 1987).

Having established that the seventy weeks began in 457 B.C. with Artaxerses' (or Cyrus') decree, it is not difficult to see the rest of the picture. The prophecy of seventy weeks (490 years) can be divided into:

1. "Seven weeks"—49 years.
2. "Threescore and two weeks"—62 weeks, or 434 years.
3. "One week"—seven years.

Some have simply combined the "seven weeks" with the "threescore and two weeks" (69 weeks), totaling 483 years from the commandment to rebuild Jerusalem until the coming of the Messiah the Prince.

"Seven weeks" (49 years) were allotted to the building of the city and the wall—from 457 B.C. to 408 B.C. The latter was the fifteenth year of Darius II (Nothus) and ended the first phase of Daniel's prophecy. The restoration of the state of the Jews in Jerusalem was finished, as recorded in Nehemiah 13:23-31.

"Threescore and two weeks" (434 more years) take us from 408 B.C. to A.D. 27 (one year must be added when going from B.C. to A.D.), when Jesus Christ the Messiah was 30 years of age (having been born in 4 B.C.)! This was the fifteenth year of Tiberius Caesar (Lk. 3:1,21-23). Some date Artaxerses' decree at 454 B.C. and take the sixty-ninth week of Daniel's prophecy to A.D. 29. Nonetheless, the Synoptic Gospels record this epochal event— the inauguration of Jesus' public ministry at His baptism in Jordan (where the Messiah received His anointing)!

Mt. 3:15-17, NIV

Jesus replied, "Let it be so now; it is proper for us to do this to fulfill all righteousness." Then John consented.

As soon as Jesus was baptized, He went up out of the water. At that moment heaven was opened, and He saw the Spirit of God descending like a dove and lighting on Him.

And a voice from heaven said, "This is My Son, whom I love; with Him I am well pleased."

Mk. 1:14-15, KJV

Now after that John was put in prison, Jesus came into Galilee, preaching the gospel of the kingdom of God,

And saying, The time is fulfilled, and the kingdom of God is at hand....

Lk. 3:21-23, KJV

Now when all the people were baptized, it came to pass, that Jesus also being baptized, and praying, the heaven was opened,

And the Holy Ghost descended in a bodily shape like a dove upon Him, and a voice came from heaven, which said, Thou art my beloved Son; in Thee I am well pleased.

And Jesus Himself began to be about thirty years of age....

Jesus was born three to four years before the beginning of the Christian Era, the year called A.D. 1. This mistake in dating arose when in A.D. 532 Dionysius

Exiguus invented the calendar of the Christian Era based upon the time of the building of the city of Rome. This kind of time was called *ab urbe condita,* or A.U.C. (or simply, U.C. time). Dionysius placed the birth of Christ U.C. 753. Later, when it was ascertained that Herod had died in U.C. 750, Jesus' birth was moved back to the latter part of U.C. 749, a little more than three years before A.D. 1. Therefore, Jesus Christ was 30 years of age in A.D. 27. The "Child" had been born in Bethlehem; the "Son" was given 30 years later at the Jordan (Is. 9:6-7)!

Dan. 9:25, KJV

> *Know therefore and understand, that from the going forth of the commandment to restore and to build Jerusalem unto the Messiah the Prince shall be seven weeks, and threescore and two weeks: the street shall be built again, and the wall, even in troublous times.*

The Hebrew word for "know" means "to ascertain by seeing" (see Dan. 1:4; 2:3; 8:19; 10:20; 11:32,38). The word for "understand" means "to be prudent, act wisely, give attention to, ponder, prosper" (see Dan. 1:4,17; 9:13,22; 11:33,35; 12:3,10).

The "commandment," or "word," to restore and rebuild Jerusalem was the decree of Artaxerses of Persia in 457 B.C. (Ezra 7). The word for "restore" is *shuwb* (Strong's #7725). It means "to turn back." *Messiah* is the Hebrew equivalent of the Greek *Christ.* Derived from the root word for "anoint" in Daniel 9:24, it is the word *mashiyach* (Strong's #4899), meaning "anointed; a conse-crated person; specifically, the Messiah," and is used 39 times in the Old Testament. The word for "prince" in Daniel 9:25-26; 11:22 is *nagiyd* (Strong's #5057). It means "a commander (as occupying the front)." It also means "prefect, chief leader" (see Gen. 32:28; Ex. 2:14; Is. 9:6; Ezek. 44:3).

Because there is no definite article preceding "messiah the prince" in the Hebrew, some commentators (according to their particular scheme of numbers and dates) have identified "messiah the prince" differently (for example, as Cyrus, mentioned in Isaiah 45:1). Besides Daniel's obvious prophetic preciseness of 483 years from 457 B.C. to A.D. 27, what does the New Testament reveal about the "Messiah"?

Jn. 4:25-26, KJV

> *The woman saith unto Him, I know that Messias cometh, which is called Christ: when He is come, He will tell us all things.*
>
> *Jesus saith unto her, I that speak unto thee am He.*

Jn. 4:42, KJV

> *And said unto the woman, Now we believe, not because of thy saying: for we have heard Him ourselves, and know that this is indeed the Christ, the Saviour of the world.*

Acts 3:15, KJV

> *And killed the Prince of life, whom God hath raised from the dead; whereof we are witnesses.*

Acts 5:31, KJV

Him hath God exalted with His right hand to be a Prince and a Saviour, for to give repentance to Israel, and forgiveness of sins.

Rev. 1:5, KJV

And from Jesus Christ, who is the...prince of the kings of the earth....

The Septuagint (LXX), the Greek Old Testament, translates Daniel 9:25, "...until Christ the prince..."

Jesus Christ was the "Messiah the Prince." Jesus, who received this anointing of the Spirit at His public baptism (A.D. 27), informed the woman at the well of His identity. Furthermore, Jesus confirmed this revelation with His own mouth at the synagogue in Nazareth (Is. 61:1; Lk. 4:16-21).

Lk. 4:21, KJV

And He began to say unto them, This day is this scripture fulfilled in your ears.

The "street" mentioned in Daniel 9:25 refers to the "width, avenue, plaza, town square" or market-place of Jerusalem. The "wall," or "ditch, moat" (the trench cut into the rock outside the city walls), points to the "troublous" times of Nehemiah. This word means "to disturb or afflict; distress or anguish" (Neh. 4:21-26; Prov. 11:17,29; 15:6,27).

The *historical* and *Messianic* fulfillment of Daniel 9:25 has been noted. Daniel's sixty-ninth week ended in

A.D. 27 when Prince Jesus stepped down into the muddy baptismal waters of the Jordan. Daniel's seventieth week began when "the Messiah the Prince" came up out of those same waters, anointed to dismantle the works of the devil (Acts 10:38; 1 Jn. 3:8)!

The *prophetic* overtone of this verse reveals the restoration of the Church from Martin Luther to the present. I have dealt with those truths and principles in depth throughout my *Principles of Present Truth From Ezra, Nehemiah, and Esther* (Richlands, NC: Tabernacle Press, 1983). The New Testament "street" can be found in Acts 9:11 and Revelation 21:21. The rebuilt spiritual "wall" can be discerned in Song of Solomon 8:10, Isaiah 60:18, Amos 7:7, Zechariah 2:5, and Revelation 21:12-19.

The People of the Prince That Shall Come

Dan. 9:26, KJV

And after threescore and two weeks shall Messiah be cut off, but not for Himself: and the people of the prince that shall come shall destroy the city and the sanctuary; and the end thereof shall be with a flood, and unto the end of the war desolations are determined.

Dan. 9:26, NIV

After the sixty-two "sevens," the Anointed One will be cut off and will have nothing. The people of the ruler who will come will destroy the city and the sanctuary. The end will come like a flood: War will continue until the end, and desolations have been decreed.

Dan. 9:26, KNOX

...Then the army of an invading leader will destroy both city and sanctuary....

Dan. 9:26, LAM

...Messiah shall be slain....

Dan. 9:26, SEPT

...the Messiah shall be cut off, though there is no crime in Him....

These final two verses mark the place where dispensationalists put a 2,000-year "gap" between the sixty-ninth and seventieth weeks of Daniel's prophecy. According to their view, at the end of that time we shall meet their notorious "prince that shall come," the future antichrist. Let's take another look at this verse in the light of fulfilled history and clear New Testament Scripture.

"Messiah" is the Hebrew equivalent for the Greek "Christ," or *Christos*, which means "the anointed one." Jesus Christ was "cut off" at the cross "after" 62 weeks (from 408 B.C. to A.D. 27). It was 69 weeks (457 B.C. to A.D. 27) "unto" the beginning of His public ministry, so He would have to be cut off "after" that (Is. 53:8; Jn. 1:41; 4:25).

The Hebrew word for "cut" is *karath* (Strong's #3772). It means "to cut (off, down, or asunder); specifically, to covenant." The words "cut off" speak of being cut off by *death*, and suggest the idea of an abrupt, violent death, or a death by the agency of others (cutting a covenant)—which took place at Calvary's cross.

Is. 53:8, KJV

> *...He was cut off out of the land of the living....*

The phrase "but not for himself" (Dan. 9:26) is literally, "and shall have nothing." Some Greek translations
of this phrase render it as "without trial" or "unjustly"
(Mt. 26–27; Acts 8:32-33). Born in another man's stable,
cradled in another man's manger with no place to lay
His head throughout His life here on earth, and buried
in another man's tomb after dying on a cursed cross, the
Christ of God and Friend of the friendless was indeed cut
off and had nothing. The Messiah would be rejected and
crucified (Is. 53:1-4; Jn. 1:11; 2 Cor. 8:9), "not for Himself"
or His own sin, but the sin of the world.

Is. 53:8, KJV

> *...for the transgression of My people was He
> stricken.*

The next part of Daniel 9:26 is most critical. Its literal
rendering is, "...and the city, and the sanctuary, the people of a prince that comes, shall lay waste...."

The word translated as "people" is the Hebrew word
am, meaning "citizens." It could imply troops or soldiers
(compare Dan. 9:24). For the word "prince," see the previous discussion on Daniel 9:25. Darby, Scofield, and
Larkin's followers say that this prince is the future antichrist. They emphasize that a natural temple will be rebuilt in Jerusalem, referencing Second Thessalonians
2:3-4 (exegeted in Chapter Eight).

But to teach that animal sacrifices will be reinstitu-
ted (even in a "memorial" sense, as taught in Scofield's

"revised" notes) ignores the Epistle to the Hebrews, the revelation of the final, "once and for all" blood sacrifice of Jesus Christ's better blood (Heb. 9–10). Compare the notes for Daniel 9:27 given below for more about this "prince." As noted, other historical views say that he was Antiochus IV Epiphanes, one of the Seleucid kings of Syria who began to rule about 175 B.C.

Daniel prophesied that the people of the prince who shall come would "destroy" the city and the sanctuary. This word means "to corrupt, spoil, ruin, mar" (Gen. 6:11-17; Dan. 8:24-25; 11:17). For "city" and "sanctuary" (the same word as "most holy"), see the notes on Daniel 9:24. The end of the city and the sanctuary is compared to an overflowing "flood" or "deluge," a gushing out-pouring of rain, a sudden inundation, carrying away everything before it (like a mighty, galloping, conquering army, sweeping everything away). Compare Job 38:25, Psalms 32:6, Daniel 11:22, and Nahum 1:8.

Daniel mentions the "end" often throughout his prophecy (see Dan. 8:17,19; 11:6,27,35,40,45; 12:4,6,9,13). Until the end of the "war" or "battle" (Dan. 11:20,25), "desolations" or "astonishments and devastations" (see Dan. 8:27; 9:17-18,27; 11:31; 12:11) are "determined" or "decided, decreed." The Hebrew margin renders the last part of Daniel 9:26 as "it shall be cut off by desolation." These words and phrases point to the complete destruction of Jerusalem in A.D. 70 (Mt. 24:2).

The *historical* and *Messianic* fulfillment of Daniel 9:26 has been noted in part above. Furthermore, this verse accurately predicts the ravaging of Jerusalem by the Roman "troops" and their "prince" Titus in A.D. 70.

Another slant of the historical view is that some variant Hebrew translations of Daniel 9:26 read, "and the prince (Messiah's) future people shall destroy the city and the sanctuary." Accordingly, the "people" of Prince Messiah would be the Jews. Josephus, the Jewish historian, blamed the complete destruction of Jerusalem upon the Zealots who resisted and continued fighting after their defenses had fallen, thinking that God would never allow the city to be conquered. These bandits caused more death and destruction than did the Romans.

Regardless, the "prince" of Daniel 9:26 is not some future antichrist.

Titus and his men "destroyed the city and the sanctuary" of the Jews. Josephus was an eye-witness to the unparalleled tribulation that brought the fall and destruction of Jerusalem, and the "end" of Judaism like a flood. His detailed and scholarly account, *Wars of the Jews*, was published about A.D. 75. His history provides a marvellous confirmation of the prophecy Jesus gave, even in fine detail. The "desolation" that Jesus decreed came to pass (Lk. 13:35). These infallible predictions by Jesus (Mt. 23:36–24:3) set the time clock for the total abomination of desolation as prophesied by Daniel.

Mt. 24:34, NIV

I tell you the truth, this generation will certainly not pass away until all these things have happened.

Jesus said, "This generation" (His own).

The marble stones of the temple, some of them 50 feet long, 24 feet wide, and 16 feet thick, cut to fit perfectly without the need of mortar, would all be thrown down and completely demolished within 40 years! After the death of Jesus, Judea had continual trouble (tribulation), especially in the harshness of their taxes. Tyranny reigned A.D. 60-62. The armies of the Roman empire, Assyria, and Egypt began a march of total destruction over the land of Israel. Wars, battles, devastation, destruction, horror, and death were everywhere. There was civil disobedience in every city (Mt. 24:4-8). Throughout Judea, thousands were killed. As noted, internal strife between rival religious factions ransacked the city of Jerusalem, doing as much or more damage than Titus' army. They would later join forces against the common Roman foe.

Emperor Vespasian sent his son Titus with elite forces (four legions) to crush the holy city in A.D. 69. Famine raged. Josephus, according to his account of Titus' siege (Wars V.-VI.), acted as a mediator between the Romans and Jews that the temple might be spared. Against Titus' wishes and in spite of what some "prophets" at that time had said, the battle culminated with the burning and desolation of the sanctuary on September 8, A.D. 70, the very month and day that Solomon's temple had been burned by the Babylonians (according to Josephus, Wars VI. iv. 8.)!

The Romans pitched their standards inside the temple court and offered sacrifice, acclaiming General Titus' victory. Later, the city was sacked and burned. Josephus said that the number of prisoners taken during this conquest was 97,000, and those who died 1,100,000 (Wars VI. ix. 3.). He notes that most of these were not natives of Jerusalem. They had come for the Feast of Unleavened Bread and had been caught in the war. The Romans set fire to outlying areas and demolished the walls to the ground, with not one stone left upon another.

Zion became a plowed field, and Jerusalem became heaps and a forest (Mic. 3:12). There was no rebuilding of Jerusalem until A.D. 180. Today's city is built upon the ruins of Titus' destruction.

Lk. 21:20, NIV

When you see Jerusalem being surrounded by armies, you will know that its desolation is near.

Lk. 21:36, NIV

Be always on the watch, and pray that you may be able to escape all that is about to happen, and that you may be able to stand before the Son of Man.

These prophecies of Jesus (Mt. 24:15-22) saved the lives of Christians who forsook the doomed city in good time and fled to the town of Pella in the Decapolis, beyond Jordan, where Herod Agrippa II, before whom Paul once stood, opened to them a safe asylum. The word for "escape" in Luke 21:36 is *ekpheugo* (Strong's #1628), and it means "to run away, to flee out of a place" (see Acts 16:27; 19:16; Rom. 2:3; 2 Cor. 11:33; 1 Thess. 5:3; and Heb. 2:3). Because of Jesus' warning, the Jerusalem Christians fled before Titus arrived.

An arch was erected in Rome to commemorate the victory of Titus and the Roman armies in the destruction of Jerusalem. Over the centuries, this monument has been a witness to the fulfillment of Jesus' words concerning the tribulation that came upon Jerusalem and Judea.

274 Whose Right It Is

For more on this, see also the *historical, Messianic* application for Daniel 9:27.

Gen. 37:9, KJV

And he dreamed yet another dream, and told it his brethren, and said, Behold, I have dreamed a dream more; and, behold, the sun and the moon and the eleven stars made obeisance to me.

Mt. 24:29, KJV

Immediately after the tribulation of those days shall the sun be darkened, and the moon shall not give her light, and the stars shall fall from heaven, and the powers of the heavens shall be shaken.

These words of Jesus reveal a picture of the twelve tribes (the sons of Jacob) and the fall of national Israel. The Jewish nation fell from their greatness, and the blessing of Abraham came upon all the nations through faith.

Daniel's prophecy of seventy weeks has been historically fulfilled. Yet, as with Matthew 24, we have seen that there are prophetic implications throughout.

The *prophetic* and spiritual overtones of Daniel 9:26 point to the life and ministry of the early Church (the people of the Prince Messiah) who brought an "end" to the old order of Judaism. This was to be especially true in the writings of the apostle Paul who replaced an earthly "city" and "sanctuary" of Jerusalem with a heavenly one (Gal. 4:21-31; Heb. 12:22-24). Thus the "people" of the Prince would be His Church. May God raise up literary apostles and prophets who will, by Spirit-anointed exegesis and exposition, dismantle the favorite teachings of the god of this world. May this be dispensationalism's "terminal generation"!

The truths found in this volume will bring a sword to the reader's traditional mind-set. There is an apostolic mandate in my spirit to destroy any focus upon a *literal* city and sanctuary—the heart and soul of Scofieldism. Beginning in 1948, through the great Charismatic renewal to the present, God has poured out His Spirit like a "flood" upon the dry ground, and men from every stream are hearing the Word (Prov. 1:23; Is. 44:3; Ezek. 37:1-14). Until the "end of the war" (Acts 20:24; 1 Tim. 4:7), God's apostles and prophets are "determined" to lay waste every emphasis other than Jesus and His Church!

He Shall Cause the Sacrifice and Oblation to Cease

Daniel pinpointed the "time" and the "hour" when Jesus would come, suffer, and die for the sins of the world (see Mt. 26:18,45; Jn. 2:4; 7:6,30; 17:1), causing the sin offering to cease.

Dan. 9:27, KJV

And He shall confirm the covenant with many for one week: and in the midst of the week He shall cause the sacrifice and the oblation to cease, and for the overspreading of abominations He shall make it desolate, even until the consummation, and that determined shall be poured upon the desolate.

Dan. 9:27, NIV

He will confirm a covenant with many for one "seven." In the middle of the "seven" He will put an end to sacrifice and offering....

Dan. 9:27, AMP

...and upon the wing or pinnacle of abominations [shall come] one who makes desolate; until the full determined end is poured out on the desolator.

Dan. 9:27, MOF

...till finally the appointed doom falls upon the sacrilegious abomination."

Dan. 9:27, JB

...until the doom assigned to the devastator.

The most critical week (seven years) in human history is the seventieth week of Daniel's prophecy! The death, burial, and resurrection of Jesus the Messiah, and the consequent outpouring of the Holy Spirit are the basis of every New Covenant reality! These great spiritual truths are now corroborated by historical fact. Satan wants this period of time to be clouded and garbled, for it was in the seventieth week of Daniel's prophecy that our adversary met his complete defeat and total demise!

Rom. 15:8-9, NIV

For I tell you that Christ has become a servant of the Jews on behalf of God's truth, to confirm the promises made to the patriarchs

so that the Gentiles may glorify God for His mercy....

In the beginning of verse 27, "He" is Messiah the Prince! Jesus is the one who "confirmed" the covenantal promises of Jeremiah's "new covenant."

This is also true, grammatically speaking. "He" (Dan. 9:27) is a singular pronoun. "Of the prince" (Dan. 9:26) is a prepositional phrase modifying "people," a plural noun. A pronoun cannot properly have as its antecedent the object of a modifying clause. "He" modifies the singular antecedent "Messiah" in verses 25 and 26. The sense of the context is as follows:

"And after threescore and two weeks shall Messiah be cut off, but not for Himself...And He [the Messiah] shall confirm the [New] covenant with many [elect Jews] for one week: and in the midst of the [seventieth] week He [the Messiah] shall cause the sacrifice and the sin offering to cease (at Calvary's cross)...."

The rest of Daniel 9:26, referencing Titus and his army, is parenthetical to the whole prophecy. It does not fit into the things that were to be done in the seventieth week, and historically, those events occurred 35 years later (A.D. 69-70).

Jesus Christ "confirmed" the Abrahamic covenant and secured the promises made to the fathers (Acts 3:13; Gal. 3:7,16,27-29). It does not say that "He" will make another covenant (as the traditional teaching says of the antichrist and the Jews). As shown, the seventieth week of Daniel's Messianic prophecy *began* immediately following Jesus' baptism. Circumcision was the covenantal seal in the Old Testament (Gen. 17), and we understand that water baptism is the covenantal seal in the New Testament (Col. 2:10-12). Jesus fulfilled or completed all righteousness when He inaugurated His public ministry at the Jordan at the age of 30 (Mt. 3:15).

Jesus' baptism occurred in the autumn of A.D. 27, marking the beginning of Daniel's seventieth week. Three-and-one-half years later brings us to the spring of A.D. 31, when the true Passover Lamb died on the cross and caused the sacrifice and oblation to cease by the shedding of His own blood!

Dispensationalists contend that a future antichrist will "make" a covenant with the Jews. It is then taught that he will "break" that covenant. The Bible teaches that Jesus Christ "confirmed" the covenant with many. The words "make" or "break" are not found in Daniel 9:27. The everlasting covenant in Jesus' blood was confirmed with the Jews for seven years before God turned to all nations.

Dan. 9:27, KJV

And He shall confirm the covenant with many....

The unusual verb (*gabar*) used for "confirm" means "to be strong; to prevail." It has the implication of making a strong "covenant" or "compact, league" (Dan. 9:4; 11:22,28,30,32) by the means of superior strength (Lk. 11:22)! The word destroys the dispensational idea that their "prince," the antichrist, will break his covenant with the Jews in the middle of the week. Daniel said that this covenant would "prevail" for an entire week, or seven years (not three-and-a-half)! Jesus Himself announced the coming of this immutable, everlasting, unbreakable New Covenant.

Mk. 1:14-15, KJV

Now after that John was put in prison, Jesus came into Galilee, preaching the gospel of the kingdom of God,

And saying, The time is fulfilled, and the kingdom of God is at hand: repent ye, and believe the gospel.

Mt. 26:28, KJV

For this is My blood of the new testament, which is shed for many....

Lk. 22:20, KJV

...This cup is the new testament in My blood, which is shed for you.

This "firm" New Covenant was made by Jesus Christ (not some future antichrist) in the redemptive work of His cross as a direct fulfillment of Daniel 9:27! There is nothing in Revelation 4–19 mentioning any antichrist making any covenant with the Jews and then breaking it.

Throughout this prophecy, Gabriel was explaining to Daniel the "covenant" that Jeremiah had predicted (Jer. 31:31-34). This was the "new" covenant with God's laws written in men's hearts. The Messiah would confirm this New Testament in His own blood with "many" of the lost sheep of the house of Israel (Mt. 10:5-6) for one week, or seven years. This is the Hebrew *rab* (Strong's #7227) which means "abundant; to cast together, increase, multiply." It is the transliteration of the Akkadian *rab*, an indication of military rank similar to our word for "general." In the first three and one-half years of the seventieth week (Jesus' public ministry), our Lord gathered together His Jewish generals (Mt. 10; Lk. 10), part of the Jewish remnant according to the election of grace (Rom. 9:21-29; 11:1-5).

Interestingly, for the past 50 years Israel and the Middle East has been the most war-torn area of the earth. To accept the confirming oath of the New Covenant (Jer. 31:31-34; Heb. 6:16-18) is to experience an end of all strife. Jerusalem's rejection of earth's Messiah has made her a "burdensome stone for all people" (Zech. 12:3).

Dan. 9:27, KJV

...and in the midst of the week He shall cause the sacrifice and the oblation to cease, and for the overspreading of abominations He shall make it desolate....

Mt. 23:38, KJV

Behold, your house is left unto you desolate.

Heb. 9:26, NIV

Then Christ would have had to suffer many times since the creation of the world. But now He has appeared once for all at the end of the ages to do away with sin by the sacrifice of Himself.

The "midst," or "half, middle," of Daniel's seventieth week was the cutting off point of Messiah's ministry after three-and-a-half years. On the *cross* "He" (Jesus the Messiah) caused the sacrifice and "oblation," or offering, to "cease" (Jn. 1:29; Eph. 2:13-15; Heb. 10:1-14), rending the veil from top to bottom (Mt. 27:51). The Hebrew word for "cease" is *shabath* (Strong's #7673), and it means "to repose; rest" (compare the English *sabbath*).

The "overspreading" of abominations in Daniel 9:27 clearly refers to increased idolatry. The word "overspreading" is literally "wing," that which covers or hides—as does the veil of flesh. It can also mean "edge or extremity" (consider the extreme evil and violence of men in Noah's day, as in Gen. 6). "Abominations" are "disgusting, filthy, loathesome, polluted things" (Dan. 11:31; 12:11). It is noteworthy that the Hebrew language is obscure here in this section. A free translation from the Hebrew text can be rendered as, "And—upon the wing—the porch of the temple—abominations! And a desolator!"

All of this is "until" (Ps. 110:1) the "consummation," the "completion or end" of this prophecy. It is interesting that the word "desolate" is literally "the desolator." If there would be a future antichrist, he would be prophetically suggested here in Daniel 9:27 and not as "the prince that shall come." The judgment "determined" (same as Dan. 9:26), the decreed ruin upon the desolator, will be "poured out," or "flow forth" (see Gen. 18:21; Ex. 11:1; 2 Chron. 12:12; Is. 10:23; 28:22; Nah. 1:8-9; Zeph. 1:18).

The *historical* and *Messianic* application of Daniel 9:27 has been noted in part. Jesus cut the New Covenant (Jer. 31:31-34) in His blood "with" ("for," or "unto") many, first of all with the Jewish remnant (to fulfill Dan. 9:24-27), and then with all men. In Matthew 23:23-38, Jesus pronounced "desolation" upon old order Judaism. He made reference to Daniel's seventy weeks only with regard to the "abomination of desolation" (Mt. 24:15; Mk. 13:14). This was the desecration of Jerusalem and its temple by

Titus and his hordes. The Pharisees had "covered" their idolatrous, systematic error and tradition, and Jesus brought an end to it all! He did this on the cross, when He was cut off in the "midst" (or "half") of the week, after three-and-a-half years of public ministry. Jesus, our peace and Lord of the sabbath, caused the Levitical offerings to "cease" or "rest" (Eph. 2:14; Heb. 3:1–4:9).

The question for all who have held to the belief of a pre-tribulation rapture is, "Where is a seven-year tribulation (historical or prophetic) period in any of this?" You can't have a pre-trib rapture without a trib! Darbyism completely rests on Daniel's prophecy—everything he taught is hooked to it!

After Jesus died on the cross, all that remained was three-and-a-half years of the seventieth week. At least that fits (numerically) the Book of Revelation—with its three-and-a-half (days) in Revelation 11:11; 42 months in Revelation 11:2; 13:5; and a time, times, and half a time in Revelation 12:14.

Regardless of one's eschatological view, what about the final half of Daniel's seventieth week, the last three-and-a-half years?

In person, Jesus came to the Jews ("thy people") and Jerusalem ("thy holy city") during the first half of Daniel's seventieth week—for three-and-a-half years. He went to the Jews, the lost sheep of the house of Israel, "first" (see Mt. 10:5-6; 15:24; Jn. 1:31; Acts 2:25-26; Rom. 1:16). Through His disciples and by His outpoured Spirit from the throne (Mk. 16:20; Gal. 4:6)—for the remaining three-and-a-half years—He confirmed the New Covenant with many elect Christian Jews for the rest of the week (A.D. 31-34).

The last three-and-a-half years of Daniel's seventieth week was Messiah's exclusive ministry to "the Jew first" (Acts 1–7; Rom. 1:16). The beginning of the Book of Acts marks the first moments of the last half of the seventieth week, all that Jesus "began to do and teach" (Acts 1:1) from the throne of grace (by the Spirit). The 120 on the Day of Pentecost were all Hebrews, as were the 3,000 that were added to the Church (Acts 2).

Acts 7:59, KJV

And they stoned Stephen....

Acts 8:5, KJV

Then Philip went down to the city of Samaria, and preached Christ unto them.

Acts 9:17, KJV

And Ananias went his way, and entered into the house; and putting his hands on him said, Brother Saul, the Lord, even Jesus, that appeared unto thee in the way as thou camest, hath sent me, that thou mightest receive thy sight, and be filled with the Holy Ghost.

Acts 10:44, KJV

While Peter yet spake these words, the Holy Ghost fell on all them which heard the word.

The first half of Daniel's seventieth week lasted from the autumn of A.D. 27 until the spring of A.D. 31. Going forward from the crucifixion three-and-a-half years, we are brought to the autumn of A.D. 34 as the grand historical terminating point of the continuous period of

Daniel's seventy weeks. This latter date is marked by the martyrdom of Stephen, the formal rejection of the gospel of Christ by the High Priest and the Jewish Sanhedrin! What soon followed was the consequent persecution of Jesus' disciples, and the turning of the apostles to all nations. The apostle Paul summed it up:

Acts 13:46, KJV

...It was necessary that the word of God should first have been spoken to you: but seeing ye put it from you, and judge yourselves unworthy of everlasting life, lo, we turn to the Gentiles.

Key events soon followed the fulfillment of Daniel's seventieth week. Philip, Peter, and John preached and ministered at Samaria (Acts 8), Saul of Tarsus was converted (Acts 9), and the Holy Ghost was poured out upon the household of Cornelius (Acts 10). The center of Christianity moved from Jerusalem (Daniel's "city") to Antioch, Paul's launching pad (Acts 11–15)! These events could only have taken place when that uninterrupted specified period (490 years), cut off for the Jews and allotted to them as a peculiar people, had expired.

Mt. 24:14, KJV

And this gospel of the kingdom shall be preached in all the world for a witness unto all nations; and then shall the end come.

Mt. 24:34, KJV

Verily I say unto you, This generation shall not pass, till all these things be fulfilled.

The "end" of Judaism came in A.D. 70! The 40 years ("this generation") from Jesus' crucifixion to the destruction of Jerusalem (A.D. 31-70) parallel the 40 years that Israel wandered in the wilderness (Ex. 16:35; Num. 14:33-34; Deut. 8:2). Just as the Old Testament people provoked the Lord with their unbelief, so Judaism stubbornly resisted the truth, having refused their Messiah (Jn. 1:11).

As noted earlier, the historical view of these things is that the sensationalized "last days" of contemporary sign-seekers was in fact the "last days" of Judaism and its animal sacrifices. A careful reflection of every reference in the Bible where the "last days" are mentioned will agree to this (see Gen. 49:1; Is. 2:2; Mic. 4:1; Acts 2:17; 2 Tim. 3:1; Jas. 5:3; 2 Pet. 3:3). There is a difference between the "last days" of the Old Covenant and the current endtimes.

Heb. 1:1-2, NIV

In the past God spoke to our forefathers through the prophets at many times and in various ways,

but in these last days He has spoken to us by His Son....

But was the gospel of the Kingdom preached in all the world for a witness unto all nations (Mt. 24:14)? What did Paul say?

Col. 1:5-6, NIV

The faith and love that spring from the hope that is stored up for you in heaven and that you have already heard about in the word of truth, the gospel that has come to you. All over the world this gospel is bearing fruit and growing....

Col. 1:23, NIV

If you continue in your faith, established and firm, not moved from the hope held out in the gospel. This is the gospel that you heard and that has been proclaimed to every creature under heaven, and of which I, Paul, have become a servant.

Compare Acts 2:5 and Romans 1:8; 10:18; 16:26.

From the facts set forth, reckoning the seventy weeks from the decree given to Ezra in the seventh year of Artaxerxes Longimanus (457 B.C.), there is perfect harmony throughout. The important, definite, historic events of the manifestation of the Messiah at His baptism, the commencement of His public ministry, His crucifixion, and the rejection by the Jews and the subsequent preaching of the gospel to all nations with the proclamation of the New Covenant—all events are in their exact place, sealing Daniel's prophecy!

Basically, Daniel's prophecy of 70 weeks has been *historically* fulfilled. Yet (as with Mathew 24), it still has spiritual implications. Like an onion, truth comes in layers. Many of the old Testament prophecies have a double reference:

1. A pertinent historical word to those to whom it was spoken.

2. A relevant prophetic word to those upon whom the end of the ages have come (Rom. 15:4; 1 Cor. 10:1-11).

The *prophetic* overtone of this final verse reveals an overcoming, glorious Church with the nature and ministry of Jesus raised up in the image of their glorious Head, the Pattern Son. Thus, these "many" of Daniel 9:27 are also found in Daniel 12:3, 10; Romans 8:29; and Hebrews 2:10.

It was Rome that desolated Jerusalem. From a broad view that covers the span of the last 2,000 years, I believe the historical "desolator" to be religious Romism, the mother of harlots (Rev. 17). All her trappings, including her many Protestant daughters and granddaughters, will be dealt with until that which has been determined is poured upon the desolator.

The "desolator" of Daniel 9:27 can also point to the spirit of antichrist as the man of sin who sits in the temple—the carnal mind, extremely religious and resistant to change (2 Thess. 2:3-4 was exegeted in Chapter Eight). This is the seat of satan, the god of this age and the energizer of all the sectarian religions inferred above. Cassette and video tapes, radio and television have brought an overspreading of these abominable concepts (most notably, Scofield's dispensationalism), which have rewoven a veil of flesh that has blinded the "in part" realm (Rom. 11:25) and corrupted the minds of men, lest they see and understand the gospel of glory and the mystery of Christ within us (2 Cor. 4:1-7; Col. 1:25-29). All this must be demolished and made desolate in the name of the Lord (2 Cor. 10:3-6).

The Devil Is Living in Denial

"And [Jesus] shall confirm the [New] covenant with many [elect Jews] for one week: and in the midst of the week [Jesus] shall cause the sacrifice and the oblation [sin offering] to cease [at Calvary]..." (see Dan. 9:27).

Daniel's "one week" (the seventieth) is the historical, chronological, moral, and redemptive fulcrum of all the ages of the human race. It heralds the period when God was manifested in the flesh, wherein He made atonement for sin and conquered satan, and also wherein the Holy Spirit came and the Kingdom of Heaven was opened to all men. To Jews throughout the world, it is irrefutable evidence that their Messiah was crucified *before* Jerusalem fell!

All time and eternity hangs on what happened during those seven years (A.D. 27-34)! As deluded as he is, satan is smarter than some Christians. He has attempted to keep Daniel 9:24-27 in obscurity. By relegating the seventieth week to the future, He has schemed to cover up the greatest seven years of human history—the death, burial, and resurrection of Jesus Christ, and the coming of the Holy Spirit to empower the Church! The time of Daniel's seventieth week is the time of all times, the time of Immanuel. No wonder the devil wants men to be confused or intimidated by this prophecy (Gen. 3:15).

The dispensational view of things, based on Daniel 9:24-27, has been satan's best shot, the most powerful weapon in his arsenal. The evil one is so deluded he thinks it didn't happen. The devil is living in denial of his own death!

He thinks, *It's not really over. I've still got one bullet left. I'll keep the Church in messy diapers, afraid of a future tribulation with its antichrist. To keep their minds off the truth that Jesus was made flesh, I'll tell them that I will be made flesh.* To that the Word replies, "No, satan, you shot and missed the mark. You met your match on a hill outside Jerusalem. It is finished! Jesus Christ, the Messiah, is Lord! He ended all Levitical sacrifice and decreed your desolation."

In nineteenth century America (preceding the historic restoration of Pentecost), the devil played his whole hand at once. As noted earlier, classical dispensationalism developed in this nation along with most of the major cults. About the same time, there were five laws enacted by the United States Congress (September 9-20, 1850) known as the Compromise of 1850; they were aimed at ending sectional disputes that threatened the Union. Margaret Macdonald, Edward Irving, and John Darby—swept along by a very powerful seducing spirit—gave us the greater compromise of 1830! In the words of Dave MacPherson, there has been an "incredible cover-up." For the remainder of the 1990s, apostles and prophets will pull the mask off satan (2 Cor. 11:13-15).

Daniel's prophecy of seventy weeks is the grandest Messianic and Christological prediction in all of Holy Writ!

My humble plea to every dispensationalist is simple— search the Scriptures. We cannot both be right. One of us is wrong—seriously wrong. If a man has erred in his doctrine, he is preaching nothing less than another gospel. This calls for genuine repentance and fruits worthy of it before the Lord Jesus Christ whom we all profess to love and serve. I challenge every minister to arise and preach what the Bible really says. In the temperament of true spiritual reformation, tell it like it is. The Pharisees will hate you, suppressing the truth in unrighteousness (Rom. 1:18). Men try to kill the message by killing the messenger. But Truth (Jn. 14:6) died and was buried. Truth arose and ascended. Truth now reigns from Heaven by the Spirit (Jn. 16:13; 1 Cor. 2:9-10).

I'm often asked, "Pastor Varner, where do you get these things that you preach and write?" My reply is simple; I tell them to check the "Acknowledgments" section at the beginning of each book (including this one). It reads, "To the Holy Spirit, who is my Teacher."

History aside, the Bible, the infallible Word of the living God, the only legitimate rule of faith and practice, is the truth (Jn. 17:17)! Learn it. Memorize it. Know it, and it will make you free (Jn. 8:31-32).

Men are tired of satan's lies, the same old cabbage. While an older generation of American fundamentalists are still being thrilled and chilled with fits of "rapture fever," there is a whole new wave of thinkers—young preachers and young people—who are finally recognizing that the future of this planet belongs to Jesus and His Church if God's people will remain faithful to His Word.

Corporate defeat and heavenly rescue are being steadily abandoned for the view that Jesus Christ is the Lord of all history and the glorious Head of His progressively triumphant Church.

Chapter Eleven

Epilogue

Ezek. 21:27, KJV

I will overturn, overturn, overturn, it: and it shall be no more, until He come whose right it is; and I will give it Him.

Eph. 4:27, KJV

Neither give place to the devil.

The last five chapters of this volume have taken a fresh historical and biblical look at dispensationalism, especially Daniel's prophecy of seventy weeks. The double witness of historical facts (for man's mind) and spiritual truths (for man's spirit) has built and established a powerful foundation with respect to eschatology, the study of "last things."

The apostolic mandate in this entire volume has addressed the current practice throughout Christendom of giving place to the devil. We must rid our lives and theology of the influence of satan. Our homes and churches should center in Jesus Christ, the one "whose right it is." Let us review what we have learned.

Chapter One introduced this Christological treatise by examining our root Messianic text (Ezek. 21:25-27). Jesus is the one "whose right it is."

Chapters Two and Three declared, "The warfare is accomplished" (Is. 40:2). The devil is not God's adversary; he is yours (1 Pet. 5:8). We have an adversary, but Jesus defeated him at the cross.

Chapters Four and Five added, "The earth is the Lord's" (Ps. 24:1), and furnished an overview of covenantal theology. Adam did not turn the earth over to satan following the transgression. The devil is the prince and god of a world system that is passing away. He has never had jurisdiction in the earth. God ruled this planet through prophets until *the* Prophet came "whose right it is" (Heb. 1:1). The earth belongs to the seed of Abraham and David—Mr. and Mrs. Jesus Christ—the Lord and His Church.

Chapters Six through Ten emphasized that the dragon still has a mouth (Rev. 12:16). He is not the thief of John 10:10 anymore; satan in the flesh was crucified. Although he is defeated, the enemy still has influence. His purpose is to abort the seed—Christ in you. His most effective weapon (word), energized by the spirit of fear, is the current stronghold of Darby's, Scofield's and Larkin's dispensationalism.

Chapter Six examined and clarified major eschatological perspectives, explaining key terms. Chapter Seven then took a fresh *historical* look at the futurist view throughout church history. Dispensationalism's nineteenth century roots and evolutionary development were examined, noting key figures such as Edward Irving, John Darby, Margaret Macdonald, C.I. Scofield, and Clarence Larkin.

Chapters Eight and Nine continued by taking a fresh biblical look at the major dispensational proof texts for the pre-tribulation rapture theory, treating many of them with a verse-by-verse exegesis (see Mt. 24:1-34; 1 Cor. 15:51-58; 1 Thess. 4:13-5:9; 2 Thess. 2:1-12).

Chapter Ten took special note of the grandfather clause underlying classical dispensationalism with its future antichrist—Daniel's prophecy of seventy weeks (Dan. 9:24-27). These verses were historically examined and compared with both the Old and New Testaments. Gabriel's words to Daniel have been fulfilled. The archangel who announced the Messiah's birth prophesied about His death. Daniel's seventieth week (A.D. 27-34) is the fulcrum and pivot of human history—the three-and-a-half year ministry of the Lord Jesus Christ consummated by His death, burial, resurrection, and ascension, and the consequent coming and outpouring of the Holy Spirit to empower the Church! The devil is living in denial of his own death. The tribulation happened in A.D. 70 and the beast (possibly Nero) is buried somewhere in the earth.

Whose Right It Is is an apostolic entreaty for Christians everywhere to stop giving place to the devil—in their preaching, singing, testifying, and living. We must return to the Christo-centric view of all things: Jesus Christ is Lord! Our purpose in life is to be conformed to His image, so as to be given dominion (Gen. 1:26-28). We have not been raised up to be evacuated from the planet or from history, but to be salt and light—witnesses and trophies of His grace.

Fresh Hope and New Vision

Hope is the seedbed of all vision. By restoring the Church's genuine expectation, men can once again boldly press toward the will of God. Aggressively running after the Lord will cause His people to pray for strength, direction, and timing. This will release the power of the Righteous One from within and activate a fresh anointing to evangelize the nations. Grace and faith will be added as believers exercise their covenantal rights in Christ. God-given purpose will be resurrected and manifested in the exploits of His glorious Church! His enemies will be made His footstool.

Acts 3:19-21, KJV

Repent ye therefore, and be converted, that your sins may be blotted out, when the times of refreshing shall come from the presence of the Lord;

And He shall send Jesus Christ, which before was preached unto you:

Whom the heaven must receive until the times of restitution of all things, which God hath spoken by the mouth of all His holy prophets since the world began.

Acts 3:21, NIV

He must remain in heaven until the time comes for God to restore everything, as He promised long ago through His holy prophets.

Jesus Christ, the Seed of Abraham and David, is the one "whose right it is." We refuse to give the devil place. Satan is not God's adversary. The warfare is accomplished. Jesus defeated the devil at the cross. The earth is the Lord's, and it always has been. Adam did not turn this earth over to satan. God rules this planet through His Son, the Heir of all things. The dragon is defeated, but he still has a mouth. The Church must arise as a second witness and enforce Jesus' triumph over the enemy.

The most powerful deterrent to this eternal purpose is the contemporary stronghold of dispensationalism, the false hope of an "any minute" rapture.

Darby and Scofield have subtly taken the prophetic covenantal promises, relegating them to the natural Jew and the future. We have been taught that anything that has to do with the Kingdom of God has yet to take place...not so. Abraham was our brother in Christ. David was our brother in Christ. Jesus secured the promises made unto the fathers: Abraham, Isaac, and Jacob.

Such is the plain teaching of Scripture, in spite of what most preachers are saying. I am not being disrespectful to people, but I have no regard...none...for religious customs. If I look or sound intense, it's because I am. I am upset with the only thing more powerful than the Word of God—man's tradition (Mk. 7:13). All true prophets are at war with things that hurt God's people, the things keeping them immature and defeated.

Jesus cannot come until the promises are fulfilled—in Christ and His Church. Jesus must remain in Heaven until the Church matures and He receives the early and latter rains. He will not come until the Bride has made herself ready.

The bulk of this writing has been based upon the New Testament Epistles. In the Gospels, Jesus gave the marching orders for His purpose. In the Book of Acts, His followers performed it. In the Epistles, they explained it. To remain apostolically orthodox and Christological, the Church must build her doctrine upon the foundation of the Pauline, Johannine, and general Epistles of the New Testament.

Many questions linger. We all have much to learn. The Lord in His wisdom has purposely veiled some of these matters until He chooses to open our eyes and ears.

The Real Issue

Eschatology is not the real issue. What counts the most is that Jesus Christ is the Lord of our lives!

Who governs the way that we live and speak? Is He our Savior but not our Lord? Are we doing His will our own way? Can His way of thinking swallow up our pre-conceived mind-sets, including previous teachings wherein our information was not necessarily wrong, just incomplete?

The only valid hermeneutic grid for God's people is the one that comes through God's own mind, eyes, and mouth by way of His Spirit.

Read and study this book again. Honest biblical investigation and unbiased scrutiny will leave us all with one fundamental, inescapable conclusion and application: There is more for us in God!

Whether one is devoutly sitting in a pew waiting for an "any minute" rapture, or playing with the Scriptures and God, there is more.

This means we must change, we must sell out, we must make a commitment to King Jesus. The heir cannot remain a child. He must come under tutors and governors, and mature.

Apostles, prophets, prophetesses...come forth!

Jesus can't come until the Church grows up. May God forgive us. We have been shallow, neither committed nor evangelical. We have not really prayed.

Jesus' second coming is not "any minute"; it's "until"...until I and you become like Him and do what He has told us to do. We have yet to see the complete fulfillment of that in our lives.

Go into the average church, convention, or Christian bookstore, or watch Christian television with all its ballyhoo and hype—millions of dollars are being wasted promoting a false hope that rolled off the lips of a fifteen-year-old kid not filled with the Spirit, not covered by a local church or a seasoned ministry. Men jumped on her "revelation" and ran with it...and still do.

Why? Because when a man preaches what people want to hear and not what they need to hear, the pay is good. There's money in it.

Ask Edward Irving about Henry Drummond's riches and Theodosa Powerscourt's palatial home. Ask C.I. Scofield about James Brookes' sponsorship and Oxford University Press' royalties. Ask any smart preacher or writer who knows when to write another slick paper-back "dispen-sensational" best-seller about the latest happenings in the Middle East. Nothing much has changed.

If the "any minute" rapture were a reality, I humbly and thankfully tell you that I am born again, Spirit-filled, and ready to go....

But what if I'm right?

I beseech you. Don't believe these things just because I or some other preacher have said them.

Pick up your Bible.

Read.

Study.

Think.

Rethink.

Then get mad enough to change...by giving your life and ministry totally to the Lord Jesus Christ, the only one "whose right it is"! Maranatha!

Appendix A

Scripture Versions

Scriptures marked (KJV) are taken from the King James Version of the Bible.

Scriptures marked (TLB) are taken from The Living Bible.

Scriptures marked (AMP) are taken from The Amplified Bible, expanded edition.

Scriptures marked (RSV) are taken from the Revised Standard Version of the Bible.

Scriptures marked (WEY) are taken from The New Testament in Modern Speech, translated by Richard Weymouth.

Scriptures marked (JB) are taken from The Jerusalem Bible.

Scriptures marked (NEB) are taken from The New English Bible.

Scriptures marked (MOF) are taken from The Bible: A New Translation, translated by James Moffatt.

Scriptures marked (PHIL) are taken from The New Testament in Modern English, translated by J.B. Phillips.

Scriptures marked (GDSP) are taken from The New Testament: An American Translation, translated by Edgar J. Goodspeed.

Scriptures marked (LAM) are taken from The Holy Bible from the Ancient Eastern Text, translated by George M. Lamsa.

Scriptures marked (KNOX) are taken from The New Testament in the Translation of Monsignor Ronald Knox.

Scriptures marked (SEPT) are taken from the Septuagint, translated into English from the collected works of the Scriptures in the Greek language.

Scriptures marked (RHM) are taken from The Emphasized Bible, translated by Joseph B. Rotherham.

Scriptures marked (WMS) are taken from The New Testament: A Translation in the Language of the People, translated by Charles B. Williams.

Appendix B
Recommended Reading

The following is a list of recommended reading for information on the historical and biblical analysis of dispensationlism:

A Closer Look at the Rapture by Bill Britton, published by The Church in Action, P.O. Box 905, Springfield, MO 65801.

Days of Vengeance by David Chilton, published by Dominion Press, P.O. Box 7999, Tyler, TX 75711, 1987.

Dispensationalism, Today, Yesterday, and Tomorrow by Curtis I. Crenshaw and Grover E. Gunn, III, published by Footstool Publications, P.O. Box 161021, Memphis, TN 38186, 1985.

The Enlightened Church: satan Who? by Dr. Karl A. Barden, published by Destiny Image, Inc., P.O. Box 310, Shippensburg, PA 17257, phone 1-800-722-6774, 1994.

The Feast of Tabernacles by George Warnock, reprinted by The Church in Action, P.O. Box 905, Springfield, MO 65801, 1951.

Forerunner of the Charismatic Movement: The Life of Edward Irving by Arnold Dallimore, published by Moody Press, Chicago, IL, 1983.

Great Prophecies of the Bible by Ralph Woodrow, published by Ralph Woodrow Evangelistic Association, Inc., P.O. Box 124, Riverside, CA 92502, 1971.

The Great Rapture Hoax by Dave MacPherson, New Puritan Library, Fletcher, NC 28732, 1987.

The Incredible Cover-up by Dave MacPherson, Omega Publications, P.O. Box 4130, Medford, OR 97501, 1975.

The Incredible Scofield by Joseph M. Canfield, Apostolic Educational Ministries, P.O. Box 49, Jefferson, OR 97352.

The Issues of Life by Kelley Varner, published by Destiny Image, Inc., P.O. Box 310, Shippensburg, PA 17257, phone 1-800-722-6774, 1992.

The Land and the Throne by Kelley Varner, published by Tabernacle Press, P.O. Box 785, Richlands, NC 28574, phone 910-324-5026, 1984.

Last Days Madness by Gary DeMar, published by American Vision, Inc., 10 Perimeter Way, B-175, Atlanta, GA 30339, 1994.

Principles of Present Truth From Ezekiel by Kelley Varner, published by Tabernacle Press, P.O. Box 785, Richlands, NC 28574, phone 910-324-5026, 1987.

Principles of Present Truth From Genesis by Kelley Varner, published by Tabernacle Press, P.O. Box 785, Richlands, NC 28574, phone 910-324-5026, 1982.

Rapture Fever by Gary North, published by Institute for Christian Economics, P.O. Box 8000, Tyler, TX 75711, 1993.

Rapture, Prophecy or Heresy by Col. H. Speed Wilson, Life Enrichment Publishers, P.O. 20050, Canton, OH 44701, 1989.

Revealing the Christ of the Revelation by Earl L. Moore, P.O. Box 33168, Indianapolis, IN 46203.

Seventy Weeks: The Historical Alternative by Robert Caringola, published by Companion Press, P.O. Box 351, Shippensburg, PA 17257, 1991.

A Study of Daniel's 70 Weeks by Charles Gilbert Weston, published by Weston Bible Ministries, Jefferson, OR 97352, 1993.

Taking a Second Look at the Second Coming by Lloyd Willhite, published by Kingdom Life Tabernacle Church, Rt. 2, Box 201A, Porter, OK 74454.

Wrongly Dividing the Word of Truth by John H. Gerstner, published by Wolgemuth & Hyatt, Inc., 1749 Mallory Lane, Suite 110, Brentwood, TN 37027, 1991.

From 1978 to the present, Pastor Varner has also taught in much detail the Scriptures studied throughout Chapters Eight and Nine. These messages and others are available on cassette tapes, including 32 tapes on "Whose Right It Is." Write or call our church office at 910-324-5026/5027 for a current catalog.

Appendix C

Books & Tapes by Kelley Varner

TAPE CATALOG

To receive a full listing of Pastor Varner's books and tapes, write or call for our current catalog:

Praise Tabernacle
P.O. Box 785
Richlands, NC 28574-0785
(910) 324-5026 or 324-5027

TAPE OF THE MONTH

Each month two cassette tapes are made available by Pastor Varner. These messages are ministered by him and others in the fivefold ministry. You may join this growing list of listeners on a monthly offering basis.

VIDEO CASSETTES

We are just beginning this new avenue of ministry. Presently available are three, two-hour video cassettes on the Book of Ruth. This teaching is a verse-by-verse exegesis concerning the Christian walk from conception to perfection, from birth to maturity. Please write or call for more information.

SEMINARS AND CONVENTIONS

There are annual meetings here in Richlands for the Body of Christ. Please inquire for information on the next meeting. There is a team of ministry here at Praise Tabernacle that is available to your local church to teach the principles of restoration and assist in the areas of praise and worship. Please contact Pastor Varner.

Available Tape Series

Jesus, Lord of the Home (12 tapes)
Are You Ready for the Third Dimension? (8 tapes)
Israel: God's Chosen People (8 tapes)
The Kingdom of God (8 tapes)
Spiritual Ministry (12 tapes)
Servant Power (8 tapes)
Four-fold Definition of the Local Church (16 tapes)
The New Testament Local Church (32 tapes)
Halloween, Christmas, Easter (8 tapes)
God's Two Greatest Mysteries (8 tapes)
The Coming of the Lord (12 tapes)
Women's Ministry (8 tapes)
The Book of Acts (8 tapes)
Principles of Kingdom Finance (8 tapes)
Bible Patterns of the Kingdom (12 tapes)
The Faith of God (8 tapes)
The Five-fold Ministry (12 tapes)
Life and Immortality (12 tapes)
Water Baptism (8 tapes)
The Day of Atonement (8 tapes)
Principles of Restoration (12 tapes)
The Will of God (8 tapes)
The Songs of Degrees (16 tapes)
The Emerging Christ (12 tapes)
Apostolic Principles (12 tapes)
Romans, Verse-by-verse (from 8 to 30 tapes)
The Feast of Tabernacles (16 tapes)
The More Excellent Ministry (8 tapes)—these are the
    original tapes preached at the House of Prayer in 1981